Two Lives to Lead: Bisexuality in Men and Women

Two Lives to Lead: Bisexuality in Men and Women

Edited by
Fritz Klein and Timothy J. Wolf

Harrington Park Press
New York • Binghamton

ISBN 0-918393-22-1

Published by

Harrington Park Press, Inc.
28 East 22 Street
New York, New York 10010

Harrington Park Press, Inc., is a subsidiary of The Haworth Press, Inc., 28 East 22 Street, New York, New York 10010.

Two Lives to Lead: Bisexuality in Men and Women was originally published by The Haworth Press, Inc., in 1985 under the title *Bisexualities: Theory and Research*. It has also been published as *Journal of Homosexuality*, Volume 11, Numbers 1/2, Spring 1985.

Library of Congress Cataloging in Publication Data

Bisexualities.
    Two lives to lead.

    Originally published as: Bisexualities.
    Bibliography: p.
    Includes index.
    1. Bisexuality. 2. Bisexuality in marriage—United States. I. Klein, Fred. II. Wolf, Timothy J. III. Title.
[HQ74.B57   1985]   306.7'65   85-5868
ISBN 0-918393-22-1

CONTENTS

A CROSS-CULTURAL PERSPECTIVE

WOMEN IN MARRIAGES

MEN IN MARRIAGES

BISEXUAL ORGANIZATIONS

BIBLIOGRAPHY

The *Journal of Homosexuality* is devoted to theoretical, empirical, and historical research on homosexuality, heterosexuality, sexual identity, social sex roles, and the sexual relationships of both men and women. It was created to serve the allied disciplinary and professional groups represented by psychology, sociology, history, anthropology, biology, medicine, the humanities, and law. Its purposes are:

    a) to bring together, within one contemporary scholarly journal, theoretical empirical, and historical research on human sexuality, particularly sexual identity;

    b) to serve as a forum for scholarly research of heuristic value for the understanding of human sexuality, based not only in the more traditional social or biological sciences, but also in literature, history and philosophy;

    c) to explore the political, social, and moral implications of research on human sexuality for professionals, clinicians, social scientists, and scholars in a wide variety of disciplines and settings.

EDITOR

JOHN P. DE CECCO, PhD, *Professor of Psychology and Human Sexuality and Director, Center for Research and Education in Sexuality (CERES), and Director, Human Sexuality Studies, San Francisco State University*

ABSTRACTS AND BOOK REVIEW EDITOR

ANA VILLAVICENCIO-STOLLER, *Center for Research and Education in Sexuality, San Francisco State University*

COPYEDITOR

NORMAN C. HOPPER, *Center for Research and Education in Sexuality, San Francisco State University*

FOUNDING EDITOR

CHARLES C. SILVERSTEIN, PhD, *New York City*

EDITORIAL BOARD

EVELYN BLACKWOOD, PhD (cand.), *Anthropology, Stanford University*
EDWARD BRONGERSMA, JD, *Founder, Dr. Edward Brongersma Foundation, The Netherlands; Former Senator, Dutch National Parliament*
ROGER BROWN, PhD, *John Lindsley Professor of Psychology, Harvard University*
VERN L. BULLOUGH, RN, PhD, *Dean, Faculty of Natural and Social Sciences, State University College at Buffalo*
ELI COLEMAN, PhD, *Assistant Professor and Coordinator of Education and Training, Program in Human Sexuality, University of Minnesota*
LOUIS CROMPTON, PhD, *Professor of English, University of Nebraska at Lincoln*
MARTIN DANNECKER, PhD, *Klinikum der Johann Wolfgang Goethe-Universitat, Abteilung fur Sexualwissenschaft, Frankfurt am Main, West Germany*
JOSHUA DRESSLER, JD, *Professor of Law, Wayne State University School of Law*
LILLIAN FADERMAN, PhD, *Distinguished Professor of English, California State University, Fresno*
DOUGLAS FUTUYMA, PhD, *Professor of Ecology and Evolution, State University of New York, Stony Brook*
JOHN GAGNON, PhD, *Professor of Sociology, State University of New York, Stony Brook*

Preface

As a contributor to the discourse on sexual identity, or sexual orientation, if you will, I have argued that the idea is essentially a biological notion pressed into the service of behavioral and social scientists (De Cecco and Shively, 1983/1984). It is biological because individuals are assigned an identity, bisexual, heterosexual, or homosexual, on the basis of the biological sex of their partners in sexual relationships or how well they fit a biological conception of femaleness or maleness. Since biological sex is the core ingredient of sexual identity, the concept inevitably implies that human sexuality basically resides in female and male genital anatomy and physiology. This "genitalization" of human sexuality, in turn, reduces it, in purpose and need, to procreation. Even as a pleasurable pursuit, the focus is narrowly genital. Sexual orientation is a biological derivative of the idea of sexual identity. It adds the notion that individuals are driven or steered by internal mechanisms or structures in the direction of female or male partners.

By pegging individuals as heterosexuals or homosexuals or, for that matter, bisexuals, the complex and fascinating ways in which human beings can be sexual in their mentality, conduct, and social relationships are crudely subsumed under a biological concept. The authors in this collection have raised their voices against this biological reductionism, which renders bisexuals as lame females or males and self-deceived or conniving heterosexuals or homosexuals.

The existence of females and males is a *biological* fact. That individuals include sexuality in their social relationships with one sex and exclude it in relationships with the other is a *social* fact. Clearly not all individuals feel the need or make the effort to maintain this sex-dichotomy and even those who would like to do so do not always succeed. Now that women often leave the hearth behind for the office and show a remarkable preference for the companionship of other women, the strict male heterosexualist, left on his own, occasionally discovers that the emotional intimacy he has experienced with women he can occasionally share with "straight" male companions. Even the dedicated female and male homosexualists, laboring side-by-side in the political struggle against discrimination, are sometimes bewildered by a sudden, mysterious attraction to their opposite-sex cohorts. Along with the vast armies of "lesbian" mothers and "gay" fathers who have turned their love and attention away from members of the opposite sexes, there are the "straight" women who glower over the nude and erect male bodies in "gay" magazines and the "straight" men who discover themselves basking in the glow of attention generously supplied by a "gay" male companion. Much that is absorbing and perplexing about social relationships into which sexual elements unwittingly intrude lies outside the boundaries imposed by the monolithic idea of sexual identity.

Dr. Klein and Dr. Wolf, as the guest editors of this special double issue on bisexuality, have marshalled an impressive array of papers to challenge conventional notions of sexual identity. Even if one were to assume that individuals were possessed of particular sexual identities, Dr. Klein's grid of variables, far more complex than the heterosexual-homosexual rating scale devised by the Kinsey group, shows that it would never be easy to assign an identity and it would have to be done repeatedly because it changes. The theoretical papers, I believe, are entirely justified in their attacking recent research on sexual identity for either blithely ignoring bisexuality or cavalierly subsuming "bisexuals" under the heterosexual or homosexual label.

I am greatly impressed by the attempts of the authors of the empirical studies in this collection to examine heterosexual marriages that exist side-by-side with homosexual relationships. The strict heterosexualist or homosexualist may find this juxtaposition of opposite-sex and same-sex love and gratification bizarre and unseemly (until, of course, it were to happen to her or him). In fact, the wives and husbands themselves were often more than a bit perplexed by the adventitious amalgamation of heterosexuality and homosexuality. Reading between the lines, however, I found absorbing the efforts of these marital partners to maintain and develop sexual relationships for which we have no descriptive or explanatory social science theory. The preoccupation of psychology and the social sciences with describing and explaining what *has* existed in the past deflects attention away from emerging structures of relationships that prefigure the future.

Among scholarly journals dealing with human sexuality, the *Journal of Homosexuality* has taken the lead in the theoretical and empirical analysis of the concept of sexual identity. Since 1983 five issues have been devoted to this topic: *Bisexual and Homosexual Identities: Critical Theoretical Issues* (Vol. 9, Nos. 2/3; *Bisexual and Homosexual Identities: Critical Clinical Issues* (Vol. 9, No. 4; and *Controversy Over the Bisexual and Homosexual Identities: Commentaries and Reactions* (Vol. 10, Nos. 3/4). The present issues, focusing particularly on bisexuality, are the latest additions to this inquiry into the idea of sexual identity.

I want to express my warmest appreciation to the guest editors for expanding the scope of that inquiry by bringing together under a single cover the research pioneers of bisexuality. I am also deeply grateful to them and the authors for preparing and stoically revising their papers

while attending to their demanding clinical practices and other professional responsibilities. My gratitude also goes to Jay Paul who, in the
difficult and sensitive role of referee and editorial adviser, perused and
commented on the manuscripts and was finally persuaded to join the con-
tributors' ranks. Finally, I thank Norman Hopper, the manuscript editor,
for relentlessly pursuing the authors for every last reference list detail and
revision.

John P. De Cecco, PhD
Editor

REFERENCE

De Cecco, J. P., & Shively, M. G. (1983/1984). From sexual identity to sexual relationships: A
contextual shift. *Journal of Homosexuality, 9*(2/3), 1-26.

Introduction

Fritz Klein, MD
Timothy J. Wolf, PhD
San Diego

The history of research into bisexuality until now could almost be characterized as nonexistent. From the outset of this project, our goal has been to stimulate inquiries into the complexities of bisexuality. We have gathered the leading sex researchers of bisexuality to explore the various facets of, until now, a practically uncharted territory.

This publication incorporates the major issues affecting bisexuals: the theoretical and psychological aspects of the bisexual orientation, the cross-cultural view, the bisexual marriage and gender roles, and the creation of bisexual subcultures. Also included is an annotated bibliography of bisexuality literature.

The four articles examining theoretical issues of bisexuality deal mainly with questions of definition. As all definitions are arbitrary, a single view of bisexuality is thus elusive. By reviewing the viewpoints of these authors, we achieve an initial understanding of the complexities of the subject. In the editors' opinion, bisexuality is different for different people, changes and evolves over time, is comprised of a number of sexual and non-sexual variables, lies in the broad spectrum between the exclusive orientations of the two "monosexualities," and for certain individuals definitely becomes a growth-inducing life pattern.

The bulk of previous research has been devoted to the psychological aspects of bisexuality. Two articles in this issue explore the problems bisexuals bring to therapy, the unique issues therapists themselves must grapple with, and the questions of psychological adjustment and self-esteem of bisexuals as compared with heterosexuals and homosexuals. Finally, Dr. Lourea's article could be useful to the professional counselor or psychotherapist assisting bisexuals.

Dr. Carrier provides us with a fascinating look at the Mexican male bisexual. The differences as compared to our American culture are great and permit us to reevaluate our conceptualizations of sexuality and gender

---

Dr. Klein is the Director of the Institute of Sexual Behavior in San Diego, where he practices psychiatry. Dr. Wolf is a consultant and psychotherapist in private practice. Correspondence can be addressed to Dr. Klein, 3821 Fourth Avenue, San Diego, CA 92103 and to Dr. Wolf, 3549 Camino del Rio South, Suite D, San Diego, CA 92108.

roles. His article points to the need for our society to explore other cultures before we can understand fully sexual differences in our own.

Studies regarding women in bisexual marriages historically have been missing in the literature. The three pioneering studies included herein deal with three different topics: women bisexuals in traditionally heterosexual marriages, married women who, at a late age, change their orientations from exclusive heterosexuality to practicing bisexuality, and married women who cope with their husband's bisexuality. These ground-breaking articles are important contributions and provide the foundations for a more balanced perspective in these areas.

We were fortunate to find many far-reaching research studies of bisexual men in marriage, a phenomenon both complex and increasingly prevalent. For the first time a substantial number of couples and individuals in marriages, encompassing both clinical and non-clinical populations, have been examined. Some of the aspects covered include disclosure to spouses, factors contributing to the preservation or dissolution of marriages, comparisons of marital and sexual satisfaction with heterosexual couples, problems of adjustment, and the differences between concealed and acknowledged bisexual husbands. We can now state that for some couples a bisexual orientation of one partner is a viable option, that a bisexual identity even enhances some marriages, that support networks and psychotherapeutic interventions aid couples in coping, and that marriages can buckle under the weight of the negative social pressure and internal dissonance.

Most bisexuals lack social support which would help validate their internal feelings and actual behaviors; there still does not exist a bisexual subculture to meet these needs. New York once had a social support network for bisexuals. Mr. Mishaan provides some hypotheses as to why it was successful for a time, but unable to take root and flourish. The exception to many bisexual groups across the country is the large flourishing and well-organized bisexual community which exists in San Francisco, serving its members socially, educationally, and even politically. The Chicago community demonstrates the similar growth difficulties experienced in many cities, including the Bisexual Forum here in San Diego.

Mr. Steir's excellent bibliography will give future researchers on bisexuality a comprehensive list of available articles and books on the subject.

It has been our pleasure to work with the contributing authors who expertly and diligently created this issue. We are extremely proud that such a high level of research has been achieved on this subject. Special thanks go to Professor De Cecco for his editorial support and encouragement of this project, and to Norman Hopper, the *Journal's* manuscript editor, for his untiring assistance. We feel this issue is an important contribution not only to professionals and researchers, but also to those who experience isolation as part of an unrecognized bisexual minority.

THEORETICAL ISSUES

Bisexuality Reconsidered: An Idea in Pursuit of a Definition

Charles E. Hansen, PhD
Anne Evans, PhD
San Diego

ABSTRACT. This paper examines the confusion and conflict stemming from the inability of sexological research to establish a reliable operational definition of the bisexual condition. An examination of current research assumptions, definitions, and limitations revealed several "errors" which predispose most investigations to controversial or insignificant results. These errors include the reseacher's: (1) erotophobia, (2) dualistic thinking, (3) use of "self-labels," and most important, (4) misuse of the Kinsey Scale as a basic definitional assumption.

This paper concludes with a description of an alternative research model and methodology for bisexuality research. This new model eschews subject labeling and proposes a two-axis system for operationally defining bisexuality and for generating testable hypotheses.

In 1948, Alfred C. Kinsey devised a simple instrument by which to describe (on a population-distribution scale) the genital-behavior patterns of his research subjects, now known as the Kinsey Scale. Originally, this scale gave researchers an opportunity to plot yet another bell-curve. However, it does not work. Given the reports by interviewees, what has continuously resulted has been a highly levoskewed and slightly bimodal curve, indicating that a dominant percentage of individuals display or report their sexual preferences and activities to be exclusively hetero-

---

Drs. Hansen and Evans are clinical psychologists in private practice. Reprint requests may be addressed to the authors, 3821 Fourth Avenue, San Diego, CA 92103.

1

sexual (mode # 1 = Kinsey 0), while another significant percentage report a predominant homosexual orientation (mode # 2 = Kinsey 6).

Such a peculiar distribution forced researchers to devise more thoughtful approaches to the study of sexuality, and, with the accumulation of data over time, sexologists used the 0 to 6 rating scale as an AXIS around which a richer and more global model of human sexuality took form; "research-sexuality" became clearly more than genitality. Thus, when sexologists consider the aspects of heterosexuality and homosexuality, conversations are rich with such concepts as developmental bonding processes, family-of-origin constellations, early adolescent trauma and rivalries, and the like. But when the topic turns to bisexuality, researchers are back to basic concepts again. The definition centers on genital behaviors and the model again becomes unilinear: a *debate* emerges, *not* around affectional issues and values, *not* around family and identity affiliations, but around genital activity or even pathological *intra*psychic incongruencies.

GENITALITY IS NOT SEXUALITY

Much of the confusion and conflict that sexologists experience when focusing on bisexuality arises from the faulty placement of emphasis on genital sexual activity, rather than on the larger issues of loving. Simply put, genitality is *not* all of sexuality. It is probable that sexuality, including bisexuality, relates to affection and affiliation as well as to genital behavior. This simple distinction is essential to an understanding of the phenomenon of bisexuality. Without it, researchers will continue to be at a loss when trying to explain the confused concepts which supposedly define the problems of bisexuals.

In earlier human sexuality research (1950-1960), it was both easy and convenient to identify a person's genital patterns (homo/hetero-) in order to sub-group and then correlate within- and between-group patterns of developmental, affectional and affiliative behaviors. However, two major factors in recent years have rendered this research approach obsolete:

1. The advent of the massive Gay Liberation Movement has produced pressure to identify with one or the other "side." As a result, it is unlikely that a bisexual will be willing to identify quickly with (or propound) yet a "third-front" in this political struggle.
2. Current conceptual models of bisexuality in the media present it as (a) a conflicted or confused identity development; (b) retarded sexual development; or (c) a defense against "true" heterosexuality or homosexuality.

Such conceptualizations may stop a bisexual from identifying as a bisexual, let alone identifying with a group for research purposes.

SOURCES OF ERROR IN CURRENT RESEARCH

At least three possible sources can be deduced for the "errors" that hinder research on bisexuality: (1) cultural "erotophobia"; (2) the law of the excluded middle; and (3) use of "self-labels" and the single-axis Kinsey continuum.

We use the term erotophobia here in a sense similar to the way "homophobia" is used. In post-Victorian western culture, the coincidence of erotic-positive attitudes with erotic-proactive behavior always provokes anxiety, even among some sexologists. Therefore, bisexuals are often seen as promiscuous. Even if one replaces this negative term with less tainted ones, such as "proactive" and "sex-positive," the threat still remains. The aspect of bisexuality which is probably the most anxiety-provoking is non-monogamy. Some would even say that bisexuality and non-monogamy (genital infidelity) are synonymous (*Playboy,* 1983). Whereas both heterosexuals and most paired homosexuals embrace some form of fidelity, the concept bisexual (virtually unresearched) suggests attraction to and sexual involvement with anyone, if not everyone. Given such an allegation of open promiscuity, few sexologists would pursue research into the labyrinth of bisexuality.

The second source of error in the bisexuality controversy is "The Law of the Excluded Middle," by which Bergler (1956) purports that once homosexual behavior commences, any subsequent heterosexual behavior must be considered "counterfeit." This psychoanalytic stance holds that one cannot eroticize two love objects or activities at the same time. Why not? Many humans practice both masturbation and coitus. These two activities should not be seen as contradictory or conflicted sexual *aims*, nor should a male and a female be considered conflicted or opposed sexual *objects*. It is astonishing that researchers have spent so many years in the field of sexuality, yet have only recently begun to formulate research approaches which *assume* "health" or normalcy among bisexuals. To continue basing their definitions of bisexuality on either the Kinsey continuum or the historic psychodynamic conceptual models, researchers are restricted by the limitations of both; the latter disposing them to "erotophobia" or dualistic thinking, the former subjecting them to the "futility of trying to sum up human sexual conduct through counting physiological events." Researchers (Gagnon, 1977, p. 260) must consider that perhaps:

> The physiological events are no more (and often less) important as indicators of what people are experiencing than the statements people make about what they (others) feel or think. (p. 261)

Furthermore, continuing to use the Kinsey Scale as a basis for their conceptualization of bisexuality creates one final trap for researchers, the same one faced in early research on homosexuality: by starting from the known (heterosexuality), one tends to define the yet unknown in terms of "what-is-not," i.e., as a deviation from a norm. Even now, research efforts continue to fall into this same trap by attempting to derive bisexuality *from* homosexuality, as "what-must-occur." Difficulties can arise when a researcher attempts to delineate bisexuality by prescribing what phenomena *must* be present to discriminate it clearly from homosexuality; identity labels, male-to-female time ratios, partner ratios, and the like.

THE PROBLEM FORMULATED

Contemporary sexological research is confronting problems in the area of bisexuality. Klein (1978, p. 61) points out the poignancy of this problem for the persons whom we seek to study:

> Many bisexuals today are in danger of choosing heterosexuality or homosexuality, because of the pressure put on them by our culture. Bisexuality is not considered a "normal" possibility by most orthodox psychiatrists. . . . Sexual labels divide us into the known "we" as opposed to the feared "them." No matter which label or behavior pattern fits our own individual inclination, we might at least entertain the notion of expanding to embrace people of all sexual orientations.

Sexologists continue to classify behaviorally their research subjects. Men whose love and loyalty for other men can match, without rivaling, their love for wives, who never engage in erotic or genital activity with men, will always be included as "heterosexuals," never questioned or described. The bisexual female who marries and chooses erotic-fidelity as a lifestyle, will also certainly be included as a "heterosexual." If she continues her fulfilling *affectional* attachments with other women but never again acts on her capacity, some researchers would call her a latent homosexual and bar her from a research sample. If, however, she does *not* marry, and the researcher encounters her during a period of her life when most of her affectional and erotic contact is with females, she almost always will be included as a "homosexual."

CONCLUSION: TOWARD A SOLUTION

Research questions relevant to bisexuality must not be derived from distinctions among heterosexuality, bisexuality and homosexuality. Again, as Gagnon writes: "The question that needs to be asked is what kind of learning histories and contexts offer scripts to people at various moments in the life cycle which make sex with both genders possible.'' (Gagnon, 1977, p. 274). Heretofore, the Kinsey continuum has served as the *sine qua non* for sexual orientation research. For exploring issues of ''pure'' homosexuality or heterosexuality, this continuum is adequate and perhaps even appropriate. It describes the quantitative aspects of sexuality—sex object and sex frequency in thought and action—and it discriminates well between the two ''pure'' orientations. But, when activities or fantasies are not preponderantly ''heterosexual'' or ''homosexual,'' this unidimensional definition (object-choice and frequency) will exclude those for whom the experiential variables of *sex aim* and *emotional quality* are central issues. (It is interesting to note that even Freud and Ellis assumed at least *two* axes: *sex-aim* and *sex-object* in their definitions of human sexuality). The aim-quality axis and its variables, if central to the assumptions of a study, would *include* the males and females described above, and such a study would *not* require ego-dystonic self-labeling by subjects.

Future bisexuality research might begin by identifying the several *aim* variations which allow for emotional erotic interaction with both genders. For example, one study might seek out a group of males who enjoy ''swinging'' with their wives and other couples to whom they feel close. Some of these males may enjoy direct erotic interaction with male partners, while some of them may feel no erotic, but only emotional, closeness with other males. Another study could seek out a group of male couples in which at least one partner enjoys occasional swinging or ''three-way'' encounters, including a female participant. Some of these males may enjoy direct erotic interaction with the female partner, while some may feel only emotional closeness with the female as she participates with them. In neither of these studies would there be consideration of such psychodynamic variables as ''latent'' heterosexuality or homosexuality. Future bisexuality research could then *begin* to examine the values and functions inherent in periodic reversals of sex-object choice. Using this approach, researchers might discover one group of ''bisexuals'' composed of both ''straights'' and ''gays'' whose mate relationships are stimulated by occasional variations in choice of both object and aim. In this context, male-to-female frequency ratios, intrapsychic conflicts, or socio-sexual deficits are completely spurious issues; thereby Gagnon's suggestions can be operationalized.

Clearly, bisexuality research premised primarily on the Kinsey Scale is futile. Researchers are indebted to Kinsey for making the world safe for sex, but they must also relegate ''The Scale'' to the pile of obsolete instrumentation. Bisexuality must be addressed, not as an intermediary status between heterosexuality and homosexuality, but as a distinct entity in which heterosexuality and homosexuality may be seen to co-mingle, but not compete. Klein is right to consider embracing, rather than labeling, people of all sexual orientations. The first and last task of all humanistic research is always to clarify and enhance human experience.

REFERENCES

Bergler, E. (1956). *Homosexuality: Disease or way of life?* New York: Hill & Wang.
Playboy readers sex survey. (1983, May). *Playboy Magazine*, pp. 126-220.
Gagnon, J. (1977). *Human sexualities*. Glenview, IL: Scott Foresman.
Klein, F. (1978). *The bisexual option*. New York: Arbor House.

Identity Conflict
or Adaptive Flexibility?
Bisexuality Reconsidered

Gary Zinik, PhD
Santa Barbara City College
Santa Barbara, CA

ABSTRACT. A definition of bisexuality is offered, followed by a discussion of two opposing models of bisexual functioning: (1) the "conflict model," which views bisexuality as problematic, stemming from identity conflict and confusion that marks a transitional stage to a homosexual orientation; and (2) the "flexibility model," which views bisexuality as the coexistence of heteroeroticism and homoeroticism, as the successful integration of homosexual and heterosexual identities into a dual sexual orientation. The Kinsey data are reviewed in an effort to determine the incidence of bisexuality in the U.S. population. Finally, specific clinical and empirical studies investigating bisexual subjects are reviewed in light of the two models.

Bisexuality has long been a misunderstood phenomenon in both academic psychology and society at large. Hundreds of research studies and scores of books have been published investigating homosexuality; in sharp contrast, the scientific community has taken little interest in bisexuality. MacDonald (1983), writing in the *Journal of Sex Research*, criticized researchers for equating bisexuality with homosexuality and asserted that "the research on homosexuality is thoroughly confounded by the inclusion of large numbers of bisexuals as homosexuals" (p. 94).

That the subject of bisexuality has generated so little interest and research is surprising if one recalls the sensational studies conducted by Alfred Kinsey and his associates in the 1940s and 1950s. The country was shocked when Kinsey discovered exceedingly high rates of homosexual behavior among American men and women. Ironically, the more noteworthy fact was (and still is) overlooked: Significantly higher percentages of people exhibit bisexual behavior than exclusively homosexual behavior.

Dr. Zinik teaches human sexuality at Santa Barbara City College and is a practicing clinician specializing in sexuality counseling. Requests for reprints may be sent to the author, P.O. Box 92226, Santa Barbara, CA 93190.

7

DEFINING BISEXUALITY

There is inconsistency in research literature between the use of the term "bisexuality," which may refer strictly to sexual behavior with both females and males (Churchill, 1967; Ford & Beach, 1951; Kinsey, Pomeroy, & Martin, 1948), and the term "bisexual," which is broader in meaning than sexual behavior, encompassing a sexual orientation and self-defined identity (Blumstein & Schwartz, 1976a, 1976b; Klein, 1978). In an attempt to simplify matters, the terms "bisexuality" and references to "bisexual" people are used interchangeably in this article to describe the broader concept of a dual-gender sexual orientation and identity, except where noted as referring to sexual behavior only.

In this article, the following criteria are used to define bisexuality: (1) eroticizing or being sexually aroused by both females and males; (2) engaging in (or desiring) sexual activity with both; and (3) adopting "bisexual" as a sexual identity label (as opposed to labeling one's self "heterosexual" or "homosexual").

Some authors also describe bisexuality as a dual "affectional preference," defined as the desire to have intimate emotional relationships with both females and males that may include sexual contact (Bode, 1976; Klein, 1978; MacInnes, 1973; Scott, 1978). However, it is possible to identify as a bisexual and have sex with both sexes without wanting emotional intimacy with either.

People who have sex with both men and women may or may not label themselves as a bisexual for many reasons. Some people may have sex with and eroticize both sexes but may prefer to identify themselves as a heterosexual or a homosexual. One's sexual identity label reflects both the organization of one's self concept and one's membership in or allegiance to a particular group or social movement (Warren, 1974). For this reason adoption of a bisexual identity is considered a necessary criterion to distinguish bisexuals from people who, while perhaps eroticizing both sexes, identify themselves as essentially heterosexual or homosexual.

Bisexuals eroticize both sexes, though not necessarily to the same degree. Nor are their sexual relations with females and males necessarily equal in number as the prefix "bi" implies. In fact these "50:50" types are believed to be quite rare (MacInnes, 1973; Money, 1980). A bisexual's proclivities usually lean toward one sex or the other in something of a 60:40 or 30:70 ratio. Hence bisexuals may have a preference for the same or the opposite sex, but continue to eroticize both or remain open to sexual involvement with both.

Individuals may exhibit simultaneous, concurrent, or serial bisexuality. *Simultaneous bisexuality* means having sex with at least one partner of the same and opposite sex at the same time. *Concurrent bisexuality* means having sex separately with females and males during the same time period of the individual's life. *Serial bisexuality* is defined as alternating male and female sexual partners over time. Individuals practicing serial bisexuality may have monogamous relationships, and thus give the appearance of living a more or less heterosexual or homosexual lifestyle.

THE BISEXUAL DEBATE

Both clinicians and sex researchers have engaged in a long-standing controversy over bisexuality. Emerging from this debate are two theories explaining the nature of bisexuality. I have called them the "conflict model" and the "flexibility model." The conflict model views bisexuality as inherently characterized by conflict, confusion, ambivalence, and the inability to decide one's sexual preference. The alternative view is the flexibility model. This view explains bisexuality as characterized by cognitive and interpersonal flexibility and, for some people, the desire for personal growth and fulfillment. The conflict model portrays bisexuals as anxious "fence-sitters," while the flexibility model describes bisexuals as experiencing the "best of both worlds."

THE CONFLICT MODEL OF BISEXUALITY

Underlying the conflict model of bisexuality is the notion that sexual orientation is a dichotomy: One is either heterosexual or homosexual. This dichotomous notion derives from the following logic. Since men and women are viewed as opposite sexes, it appears contradictory that anyone could eroticize two opposite things at the same time. Attraction to one sex would logically rule out attraction to the other, or else lead to psychological dissonance and conflict. It follows that people claiming to be bisexual are: (1) experiencing identity conflict or confusion; (2) living in an inherently temporary or transitional stage which masks the person's true underlying sexual orientation (presumably homosexual); and (3) employing the label as a method of either consciously denying or unconsciously defending against one's true homosexual preference.

In 1956, Edmund Bergler denounced bisexuality with surprising vehemence. He declared that bisexuality is an "out-and-out fraud," but conceded that male homosexuals can occasionally have "lustless mechanical sex" with women. Ruitenbeek (1973) wrote that the "mask of bisexuality" may even be "dangerous" since it prevents people from coming to terms with their own sexuality. When questioned about bisexuality, Irving Bieber (1971) stated, "A man is homosexual if his behavior is homosexual. Self-identity is not relevant" (p. 63). Some authorities admit that bisexuals exist but have weak heterosexual potency. Stern (1961) reported that people claiming to be bisexual are highly disturbed individuals with identity problems and conflicts coupled with guilt feelings. Cory and Leroy (1963) described bisexuals as "overgrown adolescents" who are confused, lack a sense of group identity, and "whose inability to differentiate one form of sexuality from another has never developed" (p. 89).

The conflict model of bisexuality is based on general assumptions about human sexuality that deserve examination. First is the notion that homosexual interests eradicate heterosexual responsiveness. Since one would cancel out the other, they cannot exist side-by-side without creating irreconcilable conflict. As mentioned earlier, this follows from the notion (based on principles of formal logic) that men and women represent opposite sexual poles; eroticizing one sex precludes eroticizing the other. Once homosexual behavior begins, subsequent heterosexual behavior is seen as hiding or denying one's homosexuality. Indeed, even heterosexual relations prior to the initial homosexual behavior are retrospectively rendered invalid by some as early instances of denial.

The second assumption underlying the conflict model is the "one drop" notion of homosexuality which states that since homosexuality is not something one would choose voluntarily in this culture in light of the social costs involved, the slightest evidence of it must indicate a deep, predispositional feature of the individual. Thus "one drop" of homosexual behavior (i.e., even one contact) is taken as evidence of an underlying homosexual orientation.

In the field of sex research, many psychological and sociological studies group bisexuals together with homosexuals; rarely are differences between the two examined (MacDonald, 1983). The common practice for sex researchers is to define people as homosexual who have had, according to the Kinsey scale (1984), "more than incidental homosexual experience" regardless of the amount of heterosexual experience.

Bisexuality is also viewed with skepticism and suspicion by the general public. This is the case in both the heterosexual and homosexual communities (Blumstein & Schwartz, 1974, 1976a, 1976b; Klein, 1978; Playboy, 1983; Tripp, 1975). In fact, skepticism by both heterosexuals and homosexuals is congruent with the conflict model of bisexuality; members of both groups may view claims to bisexuality as a failure to adjust to a homosexual orientation.

From the point of view of conventional heterosexual society, bisexuality may be considered the same as homosexuality (MacDonald, 1983; Money, 1980). Homosexuality continues to be stigmatized, and bisexuality considered just as "bad" ("Gay America," 1983). Indeed, bisexuality may even appear more threatening than homosexuality since it disrupts the conventional belief that people can be classified into two distinct sexual groups.

From the viewpoint of gay subculture, bisexuality is sometimes seen as an attempt to have one's cake and eat it too. Some gay activitists view bisexuality as an act of political betrayal. Bisexuals are seen as enjoying the privileges of heterosexual society while at the same time avoiding the stigma of homosexuality. The same is also true in the lesbian subculture.

Thus, members of both straight and gay communities often disbelieve the individual's assertions of bisexuality and attribute such claims to the inability to come to grips with a homosexual label. For this reason, a self-identified bisexual may be required to possess ample heterosexual "credentials" before a homosexual label can be avoided. Moreover, bisexuals can find themselves in a "double closet"; they hide their heterosexual activities from their homosexual peers while at the same time hiding their homosexual activities from their heterosexual peers. Bisexuals thus make an effort to appear either homosexual or heterosexual, depending on the social context, to avoid embarrassment or ostracism.

THE FLEXIBILITY MODEL OF BISEXUALITY

There is growing academic and clinical support for the validity of a bisexual orientation and lifestyle. The flexibility model portrays the bisexual as somewhat of a chameleon, capable of moving easily between the heterosexual and homosexual worlds. Bisexuality is characterized as the coexistence of heteroerotic and homoerotic feelings and behaviors, and an integration of homosexual and heterosexual identities. Both homosexual and heterosexual attractions and sexual experiences are considered genuine. Such dual experience may require a form of perceptual/cognitive flexibility which allows one to "see" seemingly opposite sexual objects as erotic and arousing. Qualities such as androgyny (sex-role flexibility) and interpersonal flexibility would aid such individuals in conducting sexually and emotionally intimate relationships in a comfortable manner (Klein, 1978).

The flexibility model has important conceptual differences from the conflict model. Rather than considering homosexual and heterosexual responses as mutually exclusive, the flexibility model posits that these two can coexist in the form of bisexual eroticism (Kinsey, Pomeroy, & Martin, 1948; Saliba, 1982; Zinik, 1983). In one sense, this is possible if males and females are no longer regarded as "opposite" sexes, hence resolving the apparent logical contradiction that one cannot eroticize two opposite sexual objects at the same time. If men and women are not considered opposites but, as it were, "variations on a theme," then sexual attraction to one sex would not necessarily preclude sexual attraction to the other. Indeed, many self-identified bisexuals report that they are attracted to qualities of particular people rather than aspects of gender per se (Bode, 1976; Coons, 1972; MacInnes, 1973; Zinik, 1983).

Unlike the conflict model, which is characterized by "either/or" thinking (one must be either heterosexual or homosexual), the flexibility model is characterized by "both/and" thinking: one can be both heterosexual and homosexual—that is, bisexual. The rationale behind the flexibility model makes it possible for homosexual and heterosexual interests to exist side-by-side without producing conflict.

The flexibility model does not, however, imply that bisexuality never produces ambivalence. Psychological confusion may accompany bisexuality, but not inevitably. Rather, the model posits that some individuals can maintain a psychologically harmonious bisexual orientation. This is in contrast to the conflict model, which views bisexuality as inherently problematic, as always characterized by confusion and conflict. Claims to bisexuality likewise do not necessarily signify a failure to adjust to an exclusive homosexual preference, though this may be true in some cases. Rather, it is possible to conceptualize bisexuality as the successful adjustment to a dual homosexual and heterosexual preference.

Sigmund Freud believed that all human beings possess bisexual potential at birth (Freud, 1953; Stoller, 1972). Steckel (1922), one of Freud's early followers, extended the bisexual period beyond the Oedipal phase of early childhood, claiming that "normal persons show a distinct bisexual period up to the age of puberty" (p. 39).

Money and Tucker (1975) also stated that all humans are born with bisexual potential, and that it is fallacious to dichotomize individuals as "pure" homosexuals or heterosexuals. During his joint research with Tucker, Money stated:

> In reality people are infinitely varied along the spectrum in between, all capable of bisexual behavior. In fact, it is safe to say that every adult human being has, in fantasy, engaged in some form of bisexual behavior, if not physical contact, to some degree at some time in his or her life. "Ambisexual" describes the human race more accurately than "heterosexual," "homosexual," or even "bisexual," although the degree of ambisexuality varies in intensity from one person to the next. (p. 16)

Klein (1978) observed that bisexuality is a relatively new term in our vocabulary, and not until recently did people even have the option of thinking of it as a way of life. Childs (1976), reporting the platform statement on women's sexuality of the Association for Women in Psychology, listed four sexual options: celibacy, lesbianism, heterosexuality, and bisexuality. Earlier, Coons (1972) and Kelly (1974), both staff clinicians at university counseling centers, had discussed the emergence of bisexuality among the youth culture as an "alternative adaptation."

Churchill (1967) described how bisexuality is discouraged by western society even more than exclusive homosexuality due to the conventional trend to dichotomize people into two sexual groups. Money and Tucker (1975) speculated that bisexuality would be much more common if encouraged, as it was in ancient Greece, by role models and cultural stereotypes.

However, society's attitude toward bisexuality appears to be changing in the 1980s. Gossip columns in newspapers, magazines, and other pop culture media leave the occasional impression that it is fashionable to be bisexual among those who live in the fast lane. More than a few celebrities and jet-setters have come out of the closet to declare their bisexuality, including singers Janis Joplin, Joan Baez, and Mick Jagger, writer Dorothy Thompson, tennis star Billy Jean King, and feminist Kate Millet (see "Bisexual Chic," 1974; Brody, 1974; Carroll, 1974; Knox, 1974; "The New Bisexuals," 1974).

SUMMARY OF THE MODELS

It should be emphasized that the foregoing discussion of the flexibility model is not meant to imply that bisexuality is somehow superior or more highly evolved than heterosexuality or homosexuality. Neither are heterosexuals or homosexuals perceived to be less generally flexible than bisexuals. While psychological and interpersonal flexibility are considered desirable traits in this culture, obviously it is not necessary to be bisexual to attain these qualities. On the other hand, to be bisexual as here defined (eroticizing and having sex with both genders and self-identifying as bisexual) may require a reasonable degree of psychological or interpersonal flexibility, as hypothesized by the model.

The terms "conflict model" and "flexibility model" were chosen because they encapsulate the opposing views on the issues of choice and decision-making: the conflict model explains bisexuality as characterized by *indecision* and the *inability to choose* a sexual/gender preference; the flexibility model characterizes bisexuality as the *conscious decision* to adopt a dual orientation, as a *free choice.*

INCIDENCE OF BISEXUALITY IN THE POPULATION

Determining how many bisexuals there are in our society is difficult. However, the Kinsey (1948, 1953) data suggest what proportion of American men and women who exhibit a combination of heterosexual and homosexual behavior in their histories. Of those between the ages of 16 and 25 who were actively sexual in any given year, 75-85% of the men and 80-90% of the women were exclusively heterosexual; 4% of the men and 2% of the women were exclusively homosexual. This leaves approximately 15% of the men and 10% of the women with bisexual histories. Gagnon (1977) also calculated that it is from this 10-15% of the population that we can draw those people with bisexual preferences. If we can assume that Kinsey's percentages remain constant over time (as corroborated by Gebhard, 1972), approximately 25 million Americans exhibit some combination of heterosexual and homosexual behavior. However, there is no way of knowing how many of these people would actually *identify* themselves as bisexual.

CLINICAL AND EMPIRICAL STUDIES OF BISEXUAL SUBJECTS

Within the past decade, bisexuality has been the subject of several magazine articles (''Bisexual Chic,'' 1974; Brody, 1974; Carroll, 1974; Knox, 1974; Mead, 1975; ''The New Bisexuals,'' 1974). and several anecdotal books (Douglas, 1970; Fast, 1975; Hurwood, 1974; MacInnes, 1973, Scott, 1978). However, much of this material is less than scholarly, leaning toward commercial sensationalism.

In *Sexual Preference: Its Development in Men and Women*, Bell, Weinberg, and Hammersmith (1981) reported perhaps the best study to date on the development of sexual orientation. Bell and associates conducted personal interviews to study the developmental histories of 979 homosexual and 477 heterosexual men and women. Most of the homosexual subjects were exclusively homosexual (Kinsey scores 5-6), but a sufficiently large number scored in the bisexual range (2-4) to permit a comparison of these two groups. The homosexuality of the exclusively homosexual subjects had emerged in childhood and early adolescence and was well established by age 19. On the other hand, experiences taking place after age 19 made a greater contribution to the development of homosexual behavior. Bell and associates hypothesized that there may be two types of homosexual development, ''predispositional homosexuality'' and ''learned homosexual responsiveness.'' They stated, ''These findings seem to suggest that *exclusive homosexuality tends to emerge from a deep-seated predisposition, while bisexuality is more subject to influence by social and sexual learning*'' (p. 201; italics in original).

Most bisexuals first eroticize the opposite sex and identify as heterosexual; later, in their 20s or 30s, they discover their homosexual interests (Bell et al., 1981; Bode, 1976; Klein, 1978; Zinik, 1983). Yet there are also cases in which life-long homosexuals spontaneously develop heterosexual interests and become bisexual. The question may be whether these individuals acquire a ''learned heterosexual responsiveness'' analogous to the ''learned homosexual responsiveness'' hypothesized by Bell et al. (1981).

Bisexuals report types of erotic fantasies different from those of hetero-sexuals and homosexuals. As might be expected, they report frequent homosexual and heterosexual fantasies, while heterosexuals report more heterosexual fantasies than homosexual fantasies, and homosexuals report more homosexual than heterosexual fantasies (Saliba, 1982; Storms, 1978, 1980; Zinik, 1983).

Bisexuals may prefer one sex over the other (the 50:50 types are ap-parently quite rare), but they are attracted to both men and women and re-main open to sexual involvement with both (Harris, 1977; Klein, 1978; *Playboy*, 1983; Rubenstein, 1982; Saliba, 1982; Zinik, 1983). Moreover, many bisexuals have maintained their erotic response pattern over time and have identified as bisexuals a large part of their adult lives. Ruben-stein (1982) found that bisexual subjects' self-esteem scores were posi-tively related to the length of time they had identified as bisexuals. These studies question the assumptions of the conflict model that homosexual in-terests necessarily eradicate heterosexual responsiveness, and that bisex-uality is a stage on the way to exclusive homosexuality.

Zinik (1983) compared male and female heterosexuals, homosexuals, and bisexuals in an anonymous survey study. He found that 138 self-identified bisexual male and female subjects reported they experienced similar levels of erotic excitement with female and male sexual partners. However, both males and females reported more emotional satisfaction with their female partners, a finding corroborated by Saliba (1982). Simi-larly, both male and female subjects reported falling in love with women more often than men, though there were a considerable number who had fallen in love with individuals of both genders at least once (Zinik, 1983). Wolff (1977) found that bisexual men frequently (but not always) re-ported their homosexual relationships tended to be of a shorter and more carnal nature than their relationships with women. Bisexual women, on the other hand, tended to have fewer but more enduring homosexual, as well as heterosexual, relationships.

Zinik (1983) also found that 79% of his bisexual subjects reported that they had experienced some degree of conflict or confusion specifically due to their bisexuality. However, most subjects reported that such confu-sion was usually due to bisexuality's inherent complexity, their need as bisexuals to balance so many variables, and their lack of social support. Many of these subjects reported that they enjoyed being bisexual in spite of the difficulties, and that being bisexual contributed to their personal fulfillment. A small minority of subjects attributed their confusion to un-certainty over whether they were really heterosexual or homosexual; they considered bisexuality a transitional stage. However, a general trend did emerge. Most subjects reported experiencing conflict and confusion when initially discovering their dual erotic interests; however, this discomfort gradually dissipated after they adopted a bisexual identity and adapted their lifestyle accordingly.

Bisexuals reported experiencing the double stigma discussed earlier; they were frequently criticized as ''fence-sitters'' by heterosexuals and homosexuals (Blumstein & Schwartz, 1974, 1976a, 1976b; Bode, 1976; Klein, 1978; *Playboy*, 1983). Bisexuality appeared to be less problematic for women than men, due perhaps to the supportive climate of the women's movement, which does not see femininity, homosexuality, and ''sisterhood'' as incompatible. Blumstein and Schwartz (1974, 1976b) reported that many of the bisexual women they interviewed met their first homosexual partners through participation in the women's movement and feminist politics. For men, however, being bisexual caused more distress because society views male bisexuals as rejecting heterosexuality and masculinity.

The ''Playboy Sex Survey'' (*Playboy*, 1983) included 2,786 self-identified bisexual males and 948 bisexual females among the 100,000 readers who mailed in completed questionnaires. The survey found that 70% of their female bisexual subjects reported happy sex lives. Almost half of the male bisexuals reported dissatisfaction with their sex lives, making them the unhappiest of all the surveyed groups. The survey concluded that bisexual women seem to be enjoying the best of both worlds; however, for bisexual men ''it's more like getting the least from either world'' (*Playboy*, 1983, p. 211). In contrast, other studies (Saliba, 1982; Zinik, 1983) found no differences in the sexual satisfaction reported by groups of heterosexual, homosexual, and bisexual subjects.

In their study of homosexuality, Masters and Johnson (1979) studied 12 ambisexual subjects, 6 men and 6 women, whom they defined as people who enjoyed sexual activities with partners of both sexes but had no interest in establishing continuing relationships with either. These subjects were seen as well-adjusted in terms of having no psychiatric or work problems, but were characterized as ''detached and lonely.''

Several clinical studies (Harris, 1977; Markus, 1981; Twichell, 1974) found that bisexuals showed no differences from heterosexual and homosexual groups on several measures of psychological adjustment (the California Psychological Inventory, the Personal Orientation Inventory, the MMPI, and the Bem Sex Role Inventory). Zinik (1983) found no differences between groups of heterosexual, homosexual, and bisexual subjects on levels of anxiety, depression, and hostility as measured by an adjective check list.

Nurius (1983) found that bisexuals scored higher than heterosexuals, but lower than homosexuals, on a measure of dysfunctional depression. Using Kinsey scores, Weinberg and Williams (1974) compared males in the bisexual range (2-4) with those more exclusively homosexual (5 & 6). They tested the notion that bisexuals would be characterized by confusion and conflict, and thus manifest more psychological problems. They found that, compared with exclusive homosexuals, bisexuals anticipated more discrimination and scored higher in "passing" as heterosexuals. Weinberg and Williams did not find the bisexuals reporting more psychological difficulties, the only exception being that they were more likely to report feeling guilt, shame, or anxiety about their homosexual behavior. However, these feelings did not seem to foster other psychological problems.

CONCLUSION

The limited clinical and empirical studies available to date indicate that bisexuals as a group are generally no more or less well-adjusted than heterosexuals or homosexuals. Bisexuality may be experienced as a conflict for some individuals, while as a desirable form of flexibility for others. It may also be experienced as both conflict and flexibility for the same person at different times in his or her life. Indeed, tentative findings (Zinik, 1983) suggest that a well-adjusted bisexual identity may develop in stages somewhat similar to the stages of healthy homosexual identity formation outlined by Cass (1979). Because of sparse social support and conventional "either/or" thinking about sexuality, bisexuality may be initially experienced as a source of confusion, as the conflict model predicts. However, when a bisexual self-identity is maintained over time, at least some individuals reach a state of balance, as described by the flexibility model, in which dual sexual interests and behavior are successfully integrated into their self-concept and lifestyle.

REFERENCES

Bell, A. P., Weinberg, M. S., & Hammersmith, S. K. (1981). *Sexual preference: Its development in men and women*. Bloomington, IN: Indiana University Press.

Bergler, E. (1956). *Homosexuality: Disease or way of life?* New York: Hill & Wang.

Bieber, I. (1971, April). Playboy Panel: Homosexuality. *Playboy Magazine*, pp. 63-67.

Bisexual chic: Anyone goes. (1974, May 27). *Time Magazine*, p. 90.

Blumstein, P. W., & Schwartz, P. (1974). Lesbianism and bisexuality. In E. Goode & R. R. Troiden (Eds.), *Sexual divorce and sexual deviants* (pp. 278-295). New York: William Morrow.

Blumstein, P. W., & Schwartz, P. (1976a). Bisexuality in men. *Urban Life, 5*, 339-358.

Blumstein, P. W., & Schwartz, P. (1976b). Bisexuality in women. *Archives of Sexual Behavior, 5*, 171-181.

Bode, J. (1976). *View from another closet: Exploring bisexuality in women*. New York: Hawthorn.

Brody, J. (1974, March 24). Bisexual life-style appears to be spreading and not necessarily among swingers. *New York Times*, p. 37.

Carroll, J. (1974, February). Bisexual chic. *Oui Magazine*, pp. 115-120.

Cass, V. C. (1979). Homosexual identity formation: A theoretical model. *Journal of Homosexuality, 4*, 219-233.

Childs, E. K. (1976). Women's sexuality: A feminist view. In S. Cox (Ed.), *Female psychology: The emerging self.* Chicago: Science Research Associates.

Churchill, W. (1967). *Homosexual behavior among males: A cross-cultural and cross-species investigation*. New York: Hawthorn Books.

Coons, F. W. (1972). Ambisexuality as an alternative adaptation. *Journal of the American College Health Association, 21*, 142-144.

Cory, D. W., & LeRoy, J. P. (1963). *The homosexual and his society*. New York: Citadel Press.

Douglas, J. (1970). *Bisexuality*. London: Canova Press.

Fast, J. (1975). *Bisexual living*. New York: M. Evans.

Ford, C. S., & Beach, F. A. (1951). *Patterns of sexual behavior*. New York: Harper.

Freud, S. (1953). Three essays on the theory of sexuality. In J. Strachey (Ed. and Trans.), *The standard edition of the complete psychological works of Sigmund Freud* (Vol. 7, pp. 125-245). London: Hogarth Press. (Original work published 1901)

Gagnon, J. (1977). *Human sexualities*. Glenview, IL: Scott Foresman.

Gay America. (1983, August 8). *Newsweek Magazine*, pp. 30-36.

Gebhard, P. H. (1972). Incidence of overt homosexuality in the U.S. and Western Europe. In J. M. Livingood (Ed.), *NIMH Task Force on Homosexuality: Final Report and Papers*, (DHEW Publication No. HSM 72-9116, pp. 22-30). Rockville, MD: National Institute of Mental Health.

Harris, D. A. I. (1977). *Social psychological characteristics of ambisexuals*. Unpublished doctoral dissertation, University of Tennessee, Knoxville, TN.

Hurwood, B. J. (1974). *Bisexuals*. New York: Fawcett World.

Kelly, G. F. (1974). Bisexuality and the youth culture. *Homosexuality Counseling Journal, 1*(2), 16-25.

Kinsey, A. C., Pomeroy, W. B., & Martin, C. E. (1948). *Sexual behavior in the human male*. Philadelphia: W. B. SAunders.

Kinsey, A. C., Pomeroy, W. B., Martin, C. E., & Gebhard, P. E. (1953). *Sexual behavior in the human female*. Philadelphia: W. B. Saunders.

Klein, F. (1978). *The bisexual option*. New York: Arbor House.

Knox, L. (1974, July). The bisexual phenomena. *Viva Magazine*, pp. 42-45, 88, 94.

MacDonald, A. P. (1983). A little bit of lavender goes a long way: A critique of research on sexual orientation. *Journal of Sex Research, 19*, 94-100.

MacInnes, C. (1973). *Loving them both: A study of bisexuality and bisexuals*. London: Martin, Brian & O'Keefe.

Markus, E. (1981). An examination of psychological adjustment and sexual preference in the female (Doctoral dissertation, University of Missouri 1980). *Dissertation Abstracts International, 41*, 4338A.

Masters, W. H., & Johnson, V. E. (1979). *Homosexuality in perspective*. Boston: Little, Brown.

Mead, M. (1975, January). Bisexuality: What's it all about? *Redbook Magazine*, pp. 29-31.

Money, J. (1980). *Love and love sickness: The science of sex, gender differentiation and pairbonding*. Baltimore: Johns Hopkins Press.

Money, J., & Tucker, P. (1975). *Sexual signatures: On being a man or a woman*. Boston: Little, Brown.

The new bisexuals. (1974, May 13). *Time Magazine*, p. 79.

Nurius, P. S. (1983). Mental health implications of sexual orientation. *Journal of Sex Research, 19*, 119-136.

Playboy readers sex survey. (1983, May). *Playboy Magazine*, pp. 126-128, 136, 210-220.

Rubenstein, M. (1982). *An indepth study of bisexuality and its relation to self-esteem*. Unpublished doctoral dissertation, Institute for Advanced Study of Human Sexuality, San Francisco, CA.

Ruitenbeek, H. M. (Ed.). (1973). *Homosexuality: A changing picture*. London: Souvenir.

Saliba, P. (1982). Research project on sexual orientation. *The bi-monthly newsletter of the Bisexual Center of San Francisco, 6*(5), pp. 3-6.

Scott, J. (1978). *Wives who love women*. New York: Walker.

Stekel, W. (1922). *Bisexual love*. New York: Emerson Books.

Stern, J. (1961). *The sixth man*. New York: Doubleday.

Stoller, R. J. (1972). The "bedrock" of masculinity and femininity: Bisexuality. *Archives of General Psychiatry, 26*, 207-212.

Storms, M. (1978). Sexual orientation and self-perception. In P. Pilner, K. R. Blansteinm, I. M. Spiegel, T. Alloway, & L. Krames (Eds.), *Advances in the study of communication and affect: Perception of emotion in self and others* (Vol. 5). New York: Plenum.

Storms, M. (1980). Theories of sexual orientation. *Journal of Personality and Social Psychology, 38*, 783-792.

Tripp, C A. (1975). *The homosexual matrix*. New York: McGraw-Hill.

Twichell, J. (1974). Sexual liberality and personality: A pilot study. In J. R. Smith & L. G. Smith (Eds.), *Beyond monogamy: Recent studies of sexual alternatives in marriage* (pp. 230-245). Baltimore: Johns Hopkins University Press.

Warren, C. A. B. (1974). *Identity and community in the gay world*. New York: John Wiley & Sons.
Weinberg, M. S., & Williams, C. J. (1974). *Male homosexuals: Their problems and adaptations*. New York: Penguin Books.
Wolff, C. (1977). *Bisexuality: A study*. London: Quartet Books.
Zinik, G. (1983). *The relationship between sexual orientation and eroticism, cognitive flexibility, and negative affect*. Unpublished doctoral dissertation, University of California, Santa Barbara, CA.

Bisexuality:
Reassessing Our Paradigms
of Sexuality

Jay P. Paul, PhD (cand.)
University of California-Berkeley

ABSTRACT. Sexuality research currently needs to re-examine critically its constructs of sexual orientation and identity for theoretical inconsistencies and simplistic assumptions about the nature of sexual desire continue to plague it. This becomes evident when one reviews how the confluence of heterosexual and homosexual desire in individuals is "explained" by theories that assume a basic dichotomy in sexual orientation. This article examines how categories such as homosexual, heterosexual, and bisexual have developed, and differentiates between their utility as social labels and as scientific constructs. The intrusion of social and political considerations into the scientific investigation of sexuality is noted, and it is suggested that the use of these labels impedes rather than advances such study.

The confluence of heterosexual and homosexual desire in individuals is a reality discrepant with many of our formulations of sexuality. Treating bisexuality as a discrete entity rather than subsuming it in discussions of homosexuality presents a set of definitional and conceptual problems that highlight the gaps between theoretical representations and the realities of human sexuality. There is far more variability and fluidity in many people's sexual patterns than theoretical notions tend to allow, suggesting that researchers have imparted an artificial consistency to an inchoate sexual universe.

It is not that science has ignored the indisputable fact that the sexual biographies of many include sexual experiences with both men and women, but rather the theoretical *meanings* given to those experiences. The tendency is to deny the legitimacy of one's erotic responsiveness to either males or females; thereby, one assumes that all people are either

---

Mr. Paul is currently completing his doctoral research in clinical psychology at the University of California, Berkeley, and is in clinical practice. He also serves as Board member and Secretary of the Bisexual Center in San Francisco, and as a consulting editor to the *Journal of Homosexuality*. Reprint requests may be sent to the author, c/o The University of California, Psychology Clinic, 2205 Tolman Hall, Berkeley, CA 94720.

basically heterosexual or homosexual. This refusal to allow for an equivalent basic bisexuality in some portion of the population leads to a variety of explanations for bisexual patterns.

MacDonald (1981) notes three interpretations that reinforce the heterosexual/homosexual dichotomy. First, bisexuality can be viewed as a transitory phenomenon; the individual eventually comes to re-establish his or her ''true'' orientation. In this case, the bisexual phase may be seen as a wish to be ''chic'' or ''trendy,'' or as an indication of disturbed interpersonal relations. Second, bisexuality can be viewed as a transitional state, with the individual shifting from one sexual pole to the other—this is primarily noted in cases where the shift is from heterosexuality to exclusive homosexuality. In this instance, the person who attempts to maintain any bisexual lifestyle is seen as ''fence-sitting,'' avoiding a true commitment to anyone (Masters & Johnson, 1979), or as a ''pathetic creature'' suffering from arrested development and identity confusion (Cory & LeRoy, 1963). And third, bisexuality is perceived as a denial of one's fundamental homosexual orientation due to internalized homophobia, or one's fears of being either socially stigmatized or socially isolated (Blair, 1974; Harry & Lovely, 1979; Schafer, 1976).

If one can ignore bisexuality, conceiving sexuality dichotomously is attractively simple. Such a binary division is rooted in the basic biological dichotomy of male/female, and assumes a similarly clear distinction between those fundamentally homosexual and those fundamentally heterosexual, based on the gender of one's sexual partners. Where there has been both heterosexual and homosexual activity, various assumptions guide the observer in the detection of the person's ''true'' orientation by one or two ''fundamental'' signs, i.e., sexual fantasies or dreams. Proposed etiologies for sexual orientation vary but tend to assume that such qualities are fixed by early childhood and possess an immutability and temporal constancy analogous to that of gender identity. This lends weight to notions of an individual's sexuality being a primary organizing principle of personality and lifestyle, bypassing the social/historical context. While the impact of social forces on the construction of specific sexual labels and roles may be acknowledged, this factor is undercut by attempts to view heterosexual and homosexual orientations as entities that both transcend a specific historical context and deal with much more than erotic and affectional desires.

Such a system is neat and clear cut in its categorization of exclusively heterosexual or homosexual persons, but it demands the grafting on of a host of assumptions to deal with the facts of bisexuality. Those who prefer the precision of such a model to the muddle of real life transfer blame from the theory to the person eroticizing both men and women. Such a person is seen as disturbed or confused. To those willing to examine the facts more critically, the strained reasoning used to dismiss bisexuality is one additional token of the inadequacy and unscientific nature of such a sexual paradigm.

This article will point out some of the critical questions that have arisen both in the attempt to fit bisexuality into current constructs of sexuality, and in current re-examinations of the issue of sexual identity. These questions emerge out of an attempt to understand the nature of sexuality and the divisions of homosexuality, heterosexuality, and bisexuality. A primary issue is the essentiality of the given sexual categories and identities, an assumption which leads to notions that sexuality and sexual desire as fixed and static in individuals. It is vital to identify our criteria for the current elements in our organization of sex. What determines the leap from behavior to identity? Furthermore, what is the justification for embellishing such an identity with non-erotic components? How appropriate are these labels as personal, integrative constructs?

In looking at this, we must be careful to disentangle the scientific construct from the idiomatic usage of these labels peculiar to our given culture and time. The difficulty of this is pointed out by Blumstein and Schwartz (1977):

> We take the simple position that personal views about sexuality in the abstract reflect wider cultural understandings, and affect, in turn, the concrete constructions people place on their own feelings and experiences, and thereby affect their behavior. So it is essential to accept cultural understandings of sexuality as crucial data, while at the same time rejecting the scientific validity of their underlying premise. (p. 31)

It is clear that acknowledging the power of the terms homosexual, bisexual, and heterosexual as *social* labels does not indicate a validity to our constructions of sexuality, which tend to be reifications of popular myths of sexuality. A review of historical conceptualizations of sexual identity highlights the culture-bound nature of our scientific understandings.

HISTORICAL PERSPECTIVES

To speak of early formulations of sexual orientation is to refer to a relatively recent scientific perspective on the basis of homosexual behavior. The 19th century saw the transformation of homosexuality from a vice (by Judaeo-Christian moral standards) into a "condition"— one that shifted focus from the act itself to the actor, from a specific point in time to a life history. Our attention has been fixed upon the person ever since.

The last century's transformation of socially censured sexual acts into signs of medical illness or pervasive biological anomalies led to the emergence of the "homosexual person," who differed constitutionally from the "normal" population. This was an extension of the then-popular concept of psychophysical parallelism, which posited a simple congruence between character and physiological traits. Socially sanctioned forms of sexual expression were reinforced by science's assertion that they were biological norms. Notions of the naturalness of the male-female configuration (justified by reproductive necessity) led to an immediate categorization of erotic desires by the biological sex of the pairing. Simplistic assumptions led to a confusion and confounding of sexual orientation, social sex-roles, and gender identity. Bisexuality was termed "psychic hermaphroditism," while those actively homosexual were labeled "inverts," the "third sex," and the "intersexes." Scientists probed, measured, and examined, expecting to find signs of physiological masculinization accompanying an assumed psychological masculinization of female homosexuals, and signs of feminization in male homosexuals. Although some physicians initially saw homosexuality as a product of moral or nervous degeneration, the primary theoretical focus was on the so-called "invert."

The simplistic notion that the homosexually active person suffered from some form of gender inversion, given the eroticizing of others of the same sex, runs into problems in dealing with the fundamentals of non-exclusive homosexuality or bisexuality. Various attempts were made to differentiate the "congenital" from the "acquired" in sexual behavior. The tendency, as in much writing on sex since then, has been to view homosexual behavior as innate and heterosexual behavior as an overlay of the homosexual substratum (Ellis, 1972). The emphasis on fundamental differences between the heterosexual and homosexual groupings led to some ludicrous ascriptions by sexologists as distinguished as Havelock Ellis (1972):

> Male inverts are sometimes unable to whistle. In both sexes a notable youthfulness of appearance is often preserved into adult age. The love of green (which is normally a preferred color chiefly by children and especially girls) is frequently observed. (p. 232)

The concept of the homosexual as intrinsically distinct from the rest of the population was a notion initially widely accepted and approved of by those open about their homoeroticism. It was the basis for arguments for decriminalization of homosexuality, since this theory could be used as a defense against charges of moral culpability for homosexual behavior, and against the apparently groundless fear of homosexuals seducing and "converting" others. The Scientific Humanitarian Committee, led by

Magnus Hirschfeld, combined goals of scientific study and social and political activism (Lauritsen & Thorstad, 1974). However, it was not recognized until later what power this construct unwittingly gave the medical profession: power to act as agents of social control under the guise of treating illness.

Freud switched the focus of etiological theories for homosexuality from biological to psycho-social developmental factors, declaring that initially the sexual instinct exists independent of a sexual object (Freud, 1905), and that the debate over "inherited" versus "acquired" forms of homosexuality was thus inappropriate (Freud, 1922). His concept of an innate bisexual disposition acting as a primary unconscious force was based upon fallacious assumptions current at the time regarding the biological bisexuality of the fetus. This pointed to his own difficulties in escaping the biological determinism and psychophysical parallelism of the period. Innate bisexuality was conceptualized as nothing more than an initial biological potential for sexual attraction to both men and women; rather than expecting it to be expressed behaviorally, it was hypothesized to be an unconscious driving force for certain psychological processes. Freud assumed a normal course of development must lead to a heterosexual object-choice; only a series of vicissitudes could lead the libido astray to a homosexual object-choice. Bisexual activity, rather than proceeding naturally from an innate bisexual disposition, was construed as a kind of inversion, of either the "amphigenic" or "contingent" variety (Freud, 1905). Although object-choice was not assumed to be innate, it was seen as established and invariant by early childhood.

These early formulations of heterosexual and homosexual patterns were based on the assumption that homosexual behavior appears in only a very small and distinct subgroup of the population. Such behavior was taken as stemming from a basic and fixed aspect of the person. As Richardson (1983/1984) points out, the publication of the Kinsey group studies of male and female sexual behavior in 1948 and 1953 posed a major definitional crisis for these scientific formulations of homosexuality. The data showed a high incidence of homosexual behavior and response (especially in the male sample), as well as apparent fluctuations of all kinds in respondents' sexual orientations.

A host of new terms emerged to safeguard the theoretical construct of a "real" homosexuality, differentiating "genuine" from "incidental," "situational," or "temporary" homosexuals. Whereas earlier formulations identified an internal state on the basis of observable behavior, the new distinctions demanded the concept of an internal state that could be in direct contradiction to behavioral signs. In a perversion of Freud's concept of latent homosexuality, it was generally assumed that practicing heterosexuals could be "latent homosexuals." Paradoxically, this apparent blurring of boundaries *maintained* the essential homosexual/

heterosexual distinction. It thus seemed that only medical experts or a retrospective analysis could determine one's "true self." This perspective left no room for the notion of someone being a "real" bisexual, as science could discredit behavioral evidence and claim to know the person better than the person could know himself or herself.

The last 20 years have led to a new set of ideas about sexual orientation, broadening the concept to that of "sexual identity." Richardson (1983/1984) sees these ideas as a consequence of an infusion of sociological research and theory in the area, the emergence of the gay liberation movement, and the increasing acceptance of homosexuality in our society. Sociological theory emphasized the social impact of labeling and deviant status, leading to the gay liberation movement's appropriation of the labeling function to create a nonpathologizing (and nonpathological) nomenclature. The emergence of the notion of the gay identity as distinct from the homosexual identity was part of this process. (The lesbian/gay distinction emerged later out of other considerations, so "gay" will be treated initially in this discussion as a genderless term, in line with historical events.)

The notion of the gay identity developed within a formulation of the "homosexual" along sociological rather than psycho(patho)logical lines. The problems facing the homosexual person were not fundamentally a product of personality or internal organization, but of society's punitive treatment of homosexuals as deviates (Weinberg, 1973). An awareness of the power of the labeling process led homosexuals to relabel themselves with a term that was positive and free of perjorative associations (Morin, 1977).

Being "gay" was initially an idealized reversal of connotations attached to being "homosexual." The individual could accept and enjoy homosexuality, while dismissing the negative societal stereotypes and attitudes about homosexuals:

> At its best it means not limiting oneself to a stereotype—a model of some previous homosexual—for one's personality, at work, at parties, with a lover. . . . It means being able to investigate one's preferences and desires in sexual roles where one chooses. . . . In essence, it means being convinced that any erotic orientation and preference may be housed in any human being. (Weinberg, 1973, p. 71)

> Homosexual is the label that was applied to Gay people as a device for separating us from the rest of the population. . . . *Gay* is a descriptive label we have assigned to ourselves as a way of reminding ourselves and others that awareness of our sexuality facilitates a capability rather than creating a restriction. It means that we are *capable* of fully loving a person of the same gender. . . . But the

label does not limit us. We who are Gay can still love someone of other gender. (Clark, 1977, pp. 103-106)

Although it might be seen as another instance of the bisexual identity being subsumed under the homosexual identity, Clark's use of "Gay" to include non-exclusively homosexual persons was in keeping with the early aspirations of the Gay Liberation movement. One of its initial ideals was the sexual liberation of all people, freeing them from categories of gender and sexual orientation to act and love as they chose (Orlando, 1984). It was anticipated that the categories of heterosexuality and homosexuality would lose their power to polarize actions, feelings and people (Altman, 1971).

Just as the emphasis of the Gay Liberation movement shifted over the course of its first decade (Altman, 1982), so did the implications of the "gay" label. Initially, it was used in a self-conscious counteracting effort to posit a healthy alternative to the sullied "homosexual" tag. The slogan "Gay is Good" was meant to offset the conventional perception of homosexuals as "sick." But "gay" soon acquired a new, more concrete meaning as an identity encompassing far more than the sexual and affectional aspects of self. In part, this reflected a shift in political tactics, as the goal of massive changes in the general population's attitudes about sex seemed unrealistic. "Gay people" were redefined in terms of being another disadvantaged minority in our society, and the image of the "gay world" of secretive sexually tinged assemblages was replaced by the "gay community" with its own culture, history, social organizations, and politics. Within that community a far more differentiated picture of the "gay identity" emerged. As a consequence, popular perceptions of homosexuality have undergone a great deal of change. In the midst of this, it is sometimes difficult to remember that the homosexual-as-an-entity is a notion that has existed in our culture only about 120 years, and is alien to most societies in which homosexuality is common (Altman, 1982; Ford & Beach, 1951).

POLITICS OF THE GAY IDENTITY

From the assumption that the "gay identity" represented a positive counterpoise to the "homosexual identity" came a set of criteria for the "truly gay" person, based both on values espoused in the gay community, and research on what factors promote a healthy integration of one's homosexuality into one's self-concept. This research has concerned itself with the "coming out" process and the developmental stages hypothesized in the formation of a "gay identity," and is reflective of the values and assumptions of certain arbiters of health and self-actualization from the ranks of "public gays" (Lee, 1977). A primary criterion is one's sense of affiliation with the gay community "in a cultural and sociable sense" (Warren, 1974, p. 149), which can be measured in as simplistic a manner as comparing the relative numbers of one's homosexual and heterosexual friends (Harry & Lovely, 1979). Being exclusively homosexual in one's sexual and affectional relationships has also been assumed to be indicative of one's "commitment" to the "gay community." Such measures place the person who is not exclusively homosexual at an immediate disadvantage. Ironically, "choosing" to keep what may be a more constricted social life is valued as emotionally and morally superior, and as politically purer.

In the process of reconstructing the homosexual as a member of a distinct minority group, not only has a positive value been placed on separatist lifestyles, but also on old beliefs in the essentiality of homosexuality. Articles on "coming out" and homosexual identity formation hint at a basic inner state of homosexual desire (almost equivalent to antiquated notions of a "homosexual sex drive") that is fixed at an early age (Berzon in Giteck, 1984; Malyon, 1981) and seems to emerge at various points in a person's life only because it has been denied, repressed, or too emotionally "loaded" to be acknowledged (Bozett, 1980; Malyon, 1981; Ross, 1971; Voeller & Walters, 1978). The idea of the emergence of homosexual feelings as indicating a belated recognition of the "true self" (Coleman, 1982; De Monteflores & Schultz, 1978; McDonald, 1982) is a recrudescence of the old invariant-inner-state/variable-behavior explanation for the Kinsey data's contradiction of biologically based theories of sexuality. The search for biological bases for homosexuality remind one of the third-sex notions of the last century; the investment in such ideas by some in the gay and lesbian communities may be similarly politically motivated.

The problem of the intrusion of political considerations into the manner in which scientists interpret data is exemplified by the arguments of Whitam (1981), who has strongly resisted any theories positing a socially constructed "homosexual role." He distinguishes homosexual activity from a biologically determined "homosexual orientation." To justify his viewpoints, he makes sweeping assertions about the universality of "basic elements appearing in homosexual subcultures," and of early appearing nonsexual "complex behavioral elements" of the homosexual orientation (p. 68). (One of these universal behavioral elements of a homosexual orientation is "the tendency toward entertainment and the arts.") Furthermore, he attacks the theoretical basis of Goode's notions of a "homosexual role" by pointing out purely political considerations:

> While sociologists may lament the misuse of sociological concepts by homophobic elements it nevertheless is true that the view that

homosexuality as an orientation is a superficial, learned, flexible aspect of one's personality feeds the primordial fears of the Anglo-Saxons that homosexuals are dangerous people and that homosexual orientations can be taught to others. . . . Such [judicial] rulings favorable to blacks and other ethnic groups, women, and the handicapped have frequently proceeded on the legal principle of "immutable characteristics," an advantage which gays will never achieve as long as the social scientific formulation of their sexuality proceeds along the lines of "sexual preference," "choice," "role," "alternative life style," and "social learning." (pp. 70-71)

Whereas the evidence of political and patently unscientific concerns intruding upon the scientific judgments of someone such as Whitam is clear, much of the influence of social and political factors in this area is far less overt because of the rudimentary level of our understanding of sexuality, especially outside of a specific familiar (and constrictive) cultural context. As a brief example of this, we can continue to examine the interpretations made by some gay-identified authors of heterosexuality comingling with homosexuality. It is not that the people singled out need to be criticized any more than any others in this field, but that owing to the large political component grafted onto the idea of homosexual or gay identity, it is easier to examine the political and social assumptions that undergird their scholarly work.

THE BISEXUAL AND THE HOMOSEXUAL COMMUNITIES

Many authors have tried to adopt a more constructionist approach to the concept of homosexual identity, emphasizing the individual as an active participant in the development of meanings for homoerotic feelings or behavior and the creation of an identity based on those meanings (Cass, 1979; Minton & McDonald, 1983/1984; Troiden, 1979; Troiden & Goode, 1980; Weinberg, 1978). However, these authors focus more on the consequences relabeling these experiences have on personal identity than they do on the interactions between the individual's understanding of his or her (1) potential for homosexual relations, (2) potential for heterosexual relations, (3) actual relationships, and (4) self-labeling. Part of the decision to adopt a homosexual identity, as opposed to a bisexual identity or a heterosexual identity, involves not only the personal significance or value one attaches to one's homosexual experience and perceived potential, but also one's simultaneous evaluation of one's heterosexuality. The authors may mention someone who went through a period of seeing himself (in these studies) as bisexual; however, there is no parallel investigation of the factors that may have led to such an identification or the need to change it. That lapse leads to an implicit discounting of the bisexual identity and to treating it as a potential intermediate identity, but not as a real option if one is to fully integrate homosexuality into one's sense of self.

Given that the self-identified bisexual can expect hostility and rejection both from the mainstream heterosexual hegemony and from self-identified homosexuals, and that social context is a powerful determinant in how one interprets behaviors and feelings (a reiterated point in these models of identity formation), there is tremendous pressure on the individual to identify as homosexual. Once one identifies as homosexual, there is then further pressure to be exclusively homosexual (especially among a subgroup of lesbian feminists) in order to be accepted (Blumstein & Schwartz, 1977). Thus, the adoption of a label for political purposes, as described in Lee (1977) and by a quoted statement in Blumstein and Schwartz (1976), may later impinge upon actual behavior. Sagarin (1973) points to that by labeling themselves as homosexual, people who are homosexually active "become entrapped in a false consciousness. They believe that they discover what they are (and by implication, since this is a discovery, they must have been this way all along). Learning their 'identity' they become . . . boxed into their own biographies" (p. 10). Altman (1982) suggests that there may be a "new style emerging among younger "gays," in which more will behave bisexually, but will continue to identify as homosexual "for political reasons" (pp. 15-16). He then goes on to undercut that identification as continuing solely for political reasons by negating the discriminatory value of sexual behavior, implying both that bisexually active "gays" will be unlikely to find significant emotional involvements with opposite-sex partners, and that the non-sexual aspects of a homosexual identification would assume greater significance.

The attempt to render the homosexual identity as a higher order construct than the bisexual identity by emphasizing its meaning for non-sexual aspects of self necessitates a belief in a biological or fixed basis for these non-erotic components. Otherwise, it requires an explanation of why the bisexual identity could not, allowed to develop alongside specifically bisexual social institutions, assume many of the non-sexual trappings the homosexual identity has taken on in the last decade. When we look longitudinally, we can see the tremendous change in the social power of the "gay community." We have no evidence to counter that a hypothetical "bisexual community" could not similarly emerge, developing its own set of personal attributions for "the bisexual." Just as the content implied by the gay label has changed over the course of a decade, so could the content of the bisexual label.

The issue of marginality for "the bisexual," caught between two sexual categories that define a clear social identity, has been outlined elsewhere (Paul, 1983/1984). The confusion between scientific and popularized meanings for sexual identity is highlighted by this conflict. The bisexual has neither a clear social identity nor a strong political voice, which results in bisexually active people not gaining appropriate recognition in scientific theory, given the history of social and political intrusions into an ostensibly scientific study of sexuality.

THE UTILITY OF THE SEXUAL IDENTITY CONSTRUCT IN RESEARCH

Articles reviewing the use of various terms of sexual identity in studies argue, with a great deal of confirmatory evidence, the research in the area of sexuality has been consistently flawed by theoretical inconsistencies and simplistic determinations of homosexual and heterosexual samples (De Cecco, 1981; De Cecco & Shively, 1983/1984; MacDonald, 1981; Paul & Weinrich, 1982). Researchers have rarely bothered with conceptual definitions of the terms gay, lesbian, homosexual, heterosexual, straight, ambisexual, or bisexual. Operational definitions have been ridiculously crude and demonstrate a serious naiveté about sexuality. As Shively, Jones, and De Cecco (1983/1984) note: "Sexual orientation was treated as if it were a palpable, unitary phenomenon although it was conceived in divergent and sometimes contradictory ways" (p. 134).

Studies may have used sexual behavior, sexual fantasy, physical location, self-report, or any number of divergent cues. When the Kinsey scale was used, it was usually reduced from a continuum to a set of categories—primarily heterosexual and homosexual (Weinberg & Williams, 1974). MacDonald (1981) points to a number of studies ostensibly of "homosexuals" which covered a range of persons who were actively homosexual and, to some degree, also heterosexually responsive. Blumstein and Schwartz (1977) point out the lack of correspondence between self-described sexual identity and the sexual biographies of those in their study sample who did not have exclusively heterosexual or exclusively homosexual histories. Part of that inconsistency appears to be a reflection of the variety of meanings attached to these labels beyond that of the biological sex of one's sexual partners: Some are perjorative and associated with social sex-role, others political in content, or diverging from the simple consideration of erotic desire.

Despite the divergent meanings given to the labels "gay" and "homosexual"—with the gay (or lesbian) identity presumably reflecting a greater political and social involvement with the so-called gay community, a higher valuation placed on one's homosexuality, and the extent to which awareness of one's homosexuality is seen as an organizing principle in various areas of one's life—it is unclear how often individuals (respondents or researchers) make the necessary distinctions between the terms. Furthermore, there is evidence that people may decide that more than one term is applicable to them (Kooden, Morin, Riddle, Rogers, Song, & Strassburger, 1979). These labels have been most often used in defining and differentiating groups in a study, a practice that still can mean tremendous variability either of subjects within a group or between studies supposedly of the same target population. Given their different meanings for the same labels, it is important for researchers to recognize the focus of their research and to look at the issues they want to examine as those between *people* rather than between categories in an artificially imposed dichotomy or trichotomy of sexuality. If one is interested in studying homosexual behavior, it is clear that studying individuals who identify as gay, lesbian, homosexual, or even bisexual will represent only a small group of those who embody homosexual desire. A common complaint is that, because "bisexuals" covers such a vast range of individuals with such varying histories and potentials, to talk about them as a unity is to invite ridicule. But that is also something that we are discovering in study after study about "homosexuals" and "heterosexuals." Given that these categories both fail to represent the total population engaged in a particular form of sexual behavior one might be studying, and also provide no clear consistency within their groupings, it is hard to understand their benefit. They tend to reduce individuals and relationships into populations about whom researchers make all sorts of assumptions. Rather than being meaningful terms for categorizing various types according to erotic and affectional factors, they tend to be merely instrumental in determining how others will initially react to and think about those individuals as *social* rather than sexual beings.

Yet an alternative is not immediately obvious. There is wisdom in stepping back from the individual and focusing instead on the various kinds of relationships individuals may form, as suggested by De Cecco and Shively (1983/1984). Rather than imposing identities on people that presumably dictate how they interact with others, researchers need to articulate a descriptive language of relationships. Authors and researchers have pointed out that it is not possible to attach a single meaning to homosexual behavior, but that it acquires its personal meaning for the participants through the relational context in which it occurs (Weinberg, 1978; Troiden, 1979; Cass, 1983/1984; Minton & McDonald, 1983/1984). Any given relationship is unique; it is not simply a summation of fixed or static qualities in the individual, but a reflection of the relationship's history, anticipated future, aims, and rules for each member. In addition, studied relationships can have an immediacy and palpability that categorized individuals do not.

CONCLUSION

The field of sexuality research is at a point where it has the resources to compare critically the current model of sexuality in western society with differing cross-cultural and trans-historical perspectives. Research theory must undergo a transition in which it sheds the accretions of folk mythologies and politically determined assumptions about sex so as to be able to reach new levels of undersatnding. In such research, those involved must be careful to separate out constructs that are popular from those that provide scientific insight. As Jonathan Katz said:

The words *heterosexual* and *homosexual* represent a particular conjunction of a gender category and an erotic category. Because of the reigning heterosexual hegemony, we're only beginning to understand that there were other basic ways of thinking about, and institutionalizing, sexuality in the past. That opens up the possibility that in the future we can have a completely different social organization of sex. (Hall, 1983, p. 41)

REFERENCES

Altman, D. (1982). *The homosexualization of America, the Americanization of the homosexual.* New York: St. Martin's Press.

Altman, D. (1971). *Homosexual oppression and liberation.* New York: Avon Books.

Blair, R. (1974). Counseling concerns and bisexual behavior. *The Homosexual Counseling Journal, 1*(2), 26-30.

Blumstein, P. W., & Schwartz, P. (1976). Bisexuality in men. *Urban Life, 5,* 339-358.

Blumstein, P. W., & Schwartz, P. (1977). Bisexuality: Some social-psychological issues. *Journal of Social Issues, 33,* 30-45.

Bozett, F. W. (1980). Gay fathers: How and why they disclose their homosexuality to their children. *Family Relations, 29,* 173-179.

Cass, V. C. (1983/1984). Homosexual identity: A concept in need of definition. *Journal of Homosexuality, 9*(2/3), 105-126.

Cass, V. C. (1979). Homosexual identity formation: A theoretical model. *Journal of Homosexuality, 4,* 219-235.

Clark, D. (1977). *Loving someone gay.* New York: Signet Books.

Coleman, E. (1982). Developmental stages of the coming-out process. In W. Paul, J. D. Weinrich, J. C. Gonsiorek, & M. E. Hotvedt (Eds.), *Homosexuality: Social, psychological, and biological issues* (pp. 149-158). Beverly Hills, CA: Sage Publications.

Cory, D. & LeRoy, J. P. (1963). *The homosexual and his society.* New York: Citadel Press.

De Cecco, J. P. (1981). Definition and meaning of sexual orientation. *Journal of Homosexuality, 6*(4), 51-67.

De Cecco, J. P., & Shively, M. G. (1983/1984). From sexual identity to sexual relationships: A contextual shift. *Journal of Homosexuality, 9*(2/3), 1-26.

De Monteflores, C., & Schultz, S. J. (1978). Coming out: Similarities and differences for lesbians and gay men. *Journal of Social Issues, 34,* 59-72.

Ellis, H. (1972). *The psychology of sex: A manual for students.* New York: Emerson Books. (Originally published 1938)

Ford, C. S., & Beach, F. A. (1951). *Patterns of sexual behavior.* New York: Harper & Row.

Freud, S. (1961). Three essays on the theory of sexuality. In J. Strachey (Ed. and Trans.), *The standard edition of the complete psychological works of Sigmund Freud* (Vol. 7). London: Hogarth Press. (Original work published 1905)

Freud, S. (1961). Psychogenesis of a case of homosexuality in a woman. In J. Strachey (Ed. and Trans.), *The standard edition of the complete psychological works of Sigmund Freud* (Vol. 18). London: Hogarth Press. (Original work published 1922)

Giteck, L. (1984, October 2). The gay theory of relativity: Family by design. *The Advocate,* pp. 28, 33, 56.

Hall, R. (1983, June 23). Historian Jonathan Katz: A new documentary for a minority in question. *The Advocate,* pp. 37-41, 79.

Harry, J. & Lovely, R. (1979). Gay marriages and communities of sexual orientation. *Alternative Lifestyles, 2,* 177-200.

Kooden, H. D., Morin, S. F., Riddle, D. I., Rogers, M., Sang, B. E., and Strassburger, F. (1979). *Removing the stigma: Final report, task force on the status of lesbian and gay male psychologists.* Washington, D.C.: American Psychological Association.

Lauritsen, J., & Thorstad, D. (1974). *The early homosexual rights movement (1864-1935).* New York: Times Change Press.

Lee, J. A. (1977). Going public: A study in the sociology of homosexual liberation. *Journal of Homosexuality, 3,* 49-78.

MacDonald, A. P., Jr. (1981). Bisexuality: Some comments on research and theory. *Journal of Homosexuality, 6*(3), 21-33.

Malyon, A. (1981/1982). Psychotherapeutic implications of internalized homophobia in gay males. *Journal of Homosexuality, 7*(2/3), 59-69.

Malyon, A. (1981). The homosexual adolescent: Developmental issues and social bias. *Child Welfare, 60,* 321-330.

Masters, W. M., & Johnson, V. E. (1979). *Homosexuality in perspective.* Boston: Little, Brown.

McDonald, G. J. (1982). Individual differences in the coming-out process for gay men: Implications for theoretical models. *Journal of Homosexuality, 8*(1), 47-60.

Minton, H. L., & McDonald, G. J. (1983/1984). Homosexual identity formation as a developmental process. *Journal of Homosexuality, 9*(2/3), 91-104.

Morin, S. F. (1977). Heterosexual bias in psychological research on lesbianism and male homosexuality. *American Psychologist, 32,* 629-637.

Orlando, L. (1984, February 25). Loving whom we choose: Bisexuality and the lesbian/gay community. Where we stand. *Gay Community News, 11,* pp. 000-000.

Paul, J. P. (1983/1984). The bisexual identity: An idea without social recognition. *Journal of Homosexuality, 9*(2/3), 45-63.

Paul, W., & Weinrich, J. D. (1982). Whom and what we study: Definition and scope of sexual orientation. In W. Paul, J. D. Weinrich, J. C. Gonsiorek, & M. E. Hotvedt (Eds.), *Homosexuality: Social, psychological, and biological issues* (pp. 23-28). Beverly Hills, CA: Sage.

Richardson, D. (1983/1984). The dilemma of essentiality in homosexual theory. *Journal of Homosexuality, 9*(2/3), 79-90.

Ross, H. L. (1971). Modes of adjustment of married homosexuals. *Social Problems, 18,* 385-393.

Sagarin, E. (1973). The good guys, the bad guys and the gay guys. *Contemporary Sociology, 2*(1), 3-13.

Schafer, S. (1976). Sexual and social problems of lesbians. *Journal of Sex Research, 12,* 50-69.

Shively, M. G., Jones, C., & De Cecco, J. P. (1983/1984). Research on sexual orientation: Definitions and methods. *Journal of Homosexuality, 9*(2/3), 127-136.

Troiden, R. R. (1979). Becoming homosexual: A model of gay identity acquisition. *Psychiatry, 42,* 362-373.

Troiden, R. R., & Goode, E. (1980). Variables related to the acquisition of a gay identity. *Journal of Homosexuality, 5,* 383-392.

Voeller, B., & Walters, J. (1978). Gay fathers. *The Family Coordinator, 27,* 149-157.

Warren, C. A. B. (1974). *Identity and community in the gay world.* New York: John Wiley & Sons.

Weinberg, G. (1973). *Society and the healthy homosexual.* New York: Anchor Books.

Weinberg, M. S., & Williams, C. J. (1974). *Male homosexuals: Their problems and adaptations.* New York: Penguin Books.

Weinberg, T. S. (1978). On "doing" and "being" gay: Sexual behavior and homosexual male self-identity. *Journal of Homosexuality, 4,* 143-157.

Whitam, F. L. (1981). A reply to Goode on "The homosexual role." *Journal of Sex Research, 17,* 66-72.

Sexual Orientation:
A Multi-Variable Dynamic Process

Fritz Klein, MD
Institute of Sexual Behavior, Inc.
San Diego

Barry Sepekoff, PhD (cand.)
New York University

Timothy J. Wolf, PhD
Institute of Sexual Behavior, Inc.
San Diego

ABSTRACT. Theory and research concerning sexual orientation has been restricted in its scope and influence by the lack of clear and widely accepted definitions of terms like heterosexual, bisexual, and homosexual. In an attempt to better demarcate and understand the complexities of human sexual attitudes, emotions, and behavior, the Klein Sexual Orientation Grid (KSOG) was developed and administered. The KSOG is composed of seven variables that are dimensions of sexual orientation, each of which is rated by the subject as applying to the present, past, or ideal. Analysis of the data from subjects who filled out the KSOG in *Forum Magazine* indicated that the instrument was a reliable and valid research tool which took into consideration the multi-variable and dynamic aspects of sexual orientation.

Theoretical positions regarding sexual orientation have been problematic because they have rigidly demarcated particular orientations, derived norms from clinical populations, and often been biased. Research instruments investigating sexual orientation tended to be as limited as the theoretical positions they were based on. Researchers have failed operationally or conceptually to define sexual orientation, by not providing clear or consistent definitions. This study gives evidence that sexual orientation cannot be reduced to a bipolar or even tripolar process, but most be recognized within a dynamic and multi-variate framework.

Rigid dichotomization of sexual orientation has been the usual practice. Most theory and research have viewed people as either heterosexual or not. The idea that bisexuality was non-existent was supported and

---

Mr. Sepekoff is a doctoral candidate in Human Sexuality at New York University.

35

perpetuated by Freud (1910), Bieber (1976), von Krafft-Ebing (1886-1939), and Ellis (1965). Although Freud believed all persons have bisexual capacities, he also believed that patients would cling to claims of bisexuality in order to avoid coming to terms with their homosexuality. As Freud (1910) stated: "A man's heterosexuality will not tolerate homosexuality" (p. 472). According to the Freudian viewpoint, the ultimate sexual adjustment of the patient was either heterosexual or homosexual.

Heterosexual bias is closely related to the strict demarcation of sexual orientation. According to Freud (1905), heterosexuality consisted of normal behavior and homosexuality of deviant behavior. Just as Freud viewed adult homosexuality as arrested development, von Krafft-Ebing (1939) viewed it as pathological and characterized congenital inversion as a "functional sign of degeneration" using degeneration in the evolutionary sense of "falling away from the genus" (pp. 70-71).

The view of homosexuality as deviance was based on data from clinical populations. Freud based much of his theory on his observations of patients, primarily female, who sought psychotherapy. Bieber, studying the factors contributing to homosexuality, arrived at his conclusions as a result of his study of male patients in psychoanalysis. The first person to question the use of clinical samples was Hooker (1969). Based on her study of the environmental components of homosexuality, Hooker concluded that inferences drawn from psychiatric samples could not be applied to a nonclinical homosexual population.

As the flaws of theoretical perspectives based on clinical samples are revealed, a less rigid and biased view of sexual orientation comes into focus. Sound psychological and cross-cultural studies support the theoretical base of bisexuality. Anna Freud (1971) argued that the sex of an individual's masturbatory fantasies is the criterion for ascertaining sexual preferences, adding that persons are capable of fantasizing about both sexes. This position is well documented in the findings of Kinsey (Kinsey, Pomeroy, & Martin, 1948). Mead (1975) referred to the normal capacity of persons to love members of both sexes. These perspectives are significant in light of empirical findings by Klein (1978) that there are between thirty and forty million persons in the United States who have either sexual attraction to or behavior with both sexes.

A less rigid view of sexual orientation is reflected in recent views of homosexuality. Wilson's (1978) sociobiological theory of sexuality includes homosexuality as necessary for species preservation. The Diagnostic and Statistical Manual of Mental Disorders (American Psychiatric Association, 1980) no longer classifies homosexuality per se as a deviance. Recent findings of Bell and Weinberg (1978) reported that the "typical" homosexual did not exist. In their studies, homosexual lifestyles varied as much as heterosexual lifestyles. A recent survey of studies comparing homosexual and heterosexual orientations revealed the generally good life adjustment of the homosexual on a wide variety of personality characteristics (Calderwood, 1981).

Although theoretical views of homosexuality have changed, the study of bisexuality continues to pose difficult problems for researchers. Blumstein and Schwartz (1976) stated that there is "little coherent relationship between the amount and 'mix' of homosexual behavior in a person's biography and that person's choice to label themselves as bisexual, homosexual, or heterosexual" (p. 339). They found that some people with no homosexual experiences considered themselves bisexual, while others who had experiences with both sexes considered themselves exclusively homosexual or heterosexual.

According to Kinsey et al. (1948), confusion concerning labeling was reflected by the polarized concept of homosexuality and heterosexuality. To address these problems, he developed the Kinsey Heterosexual-Homosexual Scale (KHHS) (Kinsey et al., 1948). This scale is an equal interval scale with continuous graduations between heterosexuality and homosexuality. An individual rating was based on relative amounts of heterosexual and homosexual response. Kinsey used the scale to rate individuals on overt experiences and psychological reactions. The ratings are as follows:

(0) Exclusively heterosexual
(1) Predominantly heterosexual, only incidentally homosexual.
(2) Predominantly heterosexual, but more than incidentally homosexual.
(3) Equally heterosexual and homosexual.
(4) Predominantly homosexual, but more than incidentally heterosexual.
(5) Predominantly homosexual, but incidentally heterosexual.
(6) Exclusively homosexual.

In the Kinsey studies (1948), 50% of males were exclusively heterosexual (0), 4% were exclusively homosexual (6), and the remaining 46% fell between 1 and 5 on the scale. While the scale displayed a less polarized view of sexual orientation, it failed to account for specific life situations, particularly those which changed over time. In this sense, the scheme still leads to labeling, viewing sexual orientation in a static fashion. Many recent studies (Saghir & Robbins, 1973; Bell & Weinberg, 1978; Masters & Johnson, 1979) have used the Kinsey scale to classify the subject as "homosexual" or "heterosexual" and generally grouped the bisexuals with the homosexuals.

The difficulty of labeling a person on the basis of a Kinsey rating, without taking into consideration the dimensions of time or the multi-variable aspects of sexual orientation (i.e., attraction, behavior, fantasy, lifestyle, emotional preference, social preference, self-identification), can be illustrated by the following examples. A married man who feels he is heterosexual is sexually involved with a male lover. A girl who breaks up with her male lover lives with a woman and then returns to the man. A woman who is in jail engages in sex with females for several years but returns to a heterosexual lifestyle once she is released. A teenager who has sex with his buddies in the locker room has sex with his girlfriend several hours later. A male nurse helps a male patient masturbate as part of the patient's rehabilitation.

Some recent research and theoretical writing has touched upon the multi-variate aspect of sexual orientation and its importance in research. As De Cecco (1981) wrote: "To depict sexuality as fixed, bifurcated states of sexual orientation, and to ignore the fact that erotic preference is labile and interpenetrated by elements of physicality, emotion, and fantasy, is to impede and even to misdirect research" (p. 51). While they virtually ignore the continuum of the Kinsey scale, using it only to classify their sample as heterosexual or homosexual, Bell and Weinberg (1978) stated: "Before one can say very much about a person on the basis of his or her sexual orientation, one must make a comprehensive appraisal of the relationship among a host of features pertaining to the person's life" (p. 329). In their programmatic research, Shively, Rudolph, and De Cecco (1978) identified the sexual orientation characteristics of physical sexual activity, interpersonal affection, and erotic fantasy on a Kinsey-type continuum.

The Klein Sexual Orientation Grid (Klein, 1980) was developed to measure a person's sexual orientation as a dynamic multi-variable process. The grid (see Figure 1) was designed to extend the scope of the Kinsey scale by including attraction, behavior, fantasy, social and emotional preference, self-identification and lifestyle. These characteristics are also measured in the past, present, and as an ideal. In the present study it was postulated that the individual's sexual orientation is composed of sexual and non-sexual variables which differ over time. By studying a large group of individuals, this study validated the theoretical model of sexual orientation as multi-variate and dynamic.

SAMPLE CHARACTERISTICS

The sample used for the analysis consisted of persons who filled out the questionnaire (KSOG) which appeared in an article entitled, "Are you sure you're heterosexual, or homosexual, or even bisexual?" in *Forum Magazine* (Klein, 1980). Of the questionnaires returned to *Forum*, 384 were usable for data analysis. Out of the 384 respondents, 351 had completed all of the questions. The fact that the sample used in this study was

Figure 1

Klein Sexual Orientation Grid

Variable	Past	Present	Ideal
A. Sexual Attraction			
B. Sexual Behavior			
C. Sexual Fantasies			
D. Emotional Preference			
E. Social Preference			
F. Self-Identification			
G. Hetero/Gay Lifestyle			

not drawn at random places significant limitations on interpretation of the data. Further limitations occur as a result of selection bias since it is not known specifically how *Forum Magazine* readers differ from other social populations. Although demographic data other than age, sex, and sexual orientation were not collected, *Forum Magazine's* readership is, according to its advertising department, largely college-educated and employed as professionals or managers.

Of the 384 respondents, 213 were male and 171 female. One hundred twenty-eight respondents identified themselves as heterosexual, 172 as bisexual, and 62 as homosexual. Twenty-two respondents did not fill out the self-identification section. For the 384 respondents the mean age was 28.2 years, the range from 14 to 72.

A Chi-square Test for Independent Samples (Siegel, 1956) showed a significant relationship between the sex of the respondents and their self-identification (Chi-square = 12.4, 2 df, p < .01). The percentage of males who identified themselves as bisexual or homosexual was greater than that of females. To study the relationship between the respondents' ages and the two independent variables of sex and self-identification, a Two-Way Uni-variate Component Analysis of Variance (Pinneau & Ault, 1974) was utilized. Results indicated a significant difference between the ages of males and females. For this sample the mean or average age of the females was significantly younger than that of the males. Secondly, there was a significant relationship between the respondents' self-identification and their age. The mean age of heterosexuals was significantly less than the mean age of bisexuals, and the mean age of the bisexuals was significantly greater than the mean age of the homosexuals. Further component analysis showed that the mean age difference between male bisexuals and homosexuals was significantly greater than the mean age difference between female bisexuals and homosexuals.

METHOD

Respondents were asked to fill out the Klein Sexual Orientation Grid, which was developed as an extension of the Kinsey Heterosexual-Homosexual Scale. The Grid is based on Klein's previous research and requires a subject to provide 21 ratings in a seven by three grid (see Figure 1). Each rating on the grid is made using the numbers 1 through 7 which correspond to the choice on the heterosexual-homosexual continuum. In addition, for each area of sexual orientation three ratings are chosen: one for the respondent's past, one for the present (defined as the preceding year), and one based on the individual's ideal choice.

The KSOG was administered with the following instructions:

A. *Sexual Attraction*

Here you (in Figure 2) will be choosing three numbers, one for each of three aspects of your life: your past, your present, and your ideal. Beginning with your past, ask yourself where you fit on this scale and select the number that best describes you. Write this number in the corresponding box marked past on the line for Variable A (Sexual Attraction) on the grid. Now, looking at Figure 2 again, select a number that describes your

Figure 2

1	2	3	4	5	6	7

| Other sex only | Other sex mostly | Other sex somewhat more | Both sexes equally | Same sex somewhat more | Same sex mostly | Same sex only |

present sexual attraction using one year as the time period you examine. For a number of people it is the same number; for others it is different. Write this number in the box marked present on the line for Variable A. Now ask yourself which number you would choose to be if it were a matter of volition. Remember there are no right or wrong numbers. When you finish writing this last number in the box marked Ideal for Variable A on the grid you should have completed the three boxes for Variable A.

B. Sexual Behavior

Here we look at actual behavior as opposed to sexual attraction. With whom do you have sex?

Use the scale in Figure 2 to rate yourself. As with the previous scale, choose a number for past, present, and ideal sexual behavior, then enter the numbers on the grid, this time under Variable B.

C. Sexual Fantasies

The third variable is sexual fantasy. Whether they occur during masturbation, while daydreaming, as a part of our real lives or purely in our imaginations, fantasies provide insight.

Rate yourself on the scale, then enter the numbers on the grid.

D. Emotional Preference

Our emotions directly influence, if not define, the actual physical act of love. Ask yourself if you love and like only the opposite sex or if you are also emotionally close to the same sex.

Find out where you fit on the scale; rate yourself as with the other scales. Enter the numbers on the grid.

E. Social Preference

Though closely allied to emotional preference, social preference is often different. You may love only women but spend most of your social life with men. Some people, of all orientations, only socialize with their own sex, while others socialize with the opposite gender exclusively.

Where are you on the scale? Choose three numbers as you have on the other scales.

F. Self-Identification

Your sexual self-definition is a strong variable since self-image strongly affects our thoughts and actions. In several cases, a person's present and past self-identification differs markedly from their ideal. Choose three numbers on the scale marked Figure 3 and fill in the numbers on the grid.

G. Heterosexual/Homosexual Lifestyle

Some heterosexuals only have sex with the opposite sex but prefer to spend the majority of their time with gay people. On the other hand, homosexual or bisexual persons may prefer to live exclusively in the gay world, the heterosexual world, or even to live in both worlds. Lifestyle is the seventh variable of sexual orientation.

Where do you tend to spend time and with whom? Choose three numbers in Figure 3 as you have on the other scales and enter them on the grid.

RESULTS

The Klein Sexual Orientation Grid consisted of 21 questions. The respondents answered each question, using a seven-point Likert-type linear scale with seven dimensions of sexual orientation and past, present, and ideal as columns, creating 21 response cells. To test for reliability of the

Figure 3

1	2	3	4	5	6	7

| Hetero only | Hetero mostly | Hetero somewhat more | Hetero/ gay equality | Gay somewhat more | Gay mostly | Gay only |

scales, Cronbach Alpha Coefficients using the Kuder-Richardson Formula 20 were computed utilizing the methods outlined by Nunally (1967). Alpha may be interpreted as the average correlation of the profile considering the items in the entire grid or each scale as a random sample of all possible measures of the same concept. The reliability estimates of the entire grid were generally excellent. Reliability estimates for the seven dimensions of sexual orientation were not as consistently high as the estimates for the past, present, and ideal scales. If the hypothesis is that a person's sexual orientation is different between the past, present and ideal, then this may account for the lower reliability estimates among the scales measuring the seven dimensions.

To test for inter-relationships among the grid variables, item-to-item correlations were computed using the procedures described by Nunally (1967) for the 21 response cells. Results of the item-to-item correlations were generally high except for the "present social preference" and "past social preference." The results suggested that a person's social preference was somewhat different from the other aspects of his or her sexual orientation.

Given the relatively high correlations among the various sexual orientation profile items, the question arises whether the different items were really measuring different dimensions of sexual orientation, or simply measuring the same dimension. One way to answer this question was to determine whether the respondent gave different responses to each of the profile questions, or tended to give the same response. Since the answers to the grid questions were ordinal in nature, a Friedman Two-Way Analysis of Variance by ranks was computed using the procedures outlined by Siegel (1956). Such an analysis takes on the look of a nonparametric one-way analysis of variance based on a randomized complete block design. The results indicated there was a significant difference between the average ranks of the 21 profile variables on the grid.

From a theoretical standpoint, the primary scales of interest are the past, present, and ideal, since it was hypothesized that a person's sexual orientation changes over time. To test whether there was a difference in the mean scale scores for the past, present, and ideal, a Hotelling T-Square Analysis was performed following the procedures outlined by Morrison (1967). Statistical analysis showed a significant difference between the three mean scale scores. Simultaneous multiple comparisons indicated a significant difference between the present scale and the past scale, but none between the ideal and present scales.

Relationships Between Variables

To study relationships among the independent variables of sex, age, and self-label, and the three scales of past, present, and ideal, several statistical analyses were performed. A Cannonical Correlation Analysis (Morrison, 1967) indicated that the vast majority of the variance (70%) between the two sets of variables was accounted for primarily by the respondent's self-identification. The second cannonical variate of age accounted for approximately 11% of the variance between the two sets of variables. This analysis also suggested that whether a respondent was male or female was more strongly related to his or her past and ideal sexual orientation than the independent variables of age or self-label.

Another method for studying relationships among the independent variables and the responses to the questions on the KSOG was the Automatic Interaction Detection as outlined by Lingwood (1981). This statistical analysis was carried out using the respondent's mean scores for all 21 questions on the grid as the dependent variables, and sex, age, and self-label as independent variables. Again, the best predictor of a respondent's mean score for the entire grid was his or her self-identification. In this analysis, the first statistical sub-populations or subgroups formed were based on the respondent's self-identification (heterosexual, homosexual, bisexual). For the most part, the respondent's sex determined the next set of sub-populations, with the exception of the heterosexual sub-population whose orientation seemed to depend more on the respondent's age rather than sex. The results of the Automatic Interaction Detection analysis supported the findings from the Cannonical Correlation analysis that the primary variable accounting for a respondent's sexual orientation on the KSOG was his or her self-identification.

Since previous analyses showed that for the sample as a whole there was a significant difference between the respondent's past, present, and ideal sexual orientation, a Multivariate Profile Analysis was conducted to determine whether the mean profiles for the three different subgroups (heterosexual, homosexual, bisexual) had the same significant differences. A One-Way Multivariate Component Analysis was carried out using the methods outlined by Pinneau and Ault (1974). The results indicated a significant difference between the mean profiles for the three subgroups in terms of their change in sexual orientation from the past, present, and ideal as measured on the KSOG. A further Univariate Analysis of Variance Test (Morrison, 1967) indicated there was a significant difference between heterosexuals, bisexuals, and homosexuals in their past, present, and ideal sexual orientation as measured on the KSOG.

To study the differences among the heterosexual, homosexual, and bisexual subgroups, a Hotelling T-Square Analysis was also performed (Morrison, 1967). The results for the heterosexual subgroup indicated a change in response between the past, present, and ideal scales. The change from past to present was not significant, but the change from present to ideal was significant. The results for the bisexual subgroup were just the reverse. Again, there was a significant overall change from past to ideal and a significant change from past to present, although there was no significant difference between the present and ideal. For the homosexual subgroup not only was the overall change from past to ideal significant, but the mean score for the present scale was also significantly higher than the mean score for the past scale, and the mean scale score for the present scale was significantly higher than the mean scale score for the ideal scale.

The results, which are illustrated in Figure 4, indicated that on the KSOG bisexuals and homosexuals had significant increases in homosexuality from the past to present histories, whereas heterosexuals remained constant. Comparing the present and ideal profiles, bisexuals and heterosexuals showed significant increase in homosexuality as an ideal. Homosexuals, in contrast, significantly decreased in homosexuality from the present to the ideal. The overall change from the past to ideal for heterosexuals, bisexuals, and homosexuals indicated significant increases in homosexuality for all three subgroups.

DISCUSSION

The data analysis encompassed several important considerations: (1) the importance of viewing sexual orientation as a process which often changes over time; (2) the importance of all seven variables on the Klein Sexual Orientation Grid in describing sexual orientation; and (3) the simplicity and inadequacy of the labels heterosexual, bisexual, and homosexual in describing a person's sexual orientation.

Analysis of the data revealed that sexual orientation was not static for this sample. Contrary to the theoretical notion that one becomes fixated in childhood, the sexual orientations of the individuals in this study often changed remarkably over the period of their adult lives. All three of the self-identified groups became significantly more homosexually oriented over time.

Since the changes from the past time-frame to the present were significant, the assumption was made that the ideal represented future changes in the sample's orientations. There was a significant trend in the direction of the bisexual norm with heterosexuals moving toward a more homosexual orientation over their lifetimes, and homosexuals moving away from a homosexual orientation. One might assume that these changes over a person's lifespan would hold true for bisexuals and homosexuals only. In this study, however, heterosexuals also changed.

Until recently the factor of change in sexual orientation has been generally ignored. Learning takes on a stronger role than genetic and hereditary factors. Many are potentially capable of travelling over a large segment of the sexual orientation continuum.

Figure 4

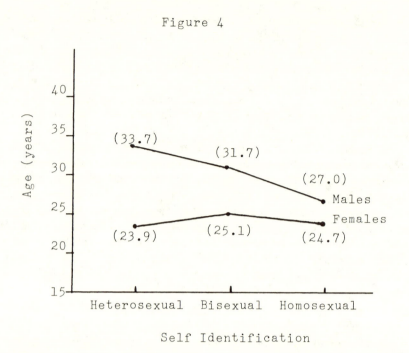

Self Identification

Theories of sexual orientation for heterosexual men and women have postulated a homosexual period during early puberty. If one remained homosexual or bisexual it often was represented as an arrested adolescent development. Our impressions of sexual orientation, obtained through hundreds of interviews over the past five years and other studies outlined in this collection, lead us to conclude that many heterosexual men and women do, in fact, experiment with homosexual behavior for the first time in later life, and thereafter some change their identification to bisexual or homosexual. Conversely, for some male and female homosexuals, such experimentation and change also occur in adulthood and lead to greater heterosexuality. Bisexual men and women not only experiment and change in adult life, but for some the changes remarkably range over the entire sexual continuum.

Alfred Kinsey was a pioneer in assessing sexual orientation as a continuous rather than discrete phenomenon. His studies, however, limited the scope of sexual orientation for the most part to behavior. In the KSOG, sexual orientation consists of several aspects. It becomes a multivariable concept comprised of three variables which directly describe the sexual self (attraction, fantasy, and behavior), three which describe aspects considered crucial to the composition of sexual orientation (emotional preference, social preference, and heterosexual or homosexual lifestyle), and also the variable of self-identification.

For example, two people with an overall average of "4" for the "present" are very different if one has the configuration 4-4-4-4-4-4-4, while the other has 2-1-3-6-7-5-4. With respect to labeling their sexual orientation, both would be considered bisexual or would be numbered as a "4" on the Kinsey scale. In actuality, we are talking about two people with extremely different outlooks, lifestyles, sexualities, and social and emotional preferences. Furthermore, both persons would surely have had very different pasts and very different orientation ideals.

The results of cross-tabulating a person's self-identification number (using the seven-part scale) with the self-label he or she gave showed the simplicity and inadequacy of labeling (heterosexual, bisexual, homosexual). A logical but arbitrary method of differentiating the three labels by the seven-part scale is to assign the numbers 1 and 2 to the label heterosexuality, 3, 4, or 5 to bisexuality, and 6 or 7 to homosexuality. On the scale, one-third of those people who labeled themselves bisexual did not fit into the categories 3, 4, or 5. For the past, 30% did not fit. In the ideal 22% did not fit. The labels of homosexuality and heterosexuality fit only in the time period of the present where 88% placed themselves into categories 6 and 7 or 1 and 2, respectively. The label for bisexuals and homosexuals was inadequate for the past time period. Interestingly, in the ideal time-frame, more bisexuals than heterosexuals fit their numbered category (77% vs. 75%) while only 66% of homosexuals wished to remain ideally in their category.

Self-identified bisexuals had the lowest predictability overall; thus, the bisexual label did not predict well or label correctly. In the ideal, only the bisexuals remained the same as the present in retaining group membership, while the heterosexuals and homosexuals dropped substantially from their present percentages. Again, bisexuals wanted to remain ideally bisexual while the self-identified heterosexuals and homosexuals wanted to change toward the bisexual center of the continuum.

Although we suggest a word of caution regarding generalizing these findings to the overall population, we think the Klein Sexual Orientation Grid proved to be a reliable and valid instrument in this study. (For validity and reliability statistics on the Klein Sexual Orientation Grid, refer to Wayson, 1983.) We see the instrument as a useful tool in differentiating persons with respect to sexual orientation by taking into consideration the meaningful dimension of time and the many related variables. Describing the individual within this framework also allows the researcher to avoid the simplistic and inadequate labeling techniques which have undermined earlier studies of bisexuality.

We do not, at this point, have clear definitions of what constitutes a bisexual, homosexual, or heterosexual. This study has attempted to point out the pitfalls of conventional labeling. In his book, *Human Sexuality*, Gagnon (1977) stated:

Whether we have expansive or narrow definitions of heterosexuality and homosexuality, love and lust, or clothed or naked sex, depends on the cultural significance that these dimensions have in both personal lives and the collective expressions of sexuality around us. Definitions should not be created to exhaust reality, to stand for all time or to account for all meanings in all circumstances. The utility of a definition is the direction it gives us for looking at the world. The definition should not be confused with the world itself. (p. 188)

The Klein Grid provides a framework for understanding sexual orientation on a theoretical level. On the practical level it enables the researcher to separate groups more precisely, to focus on the individual while noting some of the common configurations. In addition, this study directs a researcher to be more explicit in describing which aspects of sexuality and emotional/social preference are being considered as variables, and to use a multi-variate design rather than a simple contrast of distinct groups.

REFERENCES

American Psychiatric Association. (1980). *Diagnostic and statistical manual of mental disorders.* (3rd Ed.). Washington, D.C.: Author.

Blumstein, P. W., & Schwartz, P. (1976). Bisexuality in men. *Urban Life, 5,* 339-358.

Bell, A. P., & Weinberg, M. S. (1978). *Homosexualities: A study of diversity among men and women.* New York: Simon & Schuster.

Bieber, I. (1976). A discussion of "homosexuality": The ethical challenge. *Journal of Consulting and Clinical Psychology, 44,* 163-166.

Calderwood, D. (1981, December). Interview with Dr. D. Calderwood, chairperson of human sexuality, New York University.

De Cecco, J. P. (1981). Definition and meaning of sexual orientation. *Journal of Homosexuality, 6*(4), 51-67.

Ellis, A. (1965). *Homosexuality: Its causes and cures.* New York: Lyle Stuart.

Freud, A. (1971). *Problems of psychoanalytic training, diagnosis and techniques of therapy.* (Vol. 7). London: International University Press.

Freud, S. (1961). Three essays on the theory of sexuality. In J. Strachey (Ed. and Trans.), *The standard edition of the complete psychological works of Sigmund Freud* (Vol. 7). London: Hogarth Press. (Original work published 1905)

Freud, S. (1910). Three contributions to sexual theory. *New York Journal of Nervous and Mental Disorders, 7,* 472-474.

Gagnon, J. (1977). *Human sexualities.* Glenville: Scott, Foresman.

Hooker, E. (1969). Parental relations and male homosexuality in patient and non-patient samples. *Journal of Counseling and Clinical Psychology, 33,* 141-142.

Kinsey, A. C., Pomeroy, W. B., & Martin, C. E. (1948). *Sexual behavior in the human male.* Philadelphia: W. B. Saunders.

Klein, F. (1978). *The bisexual option.* New York: Arbor House.

Klein, F. (December, 1980). Are you sure you're heterosexual? or homosexual? or even bisexual? *Forum Magazine,* pp. 41-45.

Krafft-Ebing, R. von (1886-1939). Psychopathia sexualis. New York: *Pioneer Publication, 12,* 70-71.

Lingwood, D. A. (1981). *Automatic interaction detection.* Washington D.C.: Action Research Northwest.

Masters, W. H., & Johnson, V. E. (1979). *Homosexuality in perspective*. Boston: Little, Brown.

Mead, M. (1975). Bisexuality: What's it all about? *Redbook Magazine*, p. 131.

Morrison, D. F. (1967). *Multivariate statistical methods*. New York: McGraw-Hill.

Nunally, J. C. (1967). *Psychometric theory*. New York: McGraw-Hill.

Pinneau, S., & Ault, J. (1974). Univariate and multivariate component analysis. *Perceptual and Motor Skills, 39*, 955-985.

Saghir, M. T., & Robbins, E. (1973). *Male and female homosexuality: A comprehensive investigation*. Baltimore: Williams & Wilkins.

Shively, M., Rudolph, J., & De Cecco, J. P. (1978). The identification of the social sex-role stereotypes. *Journal of Homosexuality, 3*, 225-233.

Siegel, S. (1956). *Nonparametric statistics for the behavioral sciences*. New York: McGraw-Hill.

Wayson, P. (1983). *A study of personality variables in males as they relate to differences in sexual orientation*. Unpublished doctoral dissertation, California School of Professional Psychology, San Diego, CA.

Wilson, E. O. (1978). *On human nature*. Boston: Harvard University Press.

PSYCHOLOGICAL ASPECTS OF BISEXUALITY

Psycho-Social Issues Related to Counseling Bisexuals

David N. Lourea, EdD
Bisexual Counseling Services
San Francisco

ABSTRACT. An increasing number of persons who experience bisexual feelings or behaviors are seeking professional counseling. This article explores the psycho-social issues related to counseling individuals and couples concerned about their own or their partner's feelings, fantasies, or behaviors with both men and women, and the appropriateness or inappropriateness of adopting a bisexual identity or developing a bisexual lifestyle. The steps for helping individuals to differentiate problems, handle confusion, and conceptualize bisexuality are outlined. The counseling process with bisexuals includes developing support systems, examining internalized homophobia and sex-role stereotyping, helping them deal with heterosexual concerns, and with issues which affect partners when one or both is bisexual.

As more bisexual support systems develop throughout the United States, sexologists, researchers, educators, counselors and therapists must broaden their views and concepts in the scientific study of human sexuality. The professionals' tendency to perceive sexual orientation only in terms of two dichotomized monolithic extremes must change if they are to address adequately the needs and concerns of the growing number of people for whom the middle range of the sexual orientation continuum is a reality.

Dr. Lourea is one of the founders of the Bi-Center in San Francisco, Executive Director of the Bisexual Counseling Services in that city, and a counselor in private practice. Reprint requests may be sent to the author, 1761 Hayes Street, San Francisco, CA 94117.

This article will take a look at some of the psycho-social issues related to counseling individuals and couples who are concerned about their own or their partner's feelings, fantasies, or behaviors with both women and men and the viability of adopting a bisexual identity or lifestyle. The observations presented here are based on the author's personal and professional perspectives resulting from 10 years of helping to develop a self-identified bisexual community within the San Francisco Bay Area. In that light, my biases should be noted, including: (1) the belief that a bisexual self-identification is appropriate for some but not others; and (2) the belief that a positive bisexual lifestyle can be actualized, acknowledging that the complexities and ramifications of such nontraditional relationships make this lifestyle difficult for some individuals.

The first priority for counselors considering seeing clients who are concerned about their homosexual and heterosexual feelings is for counselors to evaluate honestly their own feelings. If counselors are homophobic or biphobic, they should refer clients facing those issues to a counselor who could be objective.

At the San Francisco Bisexual Center, we have found Jack Annon's PLISSIT model of behavior therapy (permission, limited information, specific suggestions, intensive therapy) a useful guideline in dealing with the people whom we have seen in the past eight years. Most client concerns have been dealt with just by giving them *permission*. "Yes, it is perfectly all right for you to fantasize about, be erotically attracted to, and to relate sexually to both women and men." "No, you don't have to act on those feelings." "You don't have to give up loving women to start loving men." The next largest group of concerns has been dealt with by giving them *limited information:* a list of books, addresses of bisexual organizations around the country, a fact sheet on commonly held myths, and basic Kinsey statistics. A smaller group of people need *specific suggestions/guidelines* on how to disclose their bisexuality to family or to heterosexual and homosexual friends, how to establish a bisexual support group in their area, and how to handle jealousy, and so forth. Only a small group of people have needed or wanted intensive therapy.

DIFFERENTIATING THE PROBLEM

When someone seeks counseling concerning sexual orientation, it is important to help that person distinguish which problems are related to their sexual orientation and which are not. Sometimes people use their bisexuality, or fear of being a "latent homosexual," as a convenient scapegoat upon which to hang all the things that go wrong in their lives. The success or failure of their relationships becomes a reflection of how well they have hidden their bisexuality. For example, most people have unresolved feelings of resentment and anger towards their parents. Sometimes these feelings are related to the dismissal or minimizing of their sexuality and sexual orientation, although most frequently they are not. A woman's fears of intimacy and her inability to form stable, committed relationships may have nothing to do with being bisexual; she could just as easily have the same problems if she were homosexual or heterosexual. In the same way, a man's compulsive sexual behavior may or may not be a manifestation of his bisexuality; however, the isolation he experiences may be due in part to his lacking a confidant with whom he can discuss his bisexuality. By every indication most bisexuals still keep their sexual orientation a secret.

While some people blame all their problems on their bisexuality, others may not be cognizant of the negative effects of keeping it secret. Many people do not recognize that their lack of spontaneity, constant state of anxiety, or fear of confrontation have anything to do with their fear of disclosing their sexual identity. It is having to keep their sexual orientation a secret, not the orientation itself, that is the problem. Conversely, counselors should not assume that a person's bisexuality is the root problem or that a client's erotic feelings for both women and men cause them distress.

CONFUSION

One of the most commonly held assumptions about bisexuals is that they are all confused. Confusion is a realistic reaction for someone who is in the first stage of "coming out." It is bewildering for a bisexual to realize that society's general assumptions about bisexuality may not be true for the individual. "How can I experience my sexual feeling as being fluid and constantly changing when everyone says they're supposed to be fixed and easily definable?" "Can I be right and everyone else wrong?" "Since no one is talking about being attracted to both women and men, then I must be the only one." "How can I be attracted to a man one day and a woman the next?" Such confusion is a reasonable reaction to society's attempt to oversimplify the human sexual experience. Confusion should be seen as a sign of mental health, not an indication of neurosis, a fact which needs to be pointed out to the bisexuals, who often blame themselves for being confused.

Ira's experience is an example of how a rigid concept of sexual orientation can lead to confusion. Ira, 55, has been married twice and is now divorced. He has been heterosexual all his life and, except for an occasional erotic dream, has never been attracted to men. Recently, however, his masturbation fantasies have been almost exclusively about men, a change which confuses him. Sally, a second example, came out as a lesbian ten years ago without much support from her family. She found love, acceptance, and respect from within the lesbian community and spent three years as a separatist living on a farm in Oregon. Recently, however, she has found herself erotically attracted to Paul, a fellow student in an English literature class. She is confused as to what to do about her feelings.

Ira and Sally need to know that it is perfectly acceptable to have those fantasies and feelings and that they do not need to act on them unless they so choose. Many things that make wonderful fantasies would not be enjoyable were they realities. For instance, people who are celibate do not stop having sexual feelings; they just choose not to act on them. Ira and Sally need to know that many people feel erotic toward both women and men, yet are content not to go beyond fantasizing. If Ira does decide to have sexual relations with men, he will need to confront homophobic stereotypes he may have previously avoided. And, if Sally decides to act on her erotic feelings for Paul, she will have to develop new ways of relating to men that incorporate the power and independence she has gained since coming out as a lesbian.

CONCEPTUALIZATION

How we conceptualize bisexuality can create problems. Whereas in general we conceive ideas by way of instantaneous, isolated images, to conceptualize bisexuality we must view it longitudinally as many images over time. We can imagine seeing a woman listening to classical music, speaking Spanish, writing with her right hand, and relating sexually to another woman. Our image of her, thus, is that of a Spanish-speaking, right-handed lesbian who enjoys listening to classical music. Yet, if she also speaks English, writes with her left hand, relates sexually to a man, and enjoys punk rock, we would see her in another time frame, as an English-speaking, left-handed, heterosexual woman who enjoys punk rock. Unless we are accustomed to conceptualize longitudinally, it would be hard to perceive her as being a bilingual, ambidextrous, and bisexual with diverse musical interests.

COMING OUT

A number of people attending the drop-in rap group in the Bi Center in San Francisco have said that they were at first very reluctant to do so. For many participants it becomes the first time they have actually met other people who consider themselves bisexual, an experience that can be overwhelming. They discover they are not the only ones who have spent years denying their bisexuality, an identity not as uncommon as they previously thought.

When people claim that "bisexuals have the best on both worlds" they do not realize that "both worlds" are closets. For example, a bisexual woman, can get support and recognition from lesbians for her homosexual feelings only if she is willing to hide her heterosexual feelings. And a bisexual man will get affirmation for his heterosexual prowess only if he can keep his homosexual desires hidden. Contrary to Woody Allen's jest that "bisexuals double their chances for a date on a Saturday night," the bisexual woman does not have the option of meeting a woman in a straight setting, and the bisexual man knows he will be chastised and possibly rejected by gay friends if he shows any interest in women.

Finding other bisexual people to talk to is a first step in coming out. After attending a number of rap groups, workshops, potlucks, discussion, dances or other social functions, some individuals want to rush out and announce to the whole world that they are bisexuals. Like the Bay Area Physicians for Human Rights, the Bi Center takes the position that closets are a health hazard. Closets leave a person vulnerable to blackmail, alienation, self-doubts, and substance abuse, as well as intensify feelings of guilt, anxiety, and paranoia. However, it is important to exercise caution in coming out, even though the eventual goal is to be able to live a life completely out of the closet.

At the Bi Center an individual is encouraged to let others know when he or she is about to come out to someone important so that the individual will have support available in case the disclosure does not go as favorably as hoped. They are reminded that just as it took them a long time to become comfortable with their own bisexuality, so it is reasonable for it to take those hearing it time to adjust to their disclosure.

ANDROGYNY AND SEX ROLE STEREOTYPES

People who are intimately involved with both men and women may become aware of how sex-role conditioning affects them since they are constantly confronted with the dichotomization of those roles. Men in this society are expected to initiate, take control, make things happen, and be responsible, especially with regard to sex; conversely, women, are encouraged to be understanding, nurturing, tender, empathetic, and supportive. For these reasons it is not surprising that in two different studies using the same questionnaire, one involving a hundred self-identified bisexual males (Lourea, 1978), and the other involving a hundred self-identified bisexual females (Rila & Reed, 1980), both study groups tended to have significantly more male than female sexual partners. Sexual connections are easily established when, between two people attracted to one another, at least one of them has been programmed by society to take risks and initiate new contacts. However, if both people in the situation make the first move, chances of a connection being made are diminished, even when strong sexual attraction exists between the two individuals. Further effects of sex-role stereotyping are seen in the Rubenstein (1982) study, wherein both bisexual women and men found themselves emotionally more satisfied with women than with men.

Obviously bisexuals are not free from the effects of societal messages regarding masculinity and femininity. They are, however, more inclined to scrutinize traditional sex-role behavior patterns and to favor an androgynous perspective. June Singer (1976) hypothesized that, while it is not necessary to be bisexual in order to be androgynous, the road may be easier for bisexuals than for others. Rubenstein's study (1976) also indicated that bisexuals were more androgynous than heterosexuals and homosexuals and were more interested in a blending of sex and friendship within their relationships.

FROM HOMOSEXUAL TO BISEXUAL

Re-entry into the world of heterosexual relations can create a dilemma for those who have been exclusively homosexual for an extended period of time. The question arises as to how they can build a relationship with someone of the other sex without falling into the trap of sex-role conditioning. For instance, a man may have learned how to attract other men and know what to expect in return. How then can he let a woman know that he is interested in her without playing the stereotypical maneuvering game?

In contrast, a homosexual woman may have learned to trust other women's timing and pacing. What will happen now with a man? If she makes the first move, will he feel threatened? Would he admit if it he did? How can she be assertive without deferring to a man, whether her assertiveness is indeed appropriate? The need to answer questions such as these was so strong that a special support group was formed at the Bi Center for lesbians and formerly identified lesbians so they could discuss what it meant to relate to men.

COUPLE COUNSELING CONCERNS

Many issues are involved when counseling a couple in which one person is bisexual and the other is either homosexual or heterosexual. If the bisexuality has not been previously acknowledged from the beginning of the relationship, issues of anger, hurt, betrayal, and trust surface and must be dealt with before further progress can be made. However, in relationships where tension and resentment have gone too long unresolved, causing damage to the relationship, the bisexual partner often assumes responsibility for its resulting demise. While the bisexual is partially responsible due to his or her lack of disclosure, it is also important to look at the verbal and nonverbal communication patterns that have developed within the relationship; for example, how unpleasant information has been permitted to surface; and whether there exists an unacknowledged agreement not to share or confront issues that are disruptive or uncomfortable. Likewise, it is important to keep in mind that relationships are multi-dimensional; the withholding of vital facts may be symptomatic of a basic disharmony between the pair, not the cause of disharmony.

Little research has been done on bisexual relationships. Data that are available seem to indicate that bisexuals become cognizant of their orientation at a later age than most heterosexuals or homosexuals; therefore, it is not uncommon for persons' bisexual nature to emerge until after they have formed a coupled relationship. In situations where the bisexuality has surfaced during a heterosexual marriage or homosexual partnership, and no deception has been involved, counseling can focus on concerns typically presented by the couple: (1) homophobia, (2) questions of choice, (3) competition that leads to insecurities, (4) monogamous versus nonmonogamous issues, (5) effects on child rearing, and (6) coming out.

(1) *Homophobia*. The homophobic feelings a heterosexual partner has are likely to incorporate societal messages about homosexual behavior. Fear, revulsion, and hostility come from those myths, i.e., homosexuality is unnatural, perverted, an abomination against God, a threat to the ideals and values of the nuclear family, or a sign of mental illness. If a husband announces that he is bisexual and is having strong feelings for other men, it could trigger unresolved homosexual feelings in his wife, feelings she may or may not be able or willing to confront. On the other hand, if a wife tells her husband she is having homosexual feelings, he may begin to question his own masculinity.

Homophobia is not just prejudice limited to the heterosexual population; it spans the entire range of the sexual continuum. One of the ways homophobia can manifest itself is in the bisexual partner's deference to heterosexual relationships. Bisexuals may feel that their lovers' heterosexual friendships should be encouraged, given priority because those relationships are "normal," and thus may see themselves as standing in the way of a healthier lifestyle for their partner.

(2) *Question of Choice*. What the monosexual partner may not realize is that erotic attraction is not a matter of choice. The bisexual person cannot turn off attractions for one sex in preference for the other, for sexual feelings cannot be filtered, and attempting to do so can lead to emotional and sexual difficulties. Persons in touch with their sexual feelings may

find that they are attracted to a number of people; deciding to relate to both men and women as opposed to either men or women is a valid option for a bisexual. Or bisexuals may choose to limit their heterosexual behavior and only act on their homosexual feelings, or vice versa, something the homophobic or heterophobic partner will find hard to believe.

(3) *Insecurities.* Competitive insecurities are fears which arise when a person is faced with possibly competing with someone of the other sex. For example, when a woman finds out that her husband is bisexual, her first reaction might be worrying how she will be able to hold on to him. "I know that I can compete with any other woman. If I lose, well, at least it was a fair fight. With a man I don't stand a chance. I've lost before I've even begun." Similarly, a male homosexual might not mind his lover relating to other men, but when it comes to his lover acting on his feelings for women, the first man's response is, "I'm in trouble. How do I compete with a woman? I can give him what any other man can but there is no way I can be a woman for him."

Sometimes these insecurities are compounded for the bisexual. Rather than dealing with the sexual difficulties between himself and his wife, a man may try to bow out of the relationship by claiming to be "more interested in men these days." A man may be frightened over the degree to which he feels bonded to his homosexual lover and thus use his heterosexuality as a shield to guard against further homosexual intimacy. If the relationship between two people is not working, it is usually because of interpersonal dynamics other than the bisexual partner's feeling more heterosexual than homosexual, or vice versa. Rather than end a relationship by admitting they are no longer in love with their partners, some people use their bisexuality as an excuse, claiming increased interest in the sex opposite to that of their partners. Such dishonesty may account for the mistrust some monosexuals feel towards bisexuals.

Competitive insecurities also surface when the spouse has to compete with someone of the same sex. A husband does not mind his wife's desires for women; however, he is upset over the idea of her wanting to relate to other men. He thinks, "If she gets it on with a woman, it doesn't reflect on me. Relating to men implies I'm not good enough or virile enough." Within a lesbian relationship of many years, one partner's feeling toward the other was "I know she can never get the kind of love I can give her from a man. It's other women that are the real threat."

(4) *Monogamy Versus Open Relationships.* Monogamy is a concept strongly rooted in our Judaeo-Christian heritage. That monogamy is seen not only as a social ideal but also as the only viable option is what creates conflict. And conflicts arising from this issue are not limited to heterosexual or bisexual couples. Many homosexual relationships also end because of the "extramarital" behavior of one of the partners.

It is also important to keep in mind that bisexuality and extramarital sex are not synonymous. Many bisexuals are perfectly content to limit their sexual behavior and keep their bisexuality restricted to fantasy, for the complexities and ramifications inherent in a non-exclusive relationship create more problems than they are willing to confront. For the bisexual, monogamy is not necessarily a possibility that is always discounted.

Objections to nonexclusivity include the fear that it means one must also go out and create other relationships. For example, a certain man does not mind that his wife sees other people, for he likes to spend time alone occasionally; he feels satisfied with the time he and his wife share. His fear is, however, that people will also expect him to have outside lovers. But he does not want to share his sexuality with anyone besides his wife. As long as it is all right for him to be monogamous, it is all right for his wife to be nonexclusive.

While many bisexuals find fulfillment and satisfaction within the confines of a monogamous relationship, many others do not. No one person is likely to satisfy all the heterosexual and homosexual needs of a bisexual. Having several relationships allows individuals to focus on what they are receiving from each partner, not what they miss in a particular individual; this relieves the burden of trying to fulfill all the needs and expectations of a single partner.

For some couples, an open relationship can be a rich, rewarding, dynamic, and emotionally satisfying way of life. Conversely, it can prove devastating to the relationship and demoralizing to the individuals involved. Much of what happens depends on guidelines which are explored ahead of time and support systems which are available. Couples having difficulties negotiating an open relationship often must also confront negative social attitudes regarding such relationships, attitudes which become more detrimental when one of the partners is bisexual.

Couples seeking counseling for opening their relationships often need to develop better communication skills; the fair fighting techniques described in George Bach's *The Intimate Enemy* (1968) and *Creative Aggression* (1974) are especially helpful in this regard. Couples need to feel comfortable with experimenting, and have a high tolerance for making mistakes. Time management issues are some of the hardest for such couples to confront. Questions arise. Who watches the children and who goes out to play? What time should one come home? Is staying out all night an option? During the holidays, how much time should be spent with another lover? When is it acceptable for a lover to stay over for the night? And in whose bed? Establishing rules is in light of such questions. And it is just as important to be able to change them when they no longer work. Flexibility and spontaneity are important characteristics if people want to maintain a successful open relationship.

(5) *The Effect on Children.* Heterosexuals are often afraid that children of homosexual or bisexual parents will be coerced, seduced, or pressured

into an alternative sexual orientation. What those same heterosexuals forget is that most homosexual and bisexual people grew up in heterosexual households with parents who tried to impose, coerce, seduce, and pressure them into heterosexuality. Studies indicate that children of homosexual or bisexual parents are no more or less likely to become heterosexual than other children. Parents who have suffered the pain of having their own sexual preferences ridiculed and denied are acutely aware of the impossibility of programming a child's future sexual orientation.

Parents living an alternative sexual lifestyle are usually committed to providing an atmosphere of respect for whichever sexual orientation emerges in the child. Sometimes, in an attempt to prove that they can be competent parents without having to be heterosexual, they assume the burden of being "supermom" or "superdad": They deny themselves the right ever to lose their tempers or to be lazy, irritable, insensitive, or moody. In addition, if their children should experience any problem, from asthma to drug abuse, from conflicts with peers to brushes with the law, the bisexual parents are likely to blame themselves and wonder if their child's problems are related to the parents' sexual orientation. These parents forget that children with heterosexual parents also have problems.

Yet, invariably, problems do arise, and people can be extremely judgemental about bisexual parents. Relatives may feel they have the right to decide if someone is a fit parent based solely on his or her sexual orientation. Grandparents or ex-spouses may try to interfere with the rearing of the children. The courts may declare the bisexual parent unfit, award custody rights, and restrict visitation privileges—all this based on homophobic, heterosexist notions such as that it is always in the best interest of the children to live with parents who are exclusively heterosexual. Counselors working with any sexual minority parent need to be aware of these issues and familiarize themselves with the custody laws in their particular area. Also, children need to be told that not everyone is going to approve of their parents' lifestyle. While children are quick to learn who they can and who they cannot talk to, it is important for them to understand why some people may react negatively. If parents have dignity and pride, have a sense of integrity about themselves, that message will come across to their children, regardless of what other people say. Such positive attitudes are the best defense against the prejudices of society. If parents are ashamed, embarrassed, or uncomfortable with their lifestyle, those nonverbal feelings will be conveyed to and internalized by their children.

(6) *Coming Out*. It is vital to the success of any relationship for couples to develop friends they can depend on for support. The complexities involved in an open relationship where at least one of the partners is bisexual can be overwhelming. Instances arise in which it is impossible for the individuals involved to be supportive of one another; having other

people to turn to can relieve pressure as well as add perspective that can help clarify issues. Often difficulties arise about the best way to come out to other people. Counselors need to remind each partner that when one of them shares personal information with family, friends, or neighbors, it affects the other partner as well. Care, sensitivity, and timing must be considered so that neither person feels exposed or betrayed by the sharing of personal information before they are ready for that information to be known. In the book *Barry and Alice: Portrait of a Bisexual Marriage* (Kohn & Matusow, 1980), Barry recalls: "I had just told a close friend from work about my bisexual feelings. Alice became furious. She said, 'You don't have the right to talk to anyone because your telling affects me too'" (pp. 161-162).

Respecting the needs of the person who is not ready to come out is important. Equally important is the burden the other partner may feel about things that need to be expressed. In *Barry and Alice*, Barry notes:

> The decision to share the truth about our lives has been a gradual, unfolding one. It was marked by a lot of struggle, and Alice and I did not always see eye to eye on it. At some point, it just became clearer to us that the costs of holding on to the secret were greater than the benefits. As we grew more comfortable with ourselves, more convinced that there was nothing wrong with the life we had chosen to lead, it came down to a question of integrity. Why hide parts of ourselves and a way of life that we considered valid? (p. 159)

Couples who take the risk of being honest about themselves and their relationships are likely to encounter hostility, fear, withdrawal, or and self-righteous pity from certain people. Some people believe that sexuality is a private matter and should never be discussed openly. Some may be offended and need to distance themselves, either temporarily or permanently, while others are honored by the confidence shared and become closer as a result. Most people have skeletons in their closets; they trust others who are willing to be open about themselves. Many couples discover that when they start opening up, their lives fill with people supportive of their lifestyle.

CONCLUSION

There are millions of people who have caring, loving, and deeply erotic feelings toward both women and men. It is not unrealistic to state that they probably far outnumber the total homosexual population. How well people are to incorporate those feelings and develop a lifestyle appropriately matched to who they really are largely depends on their ability to find accurate information and supportive environments.

People in the helping professions should examine their own fears, myths, and stereotypes regarding bisexuality before working with clients on bisexual issues. Most clients' concerns can be dealt with by giving them permission, limited information, and specific suggestions; only the smallest group of people need or want intensive therapy for their bisexual orientation. Helping individuals differentiate problems, handle confusion, and understand the problems of conceptualizing bisexuality are important first steps. Also, care must be taken in helping someone develop a support system during the stages of coming out. Examining one's homophobia, androgyny, and sex-role stereotypes are important issues that will probably arise for the therapist while counseling bisexuals. Special care and understanding must also be given to the concerns of homosexual men and women who are getting in touch with their heterosexual feelings.

When counseling couples in which one partner has hidden his or her bisexual nature, feelings of anger, hurt, betrayal, and trust between the two partners must be allowed to surface. Counseling should examine the issues of homophobia, choice, competition with either same- or opposite-sex partners, monogamy versus open relationships, child rearing, and coming out.

REFERENCES

Bach, G., & Goldberg, H. (1974). *Creative aggression*. New York: Doubleday.

Bach, G., & Wyden, P. (1968). *The intimate enemy*. New York: William Morrow.

Kohn, B., & Matusow, A. (1980). *Barry and Alice: Portrait of a bisexual marriage*. Englewood Clifts, NJ: Prentice-Hall.

Lourea, D. (1978). *100 bisexual men*. Unpublished study, Institute for the Advanced Study of Human Sexuality, San Francisco.

Rila, M., & Reed, B. (1980). *100 bisexual women*. Unpublished doctoral study, Institute for the Advanced Study of Human Sexuality, San Francisco, CA.

Rubenstein, M. (1976). *Bisexuality and androgyny: An investigative study*. Unpublished master's thesis, Lone Mountain College, San Francisco, CA.

Rubenstein, M. (1977, November/December). A bisexual perspective on androgyny. *The Bi-Monthly*, pp. 6-7.

Rubenstein, M. (1982). *An in-depth study of bisexuality and its relationship to self-esteem*. Unpublished doctoral dissertation, Institute for the Advanced Study of Human Sexuality, San Francisco.

Singer, J. (1976). *Androgyny: Toward a new theory of sexuality*. New York: Anchor Press/Doubleday.

Personality Variables
in Males as They Relate to
Differences in Sexual Orientation

Peter D. Wayson, PhD

San Diego

ABSTRACT. This study investigated personality variable differences among men of different sexual orientations. One hundred-fourteen males completed a demographic sheet, the Sexual Screening Questionnaire (SSQ), the Marlowe-Crowne Social Desirability Scale, and the Test of Attentional and Interpersonal Style (TAIS). The SSQ screened subjects into one of three categories: heterosexual, bisexual, or homosexual. It was hypothesized that, based on TAIS scores, bisexuals would describe themselves as being more attentionally unfocused and more anxious, and as having lower self-esteem than the other two groups. One-way analyses of the variance (ANOVA) of these hypotheses failed to produce significant results. A post-hoc multiple discriminant function analysis revealed that the heterosexual group was significantly more competitive both physically and interpersonally, and that the bisexual group displayed significant difficulty focusing their attention in a disciplined way.

While the existence of bisexual behavior is clearly acknowledged, little empirical research has been devoted to understanding individuals who engage in sexual behavior with both sexes. Kinsey, Pomeroy, and Martin (1948) estimated that 18% of American males had comparable amounts of heterosexual and homosexual experience, and that 37% had at least some homosexual experiences to the point of orgasm during their adult lives.

Traditionally, prevailing opinions among researchers and theorists in the area of sexual orientation assume one of two positions. The first contention is that bisexuality does not exist as a separate entity; instead, people who describe themselves as bisexual are in fact practicing homosexuals who cling to their heterosexual identity because they cannot tolerate labeling themselves homosexual (Bieber, 1971; Caprio, 1955; Ellis,

Dr. Wayson received his doctorate in clinical psychology from the California School of Professional Psychology in 1983. He currently resides in San Diego where he is in private practice and on the staff of the San Diego Academy. Correspondence may be addressed to the author, 3821 Fourth Avenue, San Diego, CA 92104.

1928; Ford & Beach, 1951). The other contention is that bisexuals exist, but that they are shallow, sociopathic individuals who have serious difficulty forming stable relationships with members of either sex and thus exist in a nether world of transient sexual encounters with both men and women (Masters & Johnson, 1979; West, 1967).

What seems clear from the literature is that both of these perspectives are highly speculative and largely unsubstantiated. They derive generally from an era when any sexual behavior other than heterosexual copulation was regarded as abnormal and psychologically pathological. Homosexuality, however, is no longer regarded by either the American Psychiatric or the American Psychological Associations as a mental illness unless it is viewed as ego-dystonic.

With this in mind, it seems that bisexuality deserves unbiased study. Research has failed to produce evidence of a pathological profile of homosexuality as compared to heterosexuality (Booth, 1977; Clark, 1973; Evans, 1970; Hooker, 1957; Siegelman, 1972; Thompson, Mc-Candless, & Strickland, 1971). Some studies however, have revealed personality differences among groups possessing different sexual orientations (Bem, 1974, 1977; Kelly & Worrell, 1976; Spence, Helmreich & Stapp, 1975; Wiggins & Holtzmuller, 1978). Most of these, however, have focused on the area of gender identity. It is important to make clear distinction between "gender identity" and "sexual orientation." Gender identity refers to qualities of personality that pertain to being either male or female and, by extension, being masculine and feminine. Sexual orientation refers specifically to the biological sex of partners with whom one has sex or to whom one is sexually attracted.

It is significant that differences between homosexual and heterosexual men and women have been determined on the basis of gender-related issues. Bernard and Epstein (1978) and Larsons (1977) found that homosexual men as a group were significantly more androgynous than heterosexual men as measured on the Bem Sex Role Inventory (BEM).

Additionally, the failure of studies to find appreciable differences between bisexuals and homosexuals has been largely due to the inadequate criteria used to define the bisexual group. Almost all empirical studies include a "bisexual" group on the basis of a particular subject's self-label. This presents the problem of how to define bisexuality, considering the numerous definitions researchers and the general population assign to the term. This study chose to use the Klein Sexual Orientation Grid (Klein, 1980) to define bisexuality as a combination of seven variables: sexual attraction, sexual fantasy, sexual behavior, emotional preference, social preference, definition of lifestyle, and self-definition.

By attempting to belong to both heterosexual and homosexual groups, bisexuals occupy a peculiar place in society. This study postulates that bisexuals have no group of their own with which to identify. This is true whether bisexuality is a transitional state for the individual or a stable one.

This study asserts that society is intolerant of the bisexual orientation and pressures such individuals to define themselves as either heterosexual or homosexual. Denied social validation, the bisexual often experiences identity confusion. The bisexual is continually confronted with the discrepancy between his or her orientation and the perspectives of the larger society. Blumstein and Schwartz (1974) discussed the intolerance of the homosexual community towards bisexuals. The intolerance of the heterosexuals to anything other than heterosexuality is too pervasive to require documentation.

Faced with society's failure to validate their sexual orientation, bisexuals may experience isolation that can have a profound impact on their personality. The confusion that results from society's denial of their existence directly affects their sense of self, and hence self-esteem. Additionally, bisexuals do not have an identifiable subculture with which to identify.

This study used the Test of Attentional and Interpersonal Style (TAIS) as a means of measuring some stresses on the bisexual. The TAIS, a personality measure that is constructed on the premise of functionality rather than pathology, focuses upon the attentional abilities and intepersonal dynamics of the individual.

This study proposed two principal hypotheses:

1. The bisexual group would report greater cognitive confusion and emotional stress, and thereby perceive themselves as more easily distracted and less able to focus than either the heterosexual or homosexual groups; and
2. The bisexual group would score lower on the self-esteem scale of the TAIS than either the heterosexual or homosexual groups.

METHOD

Subjects

One-hundred fourteen Caucasian males were recruited for the study, all over the age of 25 years (mean age 38.5 yrs.). As a group, these men were well-educated (educational mean = 16.5 years, S.D. = 5.66 yrs.) and relatively affluent (mean annual income = $38,000, S.D. = $29,400, median = $25,000). All subjects were voluntary participants, and therefore cannot be considered a random sample of the population.

On the basis of the Sexual Screening Questionnaire (SSQ) which was adapted from the Klein Sexual Orientation Grid (KSOG), the subjects were placed in one of three groups: heterosexual (n = 35), bisexual (n = 21), or homosexual (n = 58). This categorization was based on subject responses to seven questions (each using a 7-point Likert-type scale). The criteria for inclusion in any one category were the mean score for the first three scales pertaining specifically to sexuality and the mean score of seven variables. For membership in a category, both of these averages had to fall within the limits of the same sexual orientation group. These limits were 1 to 3 for heterosexuals, 3 to 5 for bisexuals, and 5 to 7 for homosexuals. Of the 165 subjects recruited, 51 were dropped because of failure to meet the study requirements.

All three groups were matched on various demographic factors including age, socioeconomic status, responses on the Marlowe-Crowne Social Desirability Scale, and the absence of either a criminal record or a current psychiatric condition requiring psychotropic medication. On only the variable of age did these groups differ significantly, and subsequent discriminant analyses indicated that age did not significantly influence results. The Marlowe-Crowne was included to control for possible response bias.

Instrumentation

Included in the packet of materials given to subjects were the Marlowe-Crowne Social Desirability Scale (Crowne & Marlowe, 1960) a demographic sheet, the SSQ (see Table 1), and the Test of Attentional and Interpersonal Style (TAIS). The TAIS explores levels of adaptive and non-adaptive functioning on the basis of attentional characteristics and in-

TABLE   1

Means and Standard Deviations on ANOVAS for

Overload Factor and Self-Esteem Scale

Group	Overload Factor		Self-Esteem Scale	
	Mean	S.D.	Mean	S.D.
Heterosexual	.03	.83	15.97	6.90
Bisexual	.04	1.05	18.81	7.92
Homosexual	.04	1.15	14.91	10.66

terpersonal dynamics. While it has never been used before to distinguish among groups on the basis of sexual orientation, the TAIS is a highly discriminating instrument. Test-retest reliability co-efficients are .83 for two weeks and .76 for over one year. Factor analytic studies of the subscales indicate the presence of seven factors which appear reliable across sex and across cultures (LaMotte, 1981; Nideffer, Wiens, & Matarazzo, 1980; Schmelzer, 1981).

The Decision-Making Factor measures the relative levels of rumination and anxiety involved in making a decision. The Competitive Factor measures levels of physical and interpersonal competitiveness. The Extroverted Factor measures the individual's relative need for and involvement with others. The Activity Level Factor describes how busy the individual perceives his world to be. The Narrowing Factor measures the individual's ability to narrow attention appropriately and thereby avoid distraction. The Overloaded Factor measures the individual's tendency to become anxious and attentionally confused in response to internal and external stimuli. Finally, the Intellectually Critical Factor measures the individual's intellectual expressiveness and his tendency to be critical.

In addition to studies already cited, construct and criterion validity has been found in a number of other studies (Nideffer, 1976; Nideffer et al., 1980). The TAIS has also proven itself effective in discriminating between heterogeneous groups, e.g., between psychiatric and non-psychiatric populations, as well as within groups which are highly homogeneous, e.g., between elite and nonelite athletes, between different psychiatric subgroups, and between musicians who play different instruments (DePalma & Nideffer, 1977; Nideffer et al., 1980).

Procedure

Subjects were males recruited from various business and professional groups. Upon completing all materials, the participant mailed the packet back to the researcher.

RESULTS

Hypothesis 1 stated that the bisexual group would describe themselves as more attentionally overloaded, by both external (OET) and internal (OIT) stimuli as measured by the TAIS. It also suggested that this fact would inhibit their ability to narrow attention effectively (low NAR) and result in a tendency to behave impulsively (high BCON). Hypothesis 2 postulated that, as a result of the attentional difficulties and in the face of minimal social validation of their sexuality, the bisexual group's self-esteem (SES) would suffer. To examine these hypotheses, two least

squares one-way analyses of variance (ANOVA) for completely randomized factor design with unequal N's were performed.

Both ANOVAs compared the three groups on the basis of their TAIS
scores on the relevant subscales described above. There were no
statistically significant differences in either analysis for the three groups.
Table 1 presents the mean scores and standard deviations for the three
groups on both dependent measures.

With respect to the hypothesized difference on self-esteem, there appeared to be a moderate trend, though not significant, in the opposite
direction from that postulated by Hypothesis 2. The bisexual group
registered a slightly higher mean score on the SES scale than did the
heterosexual and homosexual groups.

A multiple discriminant function analysis modeled after a computer
program entitled MULTIVARIANCE (Finn, 1974) was performed to examine the ability of the seven TAIS factors, as well as age and
socioeconomic status, to discriminate on the basis of sexual orientations.
This analysis resulted in two discriminant clusters which accounted for
approximately 16% of the total variance. Of these two clusters, Cluster I
explained 75% of the total variance accounted for; it alone was significant
statistically. Cluster I consisted of the TAIS factors measuring physical
competitiveness, ability effectively to narrow attention, and speed of
decision-making.

The bisexual group scored lower than either of the other two groups on
the attentional narrowing scale, thereby describing itself as least adept at
focusing and concentrating on a task. In contrast, both the heterosexual
and homosexual groups scored higher on this scale, though their scores
did not differ significantly from each other.

The TAIS factor reflecting competitiveness also discriminated among
groups. The TAIS Competitive Factor, consisting of scales measuring
physical orientation (P/O), a need for interpersonal control (CON) and
self-esteem (SES), is most clearly identified with the heterosexual group
and least associated with the homosexual group.

Finally, the Decision-Making Factor, measuring an individual's level
of rumination and anxiety (high OBS, OIT, RED) also discriminated
among groups, the homosexual group scoring highest on this factor. The
results suggest that the homosexual group is more anxious and ruminative
before coming to a decision than is the bisexual, in spite of the latter's
greater distractibility. Apparently, the bisexual group's relative difficulty
in narrowing attention and following through in a focused way does not
act to increase their anxiety.

Data were compared across group on life-history variables. Age of
first sexual experiences with men and women, length of sexual and non-
sexual relationships with men and women, and various socioeconomic indicators are summarized in Table 2.

TABLE 2

Demographic Data

	Heterosexual		Bisexual		Homosexual	
	$\overline{X}$	SD	$\overline{X}$	SD	$\overline{X}$	SD
Hollingshead Index	35.37	8.79	38.95	9.01	40.14*	10.54
Age of Sex with Female	16.94***	2.61	19.83	5.14	20.58	4.07
Age of Sex with Male	--	--	18.57	9.32	11.02	7.50
Sexual Relation with Female	9.50	7.60	11.70	7.90	6.90	8.40
Sexual Relation with Male	--	--	1.60	2.30	5.00	8.70
Nonsexual Relation with Female	10.50	9.00	12.20	9.30	13.40	9.50
Nonsexual Relation with Male	18.30	8.90	16.00	10.70	16.70	10.70

*p .05.

***p .01.

The male heterosexual group had been significantly younger than the bisexual and homosexual groups at the time of their first sexual intercourse and the first orgasm with a woman. The bisexual and homosexual group's mean age of sexual orgasm with a male, on the other hand, was not significantly different from the heterosexual group's mean age of first orgasm with a female. Also, for the bisexual group, the age of first sexual contact with a female versus that with a male did not differ significantly.

DISCUSSION

Prior to a discussion of this study's results, a word must be said about the Sexual Screening Questionnaire (SSQ) already described. To test the reliability and interrelatedness of items, a PRINCO program and Factor program with a HOW routine (Cooley & Lohmes, 1971; Ortega, 1960) was performed using four principal factors. From this process, three factors with eigen values above one accounted for approximately 74% of the total variance across all subjects. Only one of these factors will be described here since it encompasses one of the criteria for categorizing subjects into sexual orientation groups. Accounting for 44% of the total variance was the Sexuality Factor which consisted of the items pertaining to sexual attraction, fantasy, behavior, and individual sexual self-definition for past, present, and ideal response conditions.

The results suggest that distinct differences among bisexuals, heterosexuals, and homosexuals are equivocal at best. Perhaps the most interesting finding is that a psychological measure such as TAIS, which is not pathological in perspective, yields evidence of relatively minor differences.

While not reporting themselves more attentionally overloaded, bisexuals did describe themselves as less capable than either of the other two groups of narrowing attention in order to concentrate in a focused and disciplined way. It is possible that bisexuals are more distractible and less able to focus their attention because they themselves have to compensate for an acute lack of social validation, a dilemma which may create the need to maintain a false persona. This constant need to attend to the interplay between self and the environment may take its toll in terms of attentional focus, this very self-consciousness may inhibit one's ability to focus externally.

As a result of difficulties in focusing attention, the bisexual group also reports experiencing less anxiety and rumination than the other two groups. A bisexual's decision-making alacrity and inability to narrow attention may result in others seeing him as shallow and impulsive. Possibly, shallowness and impulsiveness serve to ease the burden of the bisexual's dilemma, inhibiting introspection that might lead to more confusion and distress.

Though in opposition to the initial hypothesis, the tendency to score slightly (although not significantly) higher on the self-esteem scale by the bisexual group would provide some support for this interpretation. Perhaps bisexuals cannot or will not narrow attentionally in a disciplined and focused way, and yet they react more quickly and with less anxiety than do others, and probably feel that their actions are legitimate.

Much of the extant literature, while largely speculative, has asserted that bisexuals tend to be sociopathic individuals (Bell, Weinberg, & Hammersmith, 1981; Bieber, Dain, Dince, Drellich, Grand, Gundlach, Kremer, Rifkin, Wilbur, & Bieber, 1962; Cory & Leroy, 1963; Masters & Johnson, 1979; Ross, Rogers, McCullough, & McCullough, 1978; West, 1967). The pattern of response from the bisexual group in the present study may lend some credence to this view, if sociopathy is defined as the ability to tailor one's behavior to the demands of the situation regardless of the discomfort one may experience in the process. While the sociopathic view of bisexuality is partially supported by these results, it is statistically minimal; further research is imperative for a more thorough understanding of the dynamics involved. It is possible that the need to dissemble weakens personal integrity. Certainly one of the hallmarks of the successful sociopath is the ability to discern and exploit particular situations.

The multiple discriminant function analysis of the TAIS scores revealed interesting results with regard to the Competitive factor, which measures physical orientation and competiton as well as a need for interpersonal control. Of the three scales that load on this factor, only the Physical Orientation (P/O) mean score was significantly higher (p. < 001) for the heterosexual group than for the other two groups.

An item analysis of those questions comprising the P/O scale indicates that competition is the chief ingredient of physical orientation on the TAIS. Of the eight items that load on the P/O scale, three refer directly to competition, one implies competition, and one refers to competitive experiences in elementary and high school or college. Few would argue with the premise that in American society, physical orientation often contains a strong element of competition, particularly during the educational years of an individual's (particularly a male's) life. It is important to realize that TAIS reflects just such a bias. It is reasonable to assume that heterosexual males are more physically competitive than are homosexual or bisexual males. Differentiating between physical competition and physical activity could give us a more complete understanding of the differences among the groups.

In assessing this study's results, it seems that more questions have arisen than have been answered. A study that more directly addresses impulsivity, depth of relationships, and the ability to remain narrowly focused (the sociopathy question), needs to be designed. Several alternatives theories can explain the presence of what appears to be a possible sociopathic element in the bisexual character structure.

REFERENCES

Bell, A. P., Weinberg, M. S., & Hammersmith, S. K. (1981). *Sexual preference: Its development in men and women.* Bloomington, IN: Indiana University Press.

Bem, S. L. (1974). The measurement of psychological androgyny. *Journal of Consulting and Clinical Psychology, 42,* 155-162.

Bem, S. L. (1977). On the utility of alternative procedures for assessing psychological androgyny. *Journal of Consulting and Clinical Psychology, 45,* 196-205.

Bernard, L. C., & Epstein, D. J. (1978). Androgyny scores of matched homosexual and heterosexual males. *Journal of Homosexuality, 4,* 169-178.

Bieber, I. (1971, April). Homosexuality—A symposium, the causes, and consequences, social and psychological of sexual inversion. *Playboy Magazine,* pp. 63-67.

Bieber, I., Dain, H. J., Dince, P. R., Drellich, M. G., Grand, H. G., Gundlach, R. H., Kremer, M. W., Rifkin, A. H. Wilbur, C. B., & Bieber, T. B. (1962). *Homosexuality: A psychoanalytic study of male homosexuals.* New York: Basic Books.

Blumstein, P. W., & Schwartz, P. (1974). Lesbianism and bisexuality. In E. Goode & R. R. Troiden (Eds.), *Sexual deviance and sexual deviants.* (pp. 288-297). New York: William Morrow.

Booth, H. (1977). Psychological health and sexual orientation in males (Doctoral dissertation, California School of Professional Psychology, San Francisco). *Dissertation Abstracts International,* (University Microfilms No. 77-27, 389).

Caprio, F. (1955). *Variations in sexual behavior.* New York: Grove Press.

Clark, T. R. (1973). Homosexuality as a criterion predictor of psychopathology in non-patient males. In *Proceedings of the 81st Annual Convention of the American Psychological Association, 8,* 407-408.

Cooley, W. W., & Lohmes, P. R. (1971). *Multivariate data analysis.* New York: John Wiley & Sons.

Cory, D. W., & LeRoy, J. P. (1963). *The homosexual and his society.* New York: Citadel Press.

Crowne, P., & Marlowe, D. (1960). A new scale of social desirability independent of psychopathology. *Journal of Consulting Psychology, 24,* 349-354.

DePalma, D., & Nideffer, R. M. (1977). Relationships between the test of attentional and interpersonal style and psychiatric subclassification. *Journal of Personality Assessment, 41,* 622-631.

Ellis, H. (1928). *Studies in the psychology of sex* (Vol. 2). Philadelphia: F. A. Davis.

Evans, R. B. (1970). Sixteen personality factor questionnaire scores of homosexual men. *Journal of Consulting and Clinical Psychology, 34,* 212-215.

Finn, J. D. (1974). *A general model for multivariate analysis.* New York: Holt, Rinehart & Winston.

Ford, C. S., & Beach, F. A. (1951). *Patterns of sexual behavior.* New York: Harper.

Hooker, E. (1957). The adjustment of the male overt homosexual. *Journal of Projective Techniques, 21,* 18-31.

Kelly, J. A., & Worrell, L. (1976). Parent behavior related to masculinity, femininity, and androgyny sex role orientations. *Journal of Consulting and Clinical Psychology, 44,* 843-851.

Kinsey, A. C., Pomeroy, W. B., & Martin, C. E. (1948). *Sexual behavior in the human male.* Philadelphia & London: W. B. Saunders.

Klein, F. (1980, December). Are you sure you're heterosexual? or homosexual? or even bisexual? *Forum Magazine,* pp. 41-45.

LaMotte, S. (1981). *Attentional and interpersonal style in marital relationships.* Unpublished doctoral dissertation, California School of Professional Psychology, San Diego, CA.

Larsons, P. C. (1977). Sexual identity and self-concept. *Dissertation Abstracts International, 38,* 4B.

Masters, W. H., & Johnson, V. E. (1979). *Homosexuality in perspective*. Boston: Little, Brown.

Nideffer, R. M. (1976). Test of attentional and interpersonal style. *Journal of Personality Assessment and Social Psychology, 34*, 394-404.

Nideffer, R. M., Wiens, A. N., & Matarazzo, J. D. (1980). The relevance of attentional processes to the selection and screening of police applications. In R. M. Nideffer (Ed.), *Predicting human behavior: A theory and test of attentional and interpersonal style* (pp. 000-000). San Diego: Enhanced Performance Associates.

Ortega, J. M. (1960). On strum sequences for tridiagonal matrices. *Journal of Association for Computing Machinery, 7*, 260-263.

Ross, M. W., Rogers, L. J., McCullough, D. P., & McCullough, H. (1978). Stigma, sex, and society: A new look at gender differentiation and sexual variation. *Journal of Homosexuality, 3*, 315-330.

Schmelzer, R. (1981). *Comparison of attentional and interpersonal style across two cultures, West Germany and the United States*. Unpublished doctoral dissertation, California School of Professional Psychology, San Diego.

Siegelman, M. (1972). Adjustment of male homosexuals and heterosexuals. *Archives of Sexual Behavior, 2*, 9-25.

Spence, J. T., Helmreich, R., & Stapp, J. (1975). Ratings of self and peers on sex-role attributes and their relation to self-esteem and conceptions of masculinity and femininity. *Journal of Personality and Social Psychology, 32*, 29-39.

Thompson, N. L., Jr., McCandless, B. R., & Strickland, B. R. (1971). Personal adjustment of male and female homosexuals and heterosexuals. *Journal of Abnormal Psychology, 78*, 237-240.

West, D. J. (1967). *Homosexuality*. Chicago: Aldine.

Wiggins, J. S., & Holtzmuller, A. (1978). Psychological androgyny and interpersonal behavior. *Journal of Consulting and Clinical Psychology, 46*, 40-52.

Mexican Male Bisexuality

J. M. Carrier, PhD

University of California, Irvine

ABSTRACT. Even one adult homosexual act may threaten the masculine gender identity of American males, and raise the question of their homosexuality. However, fieldwork in Northwestern Mexico revealed a different belief system. A Mestizo Mexican male's masculine gender identity is not threatened by homosexual acts as long as he plays the insertor sex role; only the male insertee, playing a female sex role, is considered homosexual. An analysis of the Mexican data suggests that bisexual behavior is thus more easily accepted by Mestizo Mexican males and is more widely practiced in that region of Mexico than in the United States.

This paper presents some preliminary observations and comments on Mexican male bisexual behavior, and on the cultural factors which appear to be related to the behavior. Some recent findings on Anglo-American male bisexual behavior will be compared with the Mexican findings. The Mexican data on which the paper is based were gathered by the author over a period of 15 years from 1968 to 1983, and include both participant-observation and interview data. Although the data were gathered primarily from mestizo males in the northwestern states of Mexico, there is some evidence (see, for example, Taylor, 1978; Zapata, 1979) that the patterns of behavior observed are similar among Mestizo males in other areas of Mexico. (Mestizos are Mexican nationals of mixed Indian and Spanish

Dr. Carrier received his degree in Social Sciences at the University of California, Irvine. He is a member of the Gender Identity Research Group at the University of California at Los Angeles, and the Anthropological Research Group on Homosexuality. Currently he is studying bisexuality in the northwestern states of Mexico. Requests for reprints should be sent to 17447 Castellammare Drive, Pacific Palisades, CA 90272.

ancestry. They make up a large majority of the population, and their culture is the dominant one.)

Few studies have focused on human bisexual behavior. This has been due, in part, to the dichotomization of sexual orientation in Anglo-American culture into heterosexuality and homosexuality. In Anglo-American culture any homosexual behavior in an individual's sexual biography, especially as an adult, raises the question of homosexuality, not bisexuality, regardless of the ratio of heterosexual to homosexual behavior or feelings. The general view in Anglo-American society, therefore, is that most people are heterosexual; those who are not are homosexual.

Data gathered by Kinsey and his associates (1948, 1953) and by anthropologists (see, for example, Davenport, 1965; and Herdt, 1981) have empirically established bisexual behavior in human populations. Based on the Human Relations Area Files, Ford and Beach (1951) presented additional cross-cultural information on bisexuality.

A major problem in evaluating the available data on bisexuality is the meaning of the sexual behavior to the individuals involved. As pointed out by Blumstein and Schwartz (1977) in a recent paper on bisexuality: "When does a pattern of sexual or other social behaviors give rise to a person's sense of his or her sexual identity, and when are they simply behaviors with no further implications?" (p. 34). In a paper on the social control of sexuality, DeLamater (1981) noted that:

> Every society has a "folk theory" (Davenport, 1977) or "commonsense theory" about sexual behavior. It includes assumptions about the purposes of sexual behavior; from these are derived beliefs or norms that specify what types of activity are appropriate and inappropriate given these purposes, and what types of partners are acceptable. The theory includes definitions or criteria for distinguishing behaviors and partners. (p. 266)

He identifies three dinstinct sexual perspectives in American society: procreational, relational, and recreational. The procreational emphasizes the reproductive aspect of sexual activity. The relational is "person-centered" sexuality and "assumes that sexual activity is an integral part of some relationships, that such behavior is a means of expressing and reinforcing emotional and psychological intimacy" (p. 266). The recreational is "body-centered" sexuality and "assumes that the purpose of sexual activity is physical pleasure . . . and is appropriate with any partner who is similarly inclined" (p. 266).

An evaluation of bisexuality in any given society must also consider the availability of sexual partners. Irrespective of individual preferences, when suitable heterosexual partners are unavailable to certain segments of a society for whatever reason, some individuals will turn to members of their own sex for sexual satisfaction. A number of sociocultural factors, operating separately or in varying combinations, may curtail or complete-ly shut off the supply of heterosexual partners. Some important factors are expectations with respect to virginity, segregation of sexes prior to marriage, age at marriage, polygamy, sex ratio, segregation of sexes as a result of incarceration, and available economic resources or distribution of income. Additionally, in some traditional Melanesian societies, male initiation rites may include homosexual behavior where semen is trans-ferred by the older males to the initiates through fellatio or anal inter-course in order to bring about growth and masculinity. All males in these societies are also expected to take wives and perform heterosexually.

Blumstein and Schwartz (1977) believe that "when more investigators have addressed themselves to the phenomenon of bisexuality, the ac-cumulated evidence will help transform the way science views human sexuality" (p. 44). The most fundamental conclusion of their research on bisexuality is that the closer they probed "such questions as how people come to define themselves sexually or how their erotic and affectional biographies are structured, the more, not less, the data defy organization in terms of the classical simplicities" (p. 31). They also made the obser-vation that:

> The implications of viewing human sexuality as being plastic and malleable have never really been exploited. Even the word *bisex-uality* gives a misleading sense of fixedness to sex-object choice, suggesting as it does a person in the middle, equidistant from heterosexuality and from homosexuality, equally erotically disposed to one gender or the other. (p. 44)

THE SOCIO-CULTURAL SETTING IN MEXICO

Those socio-cultural aspects of Mexican society which appear to be particularly relevant to male bisexuality are the lack of stigmatization of the masculine inserter role in homosexual encounters, an easily iden-tifiable group of effeminate male sexual partners, the generally per-missive attitude toward sexual behavior by males, the dual categorization of females, the proportion of single males past the age of puberty, the homosocial nature of much of male socialization, and the inequitable distribution of income.

Masculine males who play the active insertor role in homosexual en-counters generally are not conceptualized as *homosexuals* in Mexico. This lack of stigmatization provides prospective active participants with the important feeling that their masculine self-image is not threatened by their homosexual behavior. There is no doubt some level of homosexual involvement at which even a masculine male may be concerned about his self-image, particularly if he develops a pattern of non-association with females. But in Mexican society at large, as Paz (1950) has noted, "masculine homosexuality is regarded with a certain indulgence insofar as the active agent is concerned" (p. 39). Observations I made in many different parts of Mexico support the notion that those masculine males who utilize passive males as sexual outlets are greatly tolerated.

Effeminate males provide easily identifiable sexual targets for interested males in Mexico. There is the widely held belief in the society that effeminate males are homosexual, and sexually interested only in masculine males with whom they play the passive insertee sex role in anal intercourse. The beliefs linking effeminate males with homosexuality are culturally transmitted by a vocabulary which provides the appropriate labels, by homosexually oriented jokes and word games and by the mass media. From early childhood on, Mexican males are made aware of the labels used to denote male homosexuals, and the connection is always clearly made that these homosexual males (usually caled *putos* or *jotos*) are guilty of unmanly effeminate behavior.

The generally permissive attitude toward sexual behavior by Mexican males appears to be partly the result of the sexual stimuli presented them from birth onward by way of joking and the public media. They are thus sensitized to many different kinds of sexual relationships. By the time they reach puberty, they are especially aware of the availability and acceptability of effeminate males as sexual outlets. The acceptance and desirability of heterosexual intercourse is further enhanced by the fact that adolescent males, often at the first signs of puberty, may be pressured by their brothers, male cousins, friends, or all three, to prove their masculinity by having sexual intercourse with either prostitutes or available neighborhood girls. The crowded family circumstances in which a majority of the Mexican population live also contributes to a heightened awareness of the body's daily functions and needs, including those sexual. Body contact, sexual joking, or both, between male members of the family sleeping in the same bed or close together is apparently not unusual, nor is their knowledge about sexual intercourse.

Another relevant feature of Mexican society is a belief system that leads to the categorization of females as being either "good" or "bad." A good woman is conceptualized by a male as a wife and mother of his children. Prior to marriage, according to the normative cultural ideal, she must be chaste and faithful. After marriage she must continue to be faithful and should not demonstrate excessive sexual interest even in her husband. The categorization "good" thus comes down to a basic belief that a woman cannot be considered a prime sexual target and still be considered good. A woman is therefore labeled "bad" precisely because she is primarily thought of by males as being immediately exploitable as a sexual outlet.

A related aspect of the "good-bad" dichotomization of females is the double standard of sexual morality allowed Mexican males, a standard which begins prior to marriage. In the Mexican courtship system, the prospective bride is labeled a *novia*, the prospective groom a *novio*. (There is no counterpart to this system in the United States. The Mexican couple can be said to have an understanding; the arrangement is more serious than going steady, but less formal than an engagement.) The period of courtship may last as long as five years or more. Since she may one day be his wife and the mother of his children, a novia must in the eyes of her novio fall into the category "good"; she obviously cannot be considered a prime sexual target prior to marriage. Under existing mores, however, at the same time a Mexican male is courting a novia, he may also have a series of sexual contacts with whichever outlets are available. Girlfriends considered appropriate for sexual seduction are referred to as *amigas;* lovers as *amantes*. After marriage the husband may maintain the double standard and continue to seek sexual outlets in addition to his wife.

Unfortunately, I know of no sound general studies of attitudes toward sexual permissiveness in Mexico. LaBeff and Dodder (1982) briefly report a comparative study of 278 Americann and 145 Mexican college students using Reiss' Sexual Permissiveness Scale. The items rated by the students concern the acceptability of petting and sexual intercourse for females in the following affection-related states: within an engagement, with affection, and without affection. Their findings, however, are limited by the fact that their sample was confined to college students. Yet, it is nevertheless interesting to note that in all of their comparisons "the Mexican students were less permissive" (p. 286). They also note "that attitudes toward female sexual permissiveness were more complex and difficult to interpret for the Mexican sample of college students. . . some basic difference in structure were apparent" (p. 286).

Some preliminary data gathered by Taylor (1974) suggested that heterosexual anal intercourse, considered to be a common occurrence by his Mexico City respondents, may be used in Mexico as "a method of maintaining the female's status as a vaginal virgin during courtship and a common form of birth control" (p. 5).

Another relevant characteristic of Mexican society is the proportion of single males past the age of puberty. Marriage patterns in Mexico at present indicate that a sizable percentage of males do not marry until their late twenties. While single, a large majority of Mexican males, a little over 80 percent according to the 1970 census, continue to live in some kind of family grouping. This pattern apparently holds true even when single males are in their late twenties or thirties. The available data suggest that the only way a single male is able to move away from his family, even if he wants to and can afford to, is to move to a different geographical area.

Male socialization patterns in Mexico tend to be all male in character, both before and after marriage. Peer-group relationships, of particular importance in adolescence, remain essentially unchanged by marriage. Peñalosa (1968) summed it up as follows: "In social life a Mexican man's marital status is of little practical importance, as a man carries on virtually the same sort of social life after marriage as he did before—and one in which the women have little part" (p. 683).

Drinking establishments in Mexico, cantinas, bars, and nightclubs, are popular locations for Mexican males to spend some of their free time away from their families. With few exceptions, these establishments are restricted to male customers. Females who go to those establishments generally have working relationships as dance hostesses, prostitutes, or both. Thus, they obviously fall into the "bad" category. A "good" woman in Mexico would never be seen in a public drinking establishment, except possibly in cities which have designated "ladies bars," hotel bars or nightclubs for tourists. However, even there a Mexican woman would have to consider herself somewhat "liberated" to frequent such establishments on any regular basis.

The final aspect of Mexican society to be considered is distribution of income. In Mexico, inequalities in income distribution, combined with high birth rates, result in large segments of the urban as well as rural population living on incomes that barely provide the basic necessities of life. Although urban dwellers generally fare better than rural, the available data suggest that a majority in both segments of the population still tend to live in marginal situations. In recent years, the economic situation has worsened as inflation rates have climbed close to 100 percent. Less available income for males seeking sexual outlets may make effeminate males more desirable sexual targets because they are available at little or no cost, and may even be a source of income for their masculine suitors.

SOME BISEXUAL BEHAVIOR PATTERNS

The following discussion of Mexican male bisexual behavior is based on 53 structured interviews with male respondents in Guadalajara. Two-thirds (33 of 53) had had both heterosexual and homosexual experiences. In addition, there were 20 unstructured interviews with male respondents in various locations in the northwestern states of Mexico, all of whom had had both heterosexual and homosexual experiences. Participant-observation data collected by the author are also used in the discussion.

Family, peers, and the media provide strong motivation for Mexican males to become romantically involved with females from their early teens. Strong sexual needs, combined with pressure from male relatives and peers, also provide powerful motivation for males in this age group to seek sexual outlets in addition to masturbation. Societal rules governing the behavior of females who want to stay in the ''good'' category, however, present an obstacle for males interested in also receiving sexual satisfaction in their relationships with novias. A sizable percentage of Mexican males may thus rule out sexual intercourse with their novias, and seek other sexual outlets. The search for sexual outlets may last for many years because some Mexican males do not marry until their late twenties; 27% of the male population in the age group 25-29 were unmarried at the time of the 1970 census.

The search by Mexican males for sexual outlets other than their novias may focus on females or males who have established reputations for sexual availability. The sexual partners they choose depends on such obvious factors as sexual excitement, attractiveness, mutual interest, timing, and cost. Over time some may choose female partners only, others male partners only, and still others both female and male partners. Since a Kinsey-type survey of male sexual behavior has never been done in Mexico, there are no data from which an estimate can be made for any given age set of the percentage of the sexually attractive male population who at some time have utilized both female and male sexual outlets. However, judging from the sociocultural factors described above, I believe that for any given age set, a larger percentage of sexually active single males in Mexico have had sexual intercourse with both genders than have Anglo-American males. The Kinsey (1949) data suggest that about 15 percent of single sexually active Anglo-American males between 15 and 25 have mixed sexual histories. The percentage of Mexican males with mixed histories may be as high as 30 percent for the same age group.

My data suggest several patterns of bisexual behavior in Mexico. The following patterns appear to be most salient. Some post-pubertal males utilize pre-pubertal boys as sexual outlets prior to marraige, and, after marriage, continue to utilize both heterosexual and homosexual outlets. Another pattern is that some males in their first year of sexual activity initiate sexual encounters both with post-pubertal girls, and effeminate boys, they find in their neighborhoods, at school, at social outings. They continue to utilize both sexual outlets prior to marriage, but discontinue, or only occasionally use, homosexual outlets following marriage. Still another pattern exists where some males utilize both genders as sexual outlets during their first couple of years of sexual activity. They have novias and plan to marry, but they also become romantically involved with males prior to marriage. After they marry, they continue to have romantic and sexual relationships with males.

Although these patterns are the most salient ones suggested by the available data, *the data are limited*. The patterns presented above (and discussed below) thus represent perhaps only a few of the many possible patterns male bisexual behavior may follow in Mexico. They do illustrate, however, the plasticity and malleability of human sexual behavior. It should be noted that none of the males following the three patterns described above considered himself "homosexual."

Males following the first pattern described usually initiate sexual encounters with pre-pubertal effeminate boys who are relatives, nephews or cousins, or neighbors. Because of the proximity of these pre-pubertal boys, the interested post-pubertal males may maintain long-term sexual relationships with them. While these homosexual relationships are going on, the older males also have novias, and occasionally have sexual intercourse with available neighborhood girls or prostitutes. The sexual relationships with the younger males are usually terminated when the older males marry. The older males, however, may continue occasional homosexual contacts with other males after marriage.

The following presents an example of this pattern. One Mexican male initiated his first homosexual relationship at the age of 15 with his 8-year-old cousin. They slept together for one year. During that time, the younger boy played the anal insertee sex role an average of once a week. The older boy then moved to another town for one year. During that time, he had his first heterosexual contacts with prostitutes. When he returned to his younger cousin's house, they no longer shared the same bed, but they resumed their weekly sexual relationship for another three years. The relationship terminated when the informant married at the age of 20. Although the informant wanted to continue the sexual relationship with his younger cousin after marriage, the younger cousin terminated the sexual relationship by saying, "there was no longer any reason for him to feel love for him." At the age of 23, the informant reported that he is sexually satisfied with his wife, but occasionally has sexual contact with males he meets downtown.

Males following the second pattern establish durable relationships with novias between the onset of puberty and marriage. They may engage in heavy petting with their novias, and perhaps occasionally have sexual intercourse. But they do not routinely have a sexual relationship with their novias because of a general unwillingness on the part of both to go beyond heavy petting prior to marriage. Other sexual outlets are thus sought by these males wherever they can be found, and with whichever gender is available and affordable. Their interest in these sexual partners is mainly recreational. They seek additional sexual outlets after marriage only occasionally, and are more likely to seek a heterosexual outlet rather than a homosexual one if they do.

Males following the third pattern have novias and plan to marry, but the intensity of their relationships with novias is not as strong as for those males following the second pattern. They seek both female and male sexual outlets apart from their novias. Although a majority of their sexual contacts may be recreationally oriented, the males following the third pattern become emotionally as well as sexually involved with some of their male sexual partners. They generally postpone marriage until their late twenties or early thirties. The reasons given for marriage are the desire for a family or fear of loneliness as they grow older. After marriage, they maintain an extramarital relationship with a male rather than a female.

MEXICAN VERSUS ANGLO-AMERICAN BISEXUALITY

In their paper on bisexuality in Anglo-American men, Blumstein and Schwartz (1976) noted that: "Popular understanding of the concept 'masculinity' implies that one must show erotic distaste (not mere neutrality) toward other males, and that one must demonstrate competent performance in the heterosexual arena" (p. 339). They also note that: "Many homosexuals, like their heterosexual counterparts, believe that for most people 'one drop' of homosexuality makes one totally homosexual" (p. 349). They further conclude:

> The skepticism with which some of our respondents' claims to being bisexual were met reflects our dichotomous notions of sexuality, as well as the "logic" that homosexual reactions eradicate heterosexual responsiveness, and the idea that heterosexuality is superior to homosexuality (i.e., when given a free option one would always choose to be heterosexual). Therefore, most of our cultural thinking demands significant heterosexual credentials before a homosexual label can be skirted. Much of society is willing to disbelieve an uncredentialed assertion of bisexuality, and attributes such a claim to the inability to come to grips with a homosexual label. (pp. 345-346)

A major difference between the Anglo-American and Mexican cultural setting for male bisexuality is the lack of stigmatization in Mexico of the active insertor participant in homosexual encounters. As a result, most Mexican males do not believe that "one drop of homosexuality" makes one totally homosexual as long as the appropriate sexual role is played; most do not appear to believe that they must show erotic distaste toward other males as long as they are masculine, and play the insertor role in homosexual encounters. However, similar to their Anglo-American counterparts, Mexican males do feel that they must demonstrate competent performance in the heterosexual arena.

Another difference between Anglo-American and Mexican males is that Mexican males are not as concerned about homosexual reaction eradicating heterosexual responsiveness. Anal intercourse is the preferred homosexual practice between Mexican males. Males playing the insertor role often compare the anus to the vagina when talking about their male partners. There is a saying among men in Mexico, "the woman for her beauty, the man for his narrowness," the implication being that a man's tight anus is better than a woman's vagina. As noted above, it has also been reported that some Mexican males practice anal intercourse with their novias as a birth control measure, and as a means of maintaining vaginal virginity. Heterosexuality is considered superior to homosexuality in Mexico. A Mexican male's gender identity, however, is not necessarily threatened by his homosexual behavior as long as he is masculine and plays the insertor role.

CONCLUSION

One is impressed by the erotic responsiveness many Mexican males have developed to members of both genders, and by the apparent ease with which some are able to maintain sexual relations with both females and males. An important factor related to this may be that in Mexico, a male's gender identity is not linked to his sexual identity the same way it is in the Anglo-American culture. Also related, homosexuality in Mexico is talked about and joked about openly between males, and privately between some boyfriends and girlfriends. As one informant in Guadalajara put it: "Daily, practically daily, in school and outside of school and everywhere around . . . it's something to joke about; everybody talks about it . . . it just comes up all the time."

This is not to imply that maintaining sexual relationships with both genders does not generate cognitive dissonance for some Mexican males. It does. The form such dissonance takes appears to be related mainly to the *extent* of involvement in homosexuality. A major fear concerns the playing of the anal insertee sex role, which would directly threaten their masculine image. Prior to sexual intercourse, "masculine" males may do everything with their "effeminate" male partners that they do with a woman, have body contact, caress, and French kiss; however, for most, their anus is out of bounds for touching or penetration by a penis. As a preliminary sex act, fellatio is often used by anal insertees to arouse their sexual partners. The ultimate objective of the sexual encounter for both participants, however, is almost always anal intercourse.

Finally, when one considers that a large number of single Mexican males must deal with their sexuality for a long period of time, sometimes 10 to 12 years before marriage, a period in their lives when their sexual needs are the strongest, their choices of sexual partners may relate to all three of DeLamater's sexual perspectives. The ratio of person-centered to body-centered sexual relationships may vary considerably over time, and between individual males. The available data suggest that a majority of sexual outlets for most single males in Mexico are body-centered rather than person-centered. However, a cross-over point prior to marriage, perhaps in the early twenties, may exist when person-centered sexual outlets become more important. Yet even after marriage, Mexican males continue to seek outlets from a recreational perspective.

REFERENCES

Blumstein, P., & Schwartz P. (1976). Bisexuality in men. *Urban life, 5*, 339-358.

Blumstein, P., & Schwartz, P. (1977). Bisexuality: Some social psychological issues. *Journal of Social Issues, 33 (2)*, 30-45.

Davenport, W. (1965). Sexual patterns and their regulation in a society of the Southwest Pacific. In F. A. Beach (Ed.), *Sex and behavior* (pp. 164-207). New York: John Wiley & Sons.

Davenport, W. (1977). Sex in cross-cultural perspective. In F. A. Beach & M. Diamond (Eds.), *Human sexuality in four perspectives* (pp. 155-163). Baltimore: Johns Hopkins University Press.

DeLamater, J. (1981). The social control of sexuality. *Annual Review of Sociology, 7*, 263-290.

Ford, C. S., & Beach, F. A. (1951). *Patterns of sexual behavior.* New York: Harper & Row.

Herdt, G. (1981). *Guardians of the flutes: Idioms of masculinity.* New York: McGraw-Hill.

Kinsey, A. C., Pomeroy, W. B., & Martin, C. E. (1948). *Sexual behavior in the human male.* Philadelphia: W. B. Saunders.

Kinsey, A. C., Pomeroy, W. B., Martin, C. E., & Gebhard, P. E. (1953). *Sexual behavior in the human female.* Philadelphia: W. B. Saunders.

LaBeff, E., & Dodder, R. (1982). Attitudes toward sexual permissiveness in Mexico and the United States. *Journal of Social Psychology, 116*, 285-286.

Paz, O. (1950). *The labyrinth of solitude: Life and thought in Mexico.* New York: Grove.

Peñalosa, F. (1968). Mexican family roles. *Journal of Marriage & Family, 30*, 680-689.

Taylor, C. (1974, November). *Preliminary report on homosexual subculture in Mexico.* Paper presented to the American Anthropological Association Symposium on Homosexuality in Cross-cultural Perspective, Mexico City.

Taylor, C. (1978). *El ambiente: Male homosexual social life in Mexico City.* Unpublished doctoral dissertation, University of California, Berkeley.

Zapata, L. (1979). *Las aventuras, desventuras y suenos de Adonis Garcia, el vampiro de la Colonia Roma.* Mexico, D.F.: Editorial Grijalbo.

Bisexual Women in Marriages

Eli Coleman, PhD

University of Minnesota

ABSTRACT. A clinical sample of women who were currently or previously married were surveyed regarding demographics, homosexual experiences before marriage, problems in marriage, and sexual orientation. The average age of the 45 participants was 35.9. Before marriage, 21 (47%) were somewhat aware of their homosexual feelings but were much less likely to have thought of or identified themselves as homosexuals. Sexual difficulties were very common in these marriages (89%), the most cited sexual difficulty being a lack of sexual desire for their spouse (62%). Based upon Kinsey-type ratings, the sample could be described as almost exclusively heterosexual in behavior and fantasies before marriage. Some changes could be seen during marriage toward more of a homosexual orientation. The dramatic change, however, occurred following marriage, when the women reported even more of a homosexual orientation, tending toward the homosexual end of the Kinsey continuum. At the time of the study, a majority of the sample was, in fact, relating almost exclusively to other women. This study found that, compared to homosexual men who have been married, these women are more likely to marry at an earlier age, unlikely to be aware of their homosexual feelings prior to marriage, and more likely to terminate their marriage earlier because of conflicts arising as a result of their bisexual orientation and sexual dissatisfaction.

One obvious source of data for studying bisexuality is to examine individuals who are or have been married, and who engage in both homosexual and heterosexual activity. A number of studies have described homosexual men who are married (e.g., Brownfain, 1985; Coleman, 1981/1982a; Dank, 1972; Gochros, 1978; Latham & White, 1978; Mat-

Dr. Coleman is the Associate Director of the Program in Human Sexuality, Department of Family Practice and Community Health, Medical School, University of Minnesota, 2630 University Avenue, S.E., Minneapolis, MN 55414. Reprint requests may be sent to the author at that address.

teson, 1985; Ross, 1971; Wolf, 1985). A few books have also described
the lives and relationships of homosexual men who are or have been married (Klein, 1978; Kohn & Matusow, 1980; Malone, 1980; Nahas &
Turley, 1979). A number of articles and reports of gay fatherhood have
been published as well (e.g., Miller, 1979; Voeller & Walters, 1978).
Regarding bisexuality and female homosexuality in marriage, less information is available. Most research information comes from the large
scale studies of homosexuality by Saghir and Robbins (1973), Bell and
Weinberg (1978), and Masters and Johnson (1979). Some studies and articles focus on lesbian motherhood (e.g., Green, 1978; Kirkpatrick, Roy,
& Smith, 1976; Rand, Graham, & Rawlings, 1982). In addition, studies
on bisexuality (e.g., Blumstein & Schwartz, 1976; Klein, 1978) provide
researchers additional information on these women, their sexual orientation, and their marriages. However, there seems to be a gap in
knowledge and understanding of homosexual women who are or have
been married. More specifically, scant information exists on their lives as
married women dealing with their homosexual feelings.

It is not that there are fewer homosexual women in marriage. In fact,
some data suggest the opposite might be true. In their study of homosexuality, Saghir and Robbins (1973) found that 25% of the females and 18%
of the males had been previously married. Masters and Johnson (1979)
found that 32% of their female homosexual sample and 16% of their male
homosexual sample had been previously married. In the even more extensive study of homosexuality conducted by Bell and Weinberg (1978),
35% of the white and 47% of the black females had been previously married, compared to 20% of the white and 13% of the black males. In
Klein's (1978) sample of 144 people attending the New York City Bisexual Forum, 42% of the entire sample were or had been married; rather
equal numbers of males and females had had marital experience, 44
males (42%), and 16 females (39%). It should be noted there were many
more males than females in this study. A consistent pattern thus emerges
from these studies: samples of homosexual women are equally or more
likely to have been previously married than their male counterparts.

Comparisons of homosexual men and women in marriages revealed the
following differences. On the average, Bell and Weinberg (1978) found
males in their samples were married at age 24, compared to females who
were married at age 21. The females were less likely to have been aware
of their homosexuality prior to their marriage. The authors suggested the
age difference might explain why more women were likely to have been
married than the males in their sample. This fact may also be the result of
sample bias or differences in socio-cultural influences, in sexual identity
formation of males and females, or in the psycho-sexual make-up of
males and females, or a combination of all these factors.

Bell and Weinberg (1978) suggest that women may be under even greater pressure to marry because of social factors such as sex-role socialization and economics, and because they might not find a sexual relationship with a man completely intolerable or impossible. While these women may have been more likely to marry than their male counterparts, the authors found that marriages in which the female is homosexual tended not to last as long those of homosexual men. The authors concluded that females, more often than males, become aware of their homosexual feelings and develop an aversion to heterosexual relationships after their marriage, and report less satisfaction in their marriage. Males and females tended (not universally) to end their relationships for similar reasons, such as their homosexuality, involvement with a same-sex partner, and loss of sexual interest in their marital partner.

METHOD

Therapists known to the author were asked to recruit subjects through their clinical practice and personal contacts and to identify bisexual women who were or had been married and request their participation in this study. The potential participants filled out anonymously a questionnaire consisting of 26 items and returned it to the author by mail. Participation was completely voluntary. In exchange for participation, the subjects were offered a copy of the results of the study.

This population was utilized for several reasons. First, it was the most readily available sample population. Second, the author had conducted a similar study of a clinical sample of bisexual married men (Coleman, 1981/1982a), a similar female group would offer some basis for comparison. Information was gathered about demographics, awareness of homosexual feelings and behaviors before and during the marriage, the husbands' knowledge of the wives' homosexual feelings before and during the marriage, reasons for getting married, sexual difficulties or problems in marriage, attempts to eliminate homosexual feelings, attempts at counseling or therapy to deal with conflicts of their sexual orientation in their marriage, and Kinsey-type ratings of sexual orientation relating to behavior, fantasy, and emotional attachments before, during, and after marriage (if applicable).

RESULTS

Demographics

The average age of the 45 participants was 35.9 (see Table 1 for a summary of the results). The majority of the sample was highly educated: 78% graduated from a college or graduate and professional school. The

TABLE 1

SUMMARY OF DATA

N = 45	X	SD
Average Age	35.93	(4.29)
Age at First Marriage	21.60	(2.77)
Number of Children	1.24	(1.21)
Length of Current or Most Recent Marriage	8.47	(5.68)

	f	%
Awareness of Same-sex Feelings Prior to Marriage	21	(47%)
Awareness of Bisexual or Lesbian Identity Prior to Marriage	14	(31%)
Acted on Same-sex Feelings Prior to Marriage	18	(40%)
Marital Partner Knew of Same-sex Feelings Prior to Marriage	5	(11%)
Sexual Conflicts Within Marriage	40	(89%)
Extra-marital Liaisons	25	(56%)
Marital Partners' Knowledge of Same-sex Feelings During Marriage	25	(56%)
Marital Partners' Knowledge of Same-Sex Activities During Marriage	8	(24%)
Marital Partners' Consent for Extra-marital relationships	4	(9%)
Attempt to Eliminate Same-sex Feelings (other than psychotherapy)	9	(20%)
Attempts to Eliminate Same-sex Feelings Through Psychotherapy	4	(9%)

median income level for the sample was $15,001-$25,000 annually: 71% made over $15,000, 33% over $25,000. The average age of the participants when they were first married was 21.6 year olds. Thirty-one of the 45 women had children. The average number of children for the entire sample was 1.24. The average length of their current or most recent marriage was 8.47 years (range to 24 years). Two of the women in the sample had been married twice previously, were currently married, and the remainder had been married once previously.

Awareness of Homosexual Feelings Prior to Marriage

Twenty-one (47%) of the women were somewhat aware of their homosexual feelings before they were married [Yes, definitely - 9 (20%); yes, somewhat - 12 (27%)]. However, these women were less likely to have known or identified themselves as homosexuals before they were married [without question - 2 (4.5%); almost certain - 2 (4.5%); somewhat - 10 (22%); not at all - 31 (69%)]. Fourteen (31%) women were somewhat aware of their homosexuality. The majority of women had their first heterosexual experience (sexual touching, fondling, caressing, orgasm, and so on) after age 26. The age range for first homosexual experiences was as follows: younger than 6 - 1 (2%); 6-12 years - 9 (20%); 13-15 years - 3 (7%); 16-19 years - 4 (9%); 20-25 years 3 (7%); 26 or older - 25 (55%). With the average age at the time of marriage 21.6 years, it was evident that many women did not have their first homosexual experience until after they were married. Indeed, the majority (27 or 60%) indicated their first experience occurred after they were married. While some did have homosexual experiences before they were married, very few understood themselves to be bisexuals before they were married.

Reasons for Getting Married

While 47% of the women were somewhat aware of their homosexual feelings prior to marriage, very few saw this as a factor which would influence their marriage. When asked about their reasons for marrying, the majority indicated factors such as family pressures and love for their husbands. Very few reported factors such as social pressures and lack of intimacy in the homosexual world, or hoping marriage would help them overcome their homosexual feelings. (See Table 2.)

The Husbands' Knowledge

Before these women were married, 5 (11%) of their future husbands knew about their fiancees' sexual attractions toward women. Twenty-five (56%) of the husbands knew or found out about their wives' homosexual

TABLE 2

REASONS FOR MARRIAGE

	N	(%)
Societal Pressures	33	(73%)
Family Pressures	17	(38%)
Perceived Lack of Intimacy in Lesbian World	1	(2%)
Love for Husband	31	(69%)
Interest in Having and Raising Children	22	(49%)
Hoping Marriage Would Overcome Same-sex Feelings	9	(20%)

attractions during the course of marriage. While 25 (56%) of the wives had had homosexual experiences during their marriage, only 8 (24%) of the husbands knew about these experiences or relationships. Of those women who were homosexually active outside of the marriage and whose husbands knew of these experiences or relationships, only four husbands gave clear consent or approval for them. Overall, very few husbands knew of their wives' homosexual feelings before they were married, in contrast to 47% of the women knowing about their own homosexual feelings. Many of the husbands eventually found out about their wives' feelings, yet only a minority found out about actual extramarital experiences or relationships. Approval of these outside relationships occurred in only a few of these relationships. Essentially, very few open-relationships were found in these marriages.

Sexual Difficulties Experienced in Marriage

Sexual difficulties occurred to some degree in 40 (89%) of these marriages. (See Table 3.) The most frequently cited difficulty was a lack of sexual desire for their spouse (62%). In terms of actual functioning, some women experienced lubrication difficulties (36%), lack of orgasm in response to certain kinds of stimulation (31%), lack of satisfaction (29%), and pain during intercourse (20%). The respondents who experienced sexual difficulties were most likely to report a lack of desire for anyone (18%), an inability to experience orgasm at all (7%), or vaginismus (7%). Overall, the sexual difficulties experienced by most of the women were a lack of sexual desire for their spouse, and sexual dysfunctions in intercourse with their husbands.

Attempts to Eliminate Homosexual Feelings

Nine (20%) of the women reported having attempted to eliminate their homosexual feelings through various means other than psychotherapy. They listed means such as avoiding friendships with women, suppressing

TABLE 3

SEXUAL DIFFICULTIES EXPERIENCED IN MARRIAGE

	N	(%)
Yes, Definitely	18	(40%)
Yes, Somewhat	22	(49%)
No	5	(11%)
Lack of Sexual Desire for Anyone	8	(18%)
Lack of Sexual Desire for Spouse	28	(62%)
Lack of Lubrication	16	(36%)
Inability to Achieve Orgasm at All	3	(7%)
Inability to Achieve Orgasm with Certain Types Stimulation	14	(31%)
Pain During Intercourse	9	(20%)
Inability to Have Intercourse Due to Muscular Contractions	3	(7%)
No Sexual Dysfunctions, but Lack of Satisfaction	13	(29%)

homosexual thoughts and feelings, going to church, drinking and taking drugs, and having sex with numerous men. Only four women sought to change their homosexual feelings through psychotherapy.

Kinsey-Type Ratings

The subjects were asked to rate themselves in terms of sexual behavior, fantasies, and emotional attachments on a Kinsey-type scale, a continuum from 0 (exclusive heterosexuality) to 6 (exclusive homosexuality) (see Table 4). Based on these ratings, the sample could be described as almost exclusively heterosexual in behavior and fantasies before marriage. Some changes can be seen during marriage toward homosexual orientation. The dramatic change, however, occurred following marriage, when the women tended toward the homosexual end of the continuum and related almost exclusively to other women.

DISCUSSION

Comparison of Female Sample to a Male Sample

This sample of 45 women was compared to a similar sample of 31 bisexual married men previously studied by Coleman (1981/1982a). These samples are somewhat similar in that they consisted of men and women who identified themselves as bisexuals and were or had been married. However, there were several important differences. First, the samples were collected in different ways and at different times. Neither was ran-

TABLE 4

CHANGES IN KINSEY-TYPE RATINGS BEFORE, DURING, AFTER MARRIAGE

(0 = exclusive heterosexual; 6 = exclusive homosexual)

	BEFORE	DURING	AFTER
SEXUAL BEHAVIOR	.49	.91	4.49
FANTASY	1.34	2.27	4.07
EMOTIONAL ATTACHMENTS	3.53	3.47	4.78

dom and thus cannot be seen as representative of the entire population of bisexual men and women in marriage. Almost all of the female sample was not married at the time of the study, while the males were. The males had all sought psychotherapy to deal with conflicts over their homosexuality and marriage; the females were, for the most part, in therapy for other reasons. Keeping these differences in mind, one can draw a cautious comparison between the two samples. In terms of demographics, the males tended to be slightly older (males - 38.6; females -35.9). The average age at the time of marriage was younger for the females than the males (females - 21.6; males 25.5). The average number of children was less for females than males (females - 1.2; males - 2.0). The length of marraige was significantly lower for females than males (females - 8.5; males - 13.1).

The males were clearly more aware of their homosexual feelings before they were married (males - 97%; females - 47%), and were more likely to have had some previous homosexual experiences (males - 87%; females - 40%). Also, their reasons for getting married were somewhat different. Males were more likely to cite the perceived lack of intimacy in the "gay world" and negative feelings about "gay life." Again, it seems that males were more aware and concerned about their homosexual feelings prior to marriage than were females.

Before they were married, neither group was likely to tell their partners about their homosexual feelings, but males were more likely to do this than females (males - 16%; females - 11%). During marriage, the males were also more likely to tell their wives about their homosexual feelings, although it must be kept in mind that the males were encouraged to do this as part of the therapeutic process (males - 100%; females - 56%). Many of the males, however, had told their wives about their homosexual feelings even before beginning therapy. This disclosure often produced the marital crisis which brought them into therapy. Few of the males were explicit about actual extra-marital, homosexual activity which occurred, and females were similar in this regard. Partners of the males and females were often aware of homosexual feelings of their spouses; however, actual sexual experiences or relationships were rarely talked about. Also similar to the partners of the sample females, very few of the partners of the males gave their approval to outside sexual activity. It is even questionable how accepting these partners were of their husbands' or wives' outside sexual activity.

The females were more likely to report some type of sexual difficulty in the relationship (females - 89%; males - 61%). The most common type of sexual dysfunction reported by males and females was a lack of sexual desire for their spouse, both males and females reporting more difficulties in the excitement phase, erection and lubrication (males - 29%; females - 31%), than in the orgasmic phase.

In terms of eliminating homosexual feelings, the males were more likely to make such attempts than were the females. Nine (36%) of the males and four (9%) of the females reported having been through some sort of psychotherapy to eliminate their homosexual feelings. Females were also less likely to report attempting to eliminate homosexual feelings in ways other than psychotherapy. While both groups made such attempts, none were successful.

If one compares the Kinsey-type ratings of the male and female sample, some interesting observations can be made. Males were more likely to report homosexual feelings and behavior during their marraige than the females (Behavior: males - 2.42, females - .91; Fantasy: males - 4.52; females - 2.27). Females report more homosexual emotional attachments than men (males - 2.57; females - 3.47). Again, this reinforces the notion the males are more likely to report being aware of homosexual feelings, and acting on those feelings before and during their marriage than are their female counterparts.

SUMMARY AND CONCLUSIONS

This study reinforces some of the basic findings of Bell and Weinberg (1978), namely that bisexual women who have been married were more likely to marry at an earlier age, more unlikely to be aware of their homosexual feelings prior to marriage, more likely to become aware of their feelings after they married, and more likely to terminate their marriages earlier because of conflicts arising from their bisexuality and sexual dissatisfaction than were their male counterparts.

Reasons for such delayed awareness are speculative. Coleman (1981/1982b) and Grace (1979) have suggested that the lack of societal approval for a "homosexual adolescence" and society's general intolerance for homosexuality cause delays in a homosexual identity formation; research has documented this phenomenon. While the median age for awareness of homosexual feelings has been reported by Jay and Young (1979) to be 18 and by Kooden, Morin, Riddle, Rogers, Sang, and Strassburger (1979) to be 14, ranges in these samples were wide, and many research subjects did not realize these feelings until they were beyond chronological adolescence. Studies by Kooden et al. (1979) and McDonald (1982) have suggested the development of an integrated homosexual identity between 10-14 years after the first awareness of homosexual feelings. They also suggest that some people move through these stages more rapidly than others, whereas other people never progress through them, or else move more slowly from stage to stage. Kooden et al. (1979) also indicates that on the average, females have their first homosexual experiences at the age of 20 (five years later than males) and do not consider themselves to be homosexuals until 23 years of age, two years later than for males.

This delayed awareness seems to be true for this study's sample of women. In terms of developing an integrated sexual orientation identity, these women seem to be further delayed developmentally than the average population of exclusively homosexual women or men. One reason for this delay may be that these individuals seem to have an extensive bisexual history, which in turn might delay the process of developing an integrated identity. The even greater lack of societal support for bisexuality may also contribute to this developmental delay. While Coleman (1981/1982b) and others have hypothesized a developmental model for the coming-out process, and research has been conducted which generally supports this model, little theorizing and research exists on the development of a bisexual identity. This developmental delay factor may be only one of many intrapsychic, psychological and sociological factors operating in the development of a bisexual identity. Further research is needed to better understand this phenomenon. However, this apparent developmental delay does seem to explain the lack of awareness of homosexual feelings, or lack of a bisexual identity, prior to marriage for the females in this sample.

That the marriages of the females in this study seem to last for fewer years than those of the males in the previous study is also an interesting phenomenon not clearly explained, and one warranting further research, for example, research questioning the influence of sex-role socialization. Women may be less able, due to sex-role socialization, to maintain a "double-standard." As in female homosexual relationships, bisexual women seem to be less able than bisexual males to tolerate multiple relationships. So in their marital relationships they might feel a greater need to end the relationship because of the basic incompatibility they perceive between their homosexual feelings and activities and their marriage. In addition, their husbands might not be able to tolerate their wives' homosexual activity, although, with the roles reversed, such a double standard allows the males to tolerate their own outside homosexual interests and activities without much difficulty.

It is also interesting to note that few "open relationships" developed in the marriages of the women in this sample. Perhaps support for a bisexual identity or lifestyle was lacking. If many of these women were, indeed, more heterosexual rather than exclusively homosexual (as indicated by their Kinsey-type ratings), it would be interesting to know if they would experience the same constrictions in homosexual relationships as they did in their marriages. While many of the women were primarily involved in homosexual relationships at the time of the study, it is uncertain whether they would continue those relationships, revert to heterosexual relationships, or maintain both.

One of the greatest difficulties encountered in this study was finding bisexual women who were currently married. Only four currently married were found in this sample; the remainder had been previously married. The most common response from the therapists who were involved in the study was, "I just don't know of anyone who is bisexual or lesbian and is currently married. They don't seem to come to me while they are married." The sample studied, however, indicated that 39% of the women had sought out therapy to deal with conflicts in their marriage and over their bisexuality. The reason for the difficulty in locating this sample is uncertain; it may have been the result of a sampling bias due to the particular therapists involved in this study.

Finally, the overall sample difficulties of this study need to be recognized and understood. Basically, the sample is biased: it is a small clinical sample not randomized. Further studies using larger non-patient samples are needed in order to be able to validate and generalize these findings.

REFERENCES

Bell, A. P., & Weinberg, M. S. (1978). *Homosexualities: A study of diversity among men and women.* New York: Simon & Schuster.

Blumstein, P. W., & Schwartz, P. (1976). Bisexuality in women. *Archives of Sexual Behavior, 5,* 171-181.

Brownfain, J. J. (1985). A study of the married bisexual male: Paradox and resolution. *Journal of Homosexuality, 11*(1/2), 173-188

Coleman, E. (1981/1982a). Bisexual and gay men in heterosexual marriage. Conflicts and resolutions in therapy. *Journal of Homosexuality, 7*(2/3), 93-103.

Coleman, E. (1981/1982b). Developmental stages of the coming out process. *Journal of Homosexuality, 7*(2/3), 31-43.

Dank, B. M. (1972). Why homosexuals marry women. *Medical Aspects of Human Sexuality, 6,* 14-23.

Gochros, J. (1978). Counseling gay husbands. *Journal of Sex Education and Therapy, 4,* 6-10.

Grace, J. (1979, November). *Coming out alive.* Paper presented at the Sixth Biennial Professional Symposium of the National Association of Social Workers, San Antonio, TX.

Green, R. (1978). Sexual identity of 37 children raised by homosexual or transsexual parents. *American Journal of Psychiatry, 135,* 692-697.

Jay, K., & Young, A. (Eds.). (1979). *The gay report: Lesbians and gay men speak out about sexual experiences and lifestyles.* New York: Simon & Schuster.

Kirkpatrick, M., Roy, J., & Smith, K. (1976, August). A new look at lesbian mothers. *Human Behavior,* pp. 60-61.

Klein, F. (1978). *The bisexual option.* New York: Arbor House.

Kohn, B., & Matusow, A. (1980). *Barry and Alice.* Englewood Cliffs, NJ: Prentice-Hall.

Kooden, H. D., Morin, S. F., Riddle, E. I., Rogers, M., Sang, B. E., & Strassburger, F. (1979). *Removing the stigma: Final report, task force on the status of lesbian and gay male psychologists.* Washington, D.C.: American Psychological Association.

Latham, J. D., & White, G. D. (1978). Coping with homosexual expression within heterosexual marriages: Five case studies. *Journal of Sex and Marital Therapy, 4,* 198-212.

McDonald, G. J. (1982). Individual differences in the coming out process for gay men: Implications for theoretical models. *Journal of Homosexuality, 8*(1), 47-60.

Malone, J. (1980). *Straight women/gay men.* New York: Dial Press.

Masters, W. H., & Johnson, V. E. (1979). *Homosexuality in perspective.* Boston: Little, Brown.

Matteson, D. R. (1985). Bisexual men in marriage: Is a positive homosexual identity and stable marriage possible? *Journal of Homosexuality, 11*(1/2), 149-179.

Miller, B. (1979). Unpromised paternity: The lifestyles of gay fathers. In M. P. Levine (Ed.), *Gay men: The sociology of male homosexuality* (pp. 239-252). New York: Harper & Row.

Nahas, R., & Turley, M. (1979). *The new couple: Women and gay men.* New York: Seaview Press.

Rand, C., Graham, D. L. R., & Rawlings, E. I. (1982). Psychological health and factors the court seeks to control in lesbian mother custody trials. *Journal of Homosexuality, 8*(1), 27-39.

Ross, H. L. (1971). Modes of adjustment of married homosexuals. *Social Problems, 18,* 385-393.

Saghir, M. T., & Robbins, E. (1973). *Male and female homosexuality: A comprehensive investigation.* Baltimore: Williams & Wilkins.

Voeller, B., & Walters, J. (1978). Gay fathers. *The Family Coordinator, 27,* 149-157.

Wolf, T. J. (1985). Marriages of bisexual men. *Journal of Homosexuality, 11*(1/2), 135-149.

Wives' Reactions to Learning That Their Husbands Are Bisexual

Jean S. Gochros, PhD

Honolulu

ABSTRACT. Interviews with 33 women, plus data from 70 more, explored wives' reactions to being informed by their husbands that their husbands were bisexual, the consequences of disclosure, and the factors determining those reactions and consequences. Findings suggest that wives struggled less with the homosexuality itself than with problems of isolation, stigma, loss, cognitive confusion and dissonance, and lack of knowledgeable, empathic support or help in problem solving. Moreover, faulty assumptions about "disclosure" seem to have led to serious misconceptions about the wives, on the part of husbands, researchers, and therapists alike. These misconceptions and the "realities" are discussed.

After the beginning of the Gay Liberation Movement, increasing numbers of married men revealed to their wives that they were bisexual. Until very recently, however, almost no literature or research analyzed such situations; what did exist tended to focus on the husband, or to present the divorced homosexual male perspective. Often the wives were characterized as neurotics from troubled or broken families who repeatedly married bisexual men because of their poor heterosexual adjustment, who denied obvious clues to their husbands' homosexuality prior to disclosure, and then reacted neurotically to the disclosure (e.g., Hatterer, 1974; Miller, 1979).

This article will discuss findings from a 1982 exploratory study of how wives reacted to the disclosure of bisexuality, the consequences of such a disclosure for their lives, and the factors determining those reactions and consequences.

Dr. Gochros is a social worker in private practice. Correspondence may be sent to 1901 Halekoa Drive, Honolulu, HI 96821.

STUDY DESIGN

Research Questions

The scope of the study explored the following research areas:

1. How did the wife react to the disclosure?
2. What were the short, interim, and long-term consequences for her self-esteem, happiness, marital and sexual satisfaction?
3. How did she try to cope with the situation?
4. What was the effect on her attitudes toward homosexuality?
5. What problems did she face? What help did she seek and receive?

Sampling Methods

A convenience study sample of 33 wives was obtained through snowball sampling and newspaper publicity from four distinct areas: Honolulu, Portland, San Francisco, and Rochester (New York) and its adjacent rural areas. When possible, husbands, friends, relatives, or therapists were interviewed. In addition, several community therapists and divorced bisexual men whose wives were not in the study provided their own perspectives.

Overflow Respondents

An overflow of volunteers provided an unanticipated opportunity to obtain added information. Seventy more women from various states, and even overseas, were seen or provided data through telephone interviews and letters. Since there was less control over the kind and amount of data received, any descriptive statistics given here will be limited to those in the study sample. It should be emphasized, however, that while overflow respondents added to the demographic diversity, the findings, including approximate percentages, corresponded almost exactly to those of the study sample. Except for numerical figures, then, any statement made about the study sample also applies to the 70 added wives.

METHODOLOGY

Taped, semi-structured interviews were supplemented by a structured questionnaire, and four standardized validated scales measuring self-esteem (ISE), marital satisfaction (IMS), sexual satisfaction (ISS), and depression (GCS) (Hudson, 1982). Scale scores, interview responses, questionnaire responses, non-obtrusive data, and data from collateral interview with husbands, friends or therapists were compared. Content analysis was used for interview data.

SAMPLE DESCRIPTION

The sample consisted of women with a wide range of ages (23 to 59, with a median of 39), as well as a wide range of socioeconomic positions, levels of education, races, religions, and cultural backgrounds. For instance, there were Blacks, Asians, Protestants, Catholics, Jews, and Buddhists in the study. The overflow sample added a Moslem and Hindu couple, an even wider range in age and educational level, and increased cultural diversity. However, 80% of the respondents were white, Christian upper-middle class, with the wives highly educated (BAs-PhDs) and in professional or high level business careers.

Most of the 33 wives felt they had had happy childhoods with good parent-child and peer relationships. Only three had come from broken homes; only a few described parental strife. Most felt they had been sexually naive at the time of marriage due to religious proscriptions against premarital sex. Several, however, had had premarital sex with their husbands or another male partner. Only three had been previously married, and then not with a bisexual male.

Approximately 80% of the wives rated themselves above average in intelligence, assertiveness, and self-confidence. Over 50% cited ''less sexist than other men'' as one of the characteristics that had attracted them to their husbands. Over 50% had viewed themselves (and had been viewed by others) as having had unusually satisfying ''American Dream'' marriages from 1 to 27 years (median = 11) before a predisclosure build-up of tension.

Two potential sub-groups seemed underrepresented in the sample. One included distinctly lower socio-economic individuals with little education, low status jobs, and highly traditional sex-role marriages. Bisexuality was only one of many serious problems within the marriage, and in the husbands' overall life patterns. The wives remained in the marriage mainly out of financial necessity. The other included ''unconventional'' women who delighted in unconventional lifestyles, and initially reacted with enthusiasm to a disclosure of homosexuality (for purposes of this paper, the term homosexuality refers to any degree of homosexuality, no matter where a husband might fall on the Kinsey Scale, see Kinsey, 1953). Since there were only three such women, however, and since later consequences of disclosure were different for each one, any conclusions drawn from this subgroup are highly speculative.

FINDINGS

In brief, the findings to follow suggest that the situation is too complex simply to ask how a wife reacted to disclosure itself. Disclosures varied, were positive or negative depending on certain factors, and, accordingly, resulted in specific reactions followed by interim and reintegrative periods. There might be even more than one disclosure. Hence this was a "crisis-prone" situation in which one or more separate crises might arise, each with its own specific life cycle and degree of stress.

Definition of Disclosure

Disclosure is a complex event, or more accurately, a process. In the design of this study implicit and unrecognized assumptions may have entered into play, including:

1. homosexuality is easily recognized;
2. disclosure is a single, precise event, clearly specifying existence and degree of homosexuality and what it will mean for the future;
3. both immediate and future consequences of disclosure stem from the wife's immediate reaction, and from the wife's immediate reaction and ability to adjust to that one single event; and
4. all disclosures are the same. The wife is reacting purely to the knowledge that the husband is bisexual.

Although these assumptions may have been correct in some instances, they were generally simplistic, often inaccurate, and misleading.

"Disclosure" was often a process of gradually increasing awareness, sometimes covering a span of 20 years or more. It was often marked by several events that might be separated by years. An event might precipitate vague thoughts about homosexuality, or it might define such a perception more sharply. Yet, unless definitely confirmed, that event neither resolved all doubts nor necessarily offered a way of coping with those doubts. It might be an "official" disclosure by the husband or by some other person. Yet it did not necessarily help a wife assess what the homosexuality might mean for her life. Moreover, there might be several disclosures over time, each one differing in content, context, and hence in consequence.

An analogous situation is drawn to the realization that one had built a house in a geographical fault zone. The knowledge could come in many ways, either gradually or suddenly. Each tremor or quake would necessarily differ in size and nature, and have its own life cycle and effects. No single tremor would necessarily demonstrate the total effect of living in such a region, and, until the occupant moved away or died, neither the final consequences nor the time it took to reach those final consequences could be determined. Moreover, for a few women, by the time an "official" disclosure would have been made, the marital house would have crumbled, and the health of its inhabitants shattered. Disclosure would be simply a formality confirming that the damage had been related to underground seismic activity, marking the end rather than the beginning of a crisis.

Some initial disclosures, then, were like announcements in the paper that the area was in a fault zone. Without further data, the announcement simply held no meaning for the wife. Unless or until something happened to give the fact meaning, it produced little or no reaction and was considered a "disclosure" only in retrospect. In fact, many women found it difficult to determine a point of disclosure, and whether to consider it the first suspicion, the official disclosure, or the point at which the knowledge took on meaning.

This finding suggests that it is not enough to ask how a wife reacted to "the" disclosure of homosexuality. Each disclosure must be analyzed separately according to its content and context. The analysis of "final" consequences must incorporate complex interrelationships among a wide variety of factors.

FACTORS GOVERNING REACTIONS
TO ANY GIVEN DISCLOSURE

Reactions to any given disclosure depended on a combination of many factors associated with both its content and context. These factors appeared to be:

1. The degree to which content and context demonstrated a betrayal or confirmation of trust;
2. the degree to which content and context maintained, increased, decreased, or completely removed the husband's emotional/sexual commitment to the wife;
3. the wife's degree of vulnerability because of other stressful factors such as childbirth or illness;
4. the availability and use of an empathic, knowledgeable support system for both partners;
5. the degree of economic independence possible for the wife; and
6. each partner's personality, commitment to traditional views of sexuality, monogamy and husband-wife relations, and acceptance of bisexuality.

It would seem inevitable that the last factors, particularly the wife's own self-esteem, independence, assertiveness, and attitudes toward bisexuality would affect her reactions, and hence, the consequences of disclosure. However, they appeared far less important than the other factors. It seemed that how the husband coped with his bisexuality, and his subsequent behavior toward his wife were the major determinants of how she would react, either immediately or in the future.

No single factor, with the possible exception of the husband's degree of empathy and concern for his wife, determined reactions. Constellation of factors, however, could locate disclosures along a continuum from "positive" to "very negative." These factors had to do with "content" and "context" of any given disclosure. They overlapped and were not always clearcut. For example, disclosure forced by an arrest was usually a shocking experience that produced a strongly negative reaction. Yet a husband's commitment to the marriage and his empathy and concern for the wife might turn forced disclosure into a positive one. An ordinarily positive disclosure might be turned negative by the husband's insensitivity to timing, and his lack of concern for his wife's feelings.

Positive Constellations

A disclosure could be considered positive to the extent that:

1. it was given voluntarily;
2. its content was one of fantasy or infrequent and recently initiated homosexual activity. Uninvolved homosexual activity was usually less threatening to a wife than a current homosexual love relationship. However, if this relationship did not decrease commitment to the wife, even it could be positive;
3. the husband's words, affect, sensitivity to timing, and behavior demonstrated his honesty, love, concern for his wife's feelings;
4. it occurred within the context of a good marriage, or was seen as the husband's attempt to improve it. The husband's words, affect, and subsequent behavior demonstrated his emotional and sexual commitment to the wife;
5. empathic and knowlegeable peer and professional support systems were immediately available.

Initial disclosures were more apt to be positive than were later ones.

Reactions to Positive Disclosures

Positive disclosures usually led to mild shock or "stunned" reactions. The wife perceived a challenge or opportunity, a possible explanation for and solution to a problem. The wife asked just enough questions to determine that she was not to blame, and that the love and commitment of her husband were still intact. Then attention was focused mainly on maintaining (or feigning) enough calm to help diminish the husband's often severe distress.

Positive disclosures often came after what could be called a "pre-disclosure buildup" of tension, the wife often blaming herself, suspecting another woman, or suspecting homosexuality, and feeling guilty, disloyal and "crazy." In such cases, the disclosure often provided an immediate sense of relief for the wife.

Variations in reactions were evident. Content that held little meaning for a wife, for instance, led to what could be termed a "cognitive blank." The wife felt little or no anxiety, other than in perceiving that she was far less upset than her husband, and in being slightly apprehensive that she was not understanding something. Some wives were too stunned to cry, while others dissolved into uncontrolled tears. Some retreated to sort out feelings, while others deliberately did not react as a concrete way of reassuring their husbands.

No matter what the variations, positive disclosures led to positive reactions. Most wives were empathic with their husband's distress, and willingly re-negotiated the sexual contract to help meet their husbands' homosexual needs. The immediate consequences for the relationship were increased communication, a reaffirmation of love, an improvement in the sexual relationship, and a general relief of tension. For the wife there was a lifting of depression, and an increase in self esteem. Mrs. A's statement was typical:

> Actually, I was kind of proud of my reaction. I was . . . stunned, in shock, but not shocked in a moral sense. I was pretty cool and calm, all things considered. I was being understanding, flexible, a bit anxious, but willing to change the contract. I wasn't being a martyr and I wasn't denying the homosexuality. I loved him. I wanted him to be happy. I didn't want to add to the guilt he already had . . . Only . . . sometimes I wondered if I was silly to be understanding. Maybe I was just being stupid. I kept going up and down, and the more I thought about it, the more confused I got. (Gochros, 1982, p. 71)

With the word "only," most women follow a classic crisis pattern of trying to use their usual coping skills in facing a "hazardous event" (Golan, 1978). For most women, this meant trying to fill in cognitive gaps and assess their options logically and rationally. They usually started this process immediately, often within minutes or seconds. Once they did so, most women entered an "interim" period in which they were overwhelmed with conflicting thoughts and emotions. Depending on what followed, that period lasted from a few weeks to twenty years. Although positive initial disclosures were reported by over half the sample, those disclosures were often followed by more disclosures that became increasingly negative. The time between such disclosures ranged from a few weeks to several years. Description of this interval will follow discussion of negative disclosures and the reactions they produced.

Negative Disclosures

A disclosure was considered negative to the extent that it:

1. was forced rather than volunteered;
2. showed a strong betrayal of trust, plus a lack of concern for the wife's feelings or needs;
3. threatened or withdrew the husband's emotional/sexual commitment to the wife;
4. occurred within the context of a poor marriage, and spelled no chance of improvement;
5. was a later disclosure that violated the terms of an already re-negotiated contract;
6. compounded other stresses in the wife's life; and
7. was made worse by a lack of an empathic support system.

Reactions to Negative Disclosures

The more the content and context of the disclosure seemed to demonstrate a lack of concern coupled with deliberate long term deceit, the more the wife saw the disclosure as one of betrayal. She was apt to feel she had been "used." She was angry and hurt, and particularly in a "surprise" disclosure, acutely shocked. Despite common elements, content and context varied considerably. Usually a series of disclosures became increasingly negative. Later disclosures might reveal a change from fantasy to homosexual activity, increased activity, or a new lover. All these led to increased anxiety and more negative reactions. Yet if the husband maintained his commitment and engaged in empathic problem solving, the disclosure might remain in the positive category. If he did not, and the commitment and empathy decreased, the marital relationship deteriorated, and the wife's reactions grew increasingly negative.

Period Following Disclosure

Generally, wives followed Golan's (1978) "crisis" pattern of becoming increasingly confused and disoriented if both old coping skills and new emergency measures failed to resolve problems. If either the initial disclosure, or a future "last straw," created intolerable stress, the wives were thrown into acute emotional crisis. Their recovery from crisis involved the development of new resources and coping skills that served to maintain a viable marriage, helped them recover from an unwanted divorce, or prompted them to end untenable marriages.

Whether acute crisis reactions occurred immediately after disclosure or in the interim period, they always reached dangerous levels. All but a few women underwent dramatic loss of self-esteem and became seriously depressed. Almost half the wives seriously considered or actually made one or more attempts at suicide. In a few cases, they directed violence toward the husband or children. In most cases, neither suicidal or violent reactions were directly related to the homosexuality disclosure. Rather, they were precipitated by sudden, severe rejection, the disclosure of extreme deceit and betrayal, or a "last straw" in a series of rejections and betrayals. They were accompanied by confusion and a sense of powerlessness.

It is impossible to discuss these reactions without discussing the intrapsychic and interpersonal problems they stemmed from: (1) stigma and isolation; (2) cognitive confusion and dissonance; and (3) loss.

Stigma and Isolation

Almost all women reported a strong sense of isolation. They felt they were the only ones in the world faced with such a situation. The more isolated they felt, the more stigmatized they felt; the more stigmatized they felt, the more they isolated themselves. Almost all wives cited a lack of a knowledgeable support system and information as increasing their sense of stigma and isolation.

Professionals consulted were sometimes punitive toward either the husband or wife. While most wives who tried eventually found someone helpful, several did not dare confide in anyone, or else were unable to find adequate help, until after both their marriages and their own mental health had broken down.

All women reported undergoing identity and integrity crises, starting with their own questioning of what it said about them to have married a bisexual man. They worried about whether they were sexually inadequate, too masculine, too feminine, or even "latent lesbian," and so on.

While confiding in others reduced isolation and stigma, often others' reactions reinforced, rather than alleviated, their fears. One surprising finding was that once disclosure occurred, the stigma attached to the bisexual husband decreased, but then tended to be transferred to the wife. All wives reported being stigmatized to some extent by friends, homosexuals and heterosexuals, therapists, and even their own husbands. They made *a priori* and unyielding assumptions that such wives are passive-aggressive, neurotic, lesbian, vindictive, homophobic, and so on.

Cognitive Confusion and Dissonance

Cognitive confusion is defined here as the conflicting thoughts and values wives experienced while trying to assess their options. Whether from a moral, mental health, or practical viewpoint, there seemed to be at least two contradictory, equally persuasive, ways of viewing each option. For example, was willingness to accept an open sexual contract flexibility or passivity? Was refusal assertiveness or rigidity? What was a sign of self-esteem and what a lack of self-esteem?

Moreover, wives found themselves in double-binds. For example, if they tried to hide their feelings when a husband went out, they were often accused of being dishonest, or of "denying" the bisexuality. If they cried or expressed anger, they were often accused of being vindictive, too "feminine," "too masculine," or "aggressive," "guilt provoking," and so forth. If they sought or avoided divorce, they were often accused of homophobia, or of denying the husband's bisexuality.

Cognitive dissonance, defined here as the disparity between old ideas and new realities, added to the confusion. Not only was there the need to reappraise old beliefs about bisexuality and monogamy, but disparity between old and new perceptions of their husbands, or between their perceptions and those of their husbands as well. This was true not only of the area of sexual orientation, but also of the husband's total personality and behaviors.

Two syndromes, *male chauvinism* and *liberation ethics*, led to the same attitudes, i.e., that it was the husband's right, as a man or an oppressed minority, to do anything he pleased without regard for the wife's feelings, and that it was the wife's duty, as a woman or a symbolic oppressor, to help him cheerfully. Formerly sensitive, thoughtful, and non-sexist men seemed to go through a Jekyll-Hyde transformation. While few husbands were seen as villains, most were seen as unable to cope with the fact that they had created pain, unable to tolerate any expression of negative emotions, or unable to engage in problem solving. Any criticism or expressed problem by the wife was regarded as homophobia, and most men were seen to withdraw emotionally and sexually, and become highly insensitive to their wives' feelings or needs.

Trying to adapt to their husbands' sexual needs added to a sense of helplessness. Finally, disparity between the wives' old perceptions of themselves as logical, rational, decisive people, and their new confusion, indecisiveness, and helplessness, increased their loss of self-esteem.

Loss

At the time of this study, approximately two-thirds of the 33 marriages had dissolved. Of the nine still intact, four were self-defined as "struggling," the others happy, stable, and improved by disclosure. Almost all wives had suffered from the potential or real loss of someone they loved. Many divorced husbands they still loved. Many believed that divorce was needless and might not have occurred had they and their husbands had better professional help. Even more distressing than the loss of a loved one was the wives' loss of faith in their own judgment. If they had so misperceived their husbands in the past, how could they trust their judgment about other men in the future? If a husband denied having ever loved her, the wife felt she had lost her past as well as her future. During the interim period, most felt a loss of their own sense of identity.

Reintegrative Period

Despite these problems, almost all women for whom long-term effects could be assessed have returned to their original levels of self-esteem, happiness, and marital and sexual satisfaction (albeit often with another man). One of the 103 wives is now living in a satisfying lesbian relationship.

Reintegration steps differed for each wife, depending on what had happened during the interim phase. For example, for one wife, reintegration might involve reaching out to the homosexual community or having her own sexual affair. For another, reintegration might mean leaving a circle of homosexual friends or returning to traditional values.

In either case, almost all wives cited most of the following long-range positive consequences of disclosure:

1. increased self-direction and autonomy;
2. increased self-esteem based on one's own skills and attributes, rather than on a relationship with a man;
3. increased sensitivity to others' feelings;
4. increased assertiveness and communication skills;
5. increased ability to cope with crisis;
6. increased sexual, and in some cases marital, satisfaction; and
7. increased acceptance of bisexuality.

Despite criticism of "Liberation Ethics" and the militant homosexual support system's tendency to push husbands into choosing between homosexual expression and marriage, most wives felt that disclosure had had a generally positive long-range effect on their attitudes toward bisexuality. The only two who started out and remained (according to their own definition) homophobic had been given no reason to change their attitudes by their husbands, therapists, or anyone else. No wife, however she might have felt about homosexuality prior to disclosure, appeared to have divorced because of homophobia. Wives left only when they became convinced that their husbands no longer loved them, when breech of trust was so severe that to remain in the marriage was unthinkable, or when they perceived that "flexibility" and "empathy" had become one-way streets that would bring nothing but pain.

SUMMARY

My findings suggest that it is not enough to ask how a wife reacted to "a disclosure" of bisexuality. The important factors in both her immediate and future reactions did not appear to be the fact of bisexuality, learning about homosexuality, or any particular attribute of the wife. Rather, she reacted according to the content and context of several disclosures should be, what had gone before and what followed. Within the content and context lay such factors as whether the husband's behaviors and words demonstrated to wives that disclosure had affected the marriage positively. Most wives cited many long-range, positive changes in attitudes toward bisexuality.

DISCUSSION

It is generally assumed that women who inadvertently marry bisexual men differ from other women in psychosexual development and identity, emotional adjustment, parental history, and marital history. While this assumption fits a few women in this sample, there was no evidence that it was generally true. If any profile existed, it was of a highly educated, assertive, self-confident and socially skilled woman who had enjoyed a better-than-average marriage for many years. Other than that, there seemed to be nothing to distinguish this group from any other group of mainly college-educated women.

The findings also suggest that, contrary to popular opinion, wives are able to cope with the bisexual needs of their husbands, given adequate help. Considering the problems they faced, what seems surprising is not that so many marriages failed, or that so many wives fell apart, but that most wives tried so hard and recovered so well, and that some marriages were thriving from 2 to 25 years after an initial disclosure.

I believe these couples, and particularly the wives, became caught in the clash between political forces and were unable to tolerate such an ambiguous status as that of "bisexuality." Further, it would seem that sex-role stereotyping which sharply dichotomizes male and female characteristics stigmatizes not only the male who departs from the norm, but also any woman who would live with and love such a man, and who might herself depart from the norm in any way.

Further research is needed to test both the findings and the conclusions of this research. Future studies might compare this situation with that of heterosexual husbands and bisexual wives, or issues of infidelity and divorce in heterosexual couples. Guidelines are needed for helping both partners and their children. It would seem incumbent upon homosexual and heterosexual support systems, therapists, and researchers alike to guard against simplistic approaches to such highly complex situations.

REFERENCES

Gochros, J. (1982). *When husbands come out of the closet: A study of the consequences for their wives.* Unpublished doctoral dissertation, University of Denver, Denver, CO.

Golan, N. (1978). *Treatment in crisis situations.* New York: Free Press.

Hatterer, M. S. (1974). The problems of women married to homosexual men. *American Journal of Psychiatry, 4,* 275-278.

Hudson, W. (1982). *Clinical measurement package: A field manual.* Homewood, IL: Dorsey Press.

Kinsey, A. C., Pomeroy, W. B., Martin, C. E., & Gebhard, P. E. (1948). *Sexual behavior in the human male.* Philadelphia: W. B. Saunders.

Miller, B. (1979). Gay fathers and their children. *The Family Coordinator, 28,* 544-552.

Sexuality and Relationship Changes in Married Females Following the Commencement of Bisexual Activity

Joan K. Dixon, PhD
Basic Research Service
San Diego

ABSTRACT. Some of the changes in sexual behavior and relationships with spouses and other females following the commencement of bisexual activity by women after the age of 30 were studied by conducting in-depth personal interviews with 50 women. Each participant, at the time of her first sexual activity with another female: (a) was married; (b) was at least 30; (c) was, with her spouse, engaging in consensual swinging activities; (d) was enjoying sex with males; and (e) had no history, prior to age 30, of sexual attraction to females. Generally, the subjects revealed high levels of participation in, and enjoyment of, sexual activity with other females, in addition to high levels of enjoyable heterosexual activity. Their generally happy and stable marriages tended somewhat to improve, as did their overall sex lives, and they saw their relationships with other females as significantly improved. Significant changes in sexual fantasies occurred. In all cases, sexual orientation became bisexual, but overall preference for male sex partners did not change.

The issues which this study examined evolve from the concurrence of two forms of sexual behavior which the macroculture considers to be deviant and unacceptable behavior: bisexuality and swinging. Confusion and misunderstanding concerning those activities stem from a plethora of definitions which are used or assumed by researchers, other authors, and the general public, and from procedural inconsistencies in prior studies of those behaviors.

This study sought to find subjects whose bisexuality developed in adulthood out of a previous heterosexual orientation, in order to identify and examine some of the effects upon the subjects' lives which that change occasioned.

Dr. Dixon is Western Region Executive Director of the Society for the Scientific Study of Sex, and is a principal researcher at Basic Research Service in San Diego. Requests for reprints or further information may be addressed to the author, c/o Basic Research Service, P.O. Box 9591, San Diego, CA 92109.

BISEXUALITY

Freud (1905/1961) was an instrumental force in setting the stage for decades of misconceptions about bisexuality when he postulated his theory that, although all persons experience a homoerotic phase in their development toward heterosexuality as a result of their "biologically rooted" bisexual predispositions, some persons remain fixated at a homosexual level, resulting in patent homosexuality, while some other persons retain vestiges of the homosexual stage, resulting in so-called latent homosexuality. Either result, said Freud, thereafter becomes a permanent aspect of that person's personality.

That theory has led some authorities (Ruitenbeck, 1971; Saghir, 1980; Spiers, 1976) to deny that there is such a thing as bisexuality, believing rather that a person who occasionally likes sex with someone of the same sex is either a homosexual, or a heterosexual with problems. Orthodox Freudian analysts thus hold the view that bisexuality does not exist as a clinical entity, that one is either heterosexual or homosexual (Blumstein & Schwartz, 1974; Bieber, 1971).

A by-product of that bipolar concept is the scientifically unfortunate inclusion of many bisexual individuals as research subjects in studies of homosexuality. Studies by Bell and Weinberg (1978), Bell, Weinberg, and Hammersmith (1981), Coleman, Hoon, and Hoon (1983), Harry and Lovely (1979), Masters and Johnson (1979), and Saghir and Robbins (1968) are but a few of many examples where a commingling of bisexuals and homosexuals has taken place in studies ostensibly about homosexuality.

Obviously, one reason for such obfuscation is the indiscriminate use of the word "homosexual" to refer to any sexual act occurring between two or more persons of the same sex. The mere use of the word in that context is often a misuse. A term with neutral connotations of sexual orientation is preferable to one which arbitrarily stamps the act with a label.

This study assumed the existence of bisexuality as a manifestation of contemporaneous sexual desires toward one or more persons of each sex, and thus to be a concept separate and distinct from both heterosexuality and homosexuality. In the belief that one of the main reasons for the continuing confusion in scientific as well as lay circles about the nature of bisexuality is the use of the term "homosexual" to refer to a same-sex sexual act, regardless of the intent or sexual orientation of the persons involved, this study used in reference to such an act a phrase which is neutral of connotations. In order therefore to facilitate the conceptual distinction between bisexuality and homosexuality, here a sexual act involving two or more females is not referred to as a "homosexual" act but as a "multifemale sexual act," and a sexual act involving two or more males is referred to as a "multimale sexual act."

For a variety of reasons, among which the foregoing conceptual confusions are prominent, there are few reported studies of bisexuals as such (Blumstein & Schwartz, 1974, 1976a, 1976b, 1976c, 1976d; Ellis, 1962; Kenyon, 1968). Blumstein and Schwartz's reports (1974, 1976a, 1976b, 1976c, 1976d) were based on one study they conducted between 1973 and 1975 using 75 bisexual men and approximately 75 bisexual women. In their interviews with those bisexual subjects, Blumstein and Schwartz found that some of their subjects had altered their sexual behavior at various times during their lives to either include or exclude active bisexual behavior. Although no data were given, those authors summarized anecdotal accounts which seemed to give evidence of possible significant changes in self-perception and outlook experienced by some of the subjects who had begun their bisexual activity during adulthood.

This study was conducted in order to examine further what some of the changes in sexuality and relationships might be in women who commence bisexual behavior well beyond their adolescence, a point beyond which some authorities (Bell, 1980; Silverstein, 1977; Socarides, 1963; Whitam, 1977) believe one's sexual orientation *cannot* be altered.

SWINGING

The incidence of bisexual activity among women swingers is extremely high when compared to any other known and sizeable group of women. O'Neill and O'Neill (1970) reported that 60% of the swinging females in their study engaged in genital sexual activities with other women; 68% of the women in Gilmartin's (1978) study of swingers had done so. Bartell (1971) reported that when two couples swing together 75% of the females engage in sex with each other, while at large parties 92% of the females would do so.

For the purposes of this study, swinging was deemed to include the activities of a married couple who engaged in mutually consensual sexual activities with one or more other persons.

METHOD

Acquiring Participants

Potential subjects were located through several means. The author secured a booth at two alternative-lifestyles conventions and solicited volunteer participants there, and also answered appropriate ads in swinging publications from women or couples. Participation and referrals were sought in person and by mail from other persons, including operators of "swing party houses" and swingers' social organizations, and from friends and acquaintances of the author. Referrals were also sought from participants.

Because of the difficulties acquiring a properly stratified random sample of underground populations, such as sexually variant minorities (Bell, 1974; Blumstein & Schwartz, 1976d; Ramey, 1975; Weinberg, 1970), and the inherently restricted population from which the sample was being drawn, in-depth interviews were conducted with the first 50 women who met all participation requirements. All subjects were residents of California, Oregon, or Washington.

Participation Requirements

To satisfy, with some reasonable assurance, the research requirement that each subject was in fact exclusively heterosexual in behavior and psychosexual feelings prior to her first significant sexual act with another female, a series of qualifying requirements was set for prospective participants. Each subject had to have a history of satisfying and exclusively heterosexual sexual activity before engaging in her first significant multi-female sexual activity.

Thus, each participant reported that she had engaged in sexual activities with another female for the first time: (a) at or after the age of 30; (b) while married; (c) while engaged in a personally satisfying swinging lifestyle, involving access to and sexual contact with a number of different males; (d) with no history prior to age 30 of any conscious sexual desire or significant amount of erotic fantasy involving her and any other female.

To satisfy other requirements of the study, about which a report has been made elsewhere (Dixon, 1984), having to do with an actual change in sexual orientation and its etiological factors (as opposed to a mere change in sexual behavior), participation was additionally limited to only those women meeting the above criteria who also were currently engaging in or desirous of engaging in sex with partners of each sex.

Interviews

All interviews were conducted by the author. Subjects were assured that their responses would be treated as confidential and that their identities would not be divulged. Interviews were semi-structured around an outline which included, in addition to demographic items, a broad spectrum of sociosexual attitudinal and behavioral questions designed to elicit an overall history of the subjects' past and present sexuality and their subjective assessments of it. Interviews averaged about one hour in length.

In determining whether or not subjects had had sexual activity with another female prior to being 30, married, and swinging, it was decided to mark first multifemale sexual activity as the first time cunnilingus took place with another female. That particular activity was chosen because it more commonly was the event best remembered as significant.

Sample

Although this is not a stratified or random sample, the variety of sources from which the sample was gathered is believed to include all major types in the geographical area covered. The average age of the sample makes this the oldest sample of swingers about which the author has found any report ($M = 42.9$, $SD = 7.7$, $R = 32-60$). Subjects were predominantly of the socioeconomic middle-class; 96% were Caucasian, 4% Black. At the time of the interviews, 90% were married, 4% widowed, 4% divorced, and 2% separated. A 58% majority of subjects had been married only once; another 32% had been married twice; 8% reported three marriages; and the remaining 2% had been married five times. The mean length of current marriages was 15.3 years ($SD = 8.5$). Twenty percent of the subjects were childfree, and the remaining 80% had among them 100 children.

Religious preference was listed by 34% of the sample as Protestant, 16% as Catholic, and 12% as Jewish; however, the largest segment (38%) said "none." In describing the formal expression of their religious beliefs only 4% indicated they were "very" religious; another 12% indicated they were "moderately" religious. The rest were only mildly religious or seemed not to be religious at all.

To put in perspective the changes in behavior which are examined and discussed later in this report, it is useful to note the age at which subjects had their first sexual experience with another female. The mean age was 37 ($SD = 6.5$), with a range of 30 to 56.

Subjects typically found themselves engaging in sex with another female within 3 years after they began swinging ($M = 2.9$, $SD = 2.3$, median $= 2$), yet the length of time in swinging before experiencing sex with another female ranged all the way from immediately to 11 years. A mean of 6 years ($SD = 3.9$) had elapsed since the subjects had had that first multifemale sexual experience; the length of time ranged from less than one year to 21 years.

The median number of female sex partners was 12; the range was from 3 to 250. Because of skewing from the wide range, the mean is not being reported. As was to be expected from a sample of women of such age and past heterosexual history, Table 1 reveals this sample having had, in addition to their sizeable numbers of female sex partners, even larger numbers of male sex partners.

RESULTS

The settings in which swinging multifemale sexual behavior began and continued were investigated. Although some researchers have at times commented on the situations (4-somes, 3-somes, and so on) in which multifemale sexual activity occurs among female swingers (Barkas, 1974; Bartell, 1971; Blumstein & Schwartz, 1974; Gilmartin, 1978), there appears to be no previously reported figures with which to compare the data in Table 2.

Relatively little multifemale sexual activity occurring in a purely female environment was reported. Yet that type of setting shows a substantial "current" increase over "first experience" data. The preeminence of the social aspect of the setting in which the multifemale sexual activity occurs is, though apparent in Table 2, only partly revealed there, for not one subject indicated that her sexual activities with other

Table 1

Numbers of Female and Male Sexual Partners: Percentages of

Sample

($\underline{N}$ = 50)

	Sexual Partners	
Number of Partners	Female	Male
3 – 5	14%	0%
6 – 10	24	0
11 – 20[a]	26	6
25 – 50	20	12
51 – 250	16	46
251 – 500	0	14
501 – 1000	0	12
1000+	0	10

[a]Gap between groups is due to space between numbers reported.

Table 2

Comparison of First and Current Multifemale Swinging Sexual

Experiences

($\underline{N}$ = 50)

	Swing Party	Two-Couple 4-Some	3-Some with Spouse and Another Female	Subject and One Other Female	Group of Only Woman
First Experience	50%	32%	10%	4%	4%
Current Experience[a]	84	86	54	20	14

[a]Totals over 100% because many subjects engaged currently in more than one such activity.

women were currently limited to one-on-one situations where the two females were alone.

Of the 50 women interviewed, the vast majority (82%) participated only as receivers in their first multifemale sexual experience, whereas 6% participated as oralists, and 12% participated as both oralists and receivers. In contrast, 80% of the women reported current participation as both oralists and receivers, with just 20% participating as receivers only, evidencing the subjects' movement toward full participation in multifemale cunnilingus.

The generally positive reactions of these subjects to their first sexual experience with another female after a previous history as strictly heterosexual are shown in Table 3. Reactions appeared to have progressed with repeated experiences to a general rating of excellent.

Ninety-six percent of the sample were currently masturbating, compared to only 44% of the married women up to age 45 (the oldest agebracket for which figures were given) in Kinsey, Pomeroy, Martin, and Gebhard's (1953) sample. Only one subject (2%) had never masturbated.

Table 3

Subjects' Ratings of First and Current Multifemale Sexual
Experiences Compared
(N = 50)

	Excellent	Fair	Neutral	Somewhat Negative	Very Negative
First Experience	16%	36%	24%	14%	10%
Current Experiences	64	26	8	2	--

Currently masturbating subjects had a mean frequency of that activity of 1.8 times a week (*SD* = 1.4). The median frequency of 2 times a week for that activity is exactly 10 times the 0.2 per week median frequency found by Kinsey et al. among masturbating married women 21-55.

Prior to having their first sexual experience with another female, 44.9% of the 49 subjects who reported having masturbated during that time fantasized occasionally while masturbating. Only one subject (4.5% of those fantasizing while masturbating) included a female other than herself in those fantasies. By contrast to the latter figure, the Kinsey group found that 10% of the women in their study who fantasized while masturbating sometimes included women in those fantasies. The Kinsey data included single women, a group known to have a larger homosexual subpopulation than do married women. In his national population study, Hunt (1974) found that 11% of the women in his study who currently masturbated at sometime employed "homosexual" fantasies while masturbating. By contrast, a mere 2% of the subjects in this study employed such fantasies prior to their first multifemale sexual experience.

After having experienced several incidents of sex with other women, 68.8% (up from 44.9%) of the subjects who were currently masturbating fantasized at some time while doing so, and 61% of those who were at times masturbating with fantasies (up from 4.5%) included other women as erotic sex objects in those fantasies.

For such a quantum change in adult human sexual behavior, figures alone are sometimes an inadequate index of the change as it is perceived by the people experiencing the change. Here are some typical quotes taken from statements by subjects regarding the changes in their fantasies subsequent to their commencement of sexual activities with other women:

> I never before fantasized about women. My whole fantasy world has changed . . . I learned how great they [women lovers] are.
> Now I fantasize women together sometimes—before I had no fantasies.
> Now while masturbating I fantasize two women actively involved . . . never had women in fantasies before.
> I fantasize beautiful women when masturbating and fucking.
> After 2-3 years [following first multifemale sex activity] I began to include females in my fantasies with males.

The data in Table 4 were broken down to show the increased frequencies (the median increased over 2-1/2 times) by which subjects who were not currently married or living with their spouses engaged in sex with another female, compared to the frequencies of the subjects who were still living (and swinging) with a spouse.

Table 5 indicates that a majority of the subjects typically had coitus with their husbands more often than 3.5 times a week. In comparison, Ramey (1975) cited a national average-frequency (no age-group breakdowns given) of 2.5 times per week for marital coitus.

Of the 15 subjects (30%) in this study with a prior marriage, for whom data for frequency of marital coitus in prior marriages were recorded and who were presently married, the mean frequency of marital coital activity increased from 2.6 times per week (SD = 2.6) in prior marriages (right at Ramey's national average) to 4.8 times per week (SD = 3.0) in the present marriages—an 84.6% increase. Eighty percent of this subsample began swinging and began sexual activity with other females during current marriages.

Sexual satisfaction in 76% of current marriages (n = 46) was rated as excellent or good, and as fair in 22%; marital compatibility was rated excellent or good in 80% of current marriages, as fair in 13%. Significantly, only 4% of the sample had divorced subsequent to their commencement of multifemale sexual activity.

Of those 20 (40%) previously married subjects who were currently married, only 5% rated the sexual satisfaction of the current marriage below that of a prior marriage, 10% rated it equal to at least one prior marriage, and 85% rated it higher than any prior marriage. All 45 (90%) subjects who were presently married and cohabiting with their spouses engaged in coitus and oral sex with their husbands, 68% in penile/anal sex, and 8% in bondage and discipline activities. A large majority of subjects listed, in addition to sexual activities, five or more other activities which they shared regularly or often with their spouses, indicating a fairly wide community of interests, and coincidentally a fairly large amount of shared time.

At the time of the interviews, 84% of the subjects subjectively rated their spouses' present attitude about their wives' multifemale sexual activity as "highly approving," while 12% rated it as "approving," and 4% said it was "neutral." Currently divorced, widowed, and separated subjects gave their former spouses' last known attitude.

The subjects who were then cohabiting with their spouses ($n = 45$) were questioned as to what level of discomfort their husbands might have toward multimale sexual activity, in view of their wives' venture into bisexuality. One-fifth of those wives said that their husbands were also bisexual; 29% had husbands with neutral feelings about multimale sexual

Table 4

Current Frequencies of Multifemale Sexual Experiences

	Mean (per month)	SD (per month)	Median (per month)	Range
N = 50	1.5	1.8	1.0	2 per week to 2 per year
n = 45[a]	1.4	1.9	0.9	2 per week to 2 per year
n = 5[b]	2.4	1.4	2.5	1 per week to 6 per year

[a]Subjects currently married and cohabiting with their spouses.
[b]Subjects currently divorced, widowed, or separated.

Table 5

Marital Coital Frequencies Compared

	Number Per Month					
	0	1-5	6-10	11-15	16-20	20+
This Study	0%	4%	5%	38%	20%	33%
Tavris & Sadd[a]	2	26	32	21	11	8
Gilmartin[b]	(------11%------)			34	32	23

[a]Tavris and Sadd (1975, p. 67) reported results of a national survey of married female Redbook magazine readers without age breakdowns shown for the above figures.

[b]Gilmartin (1978, p. 312) reported above figures for swinging wives--no age breakdowns given. Sixty-eight percent had at sometime had sex with another woman.

activity; 18% indicated the level of their husband's discomfort with that behavior as slightly phobic; 20% revealed their husbands to be very phobic about it; and 9% did not know their spouses' feelings about the subject.

Table 6 indicates the reduced discomfort which the sample felt regarding multifemale and multimale sexual activity as subjects began to experience their own bisexuality. Most subjects indicated that before their first multifemale sexual experience they felt more discomfort with the subject of multimale sexual activity than did their spouses. Even though more than one out of five subjects remained significantly uncomfortable with the subject of multimale sexual activity, the sample as a whole moved from being less tolerant to more accepting of multimale sexual activity than were their husbands.

Perhaps the most profound changes eventually occurring in these subjects subsequent to the onset of multifemale sexual activity were changes of attitude toward and relationships with other women. Those changes, which in some instances were quite dramatic, were reported by every subject and in all cases seen as positive.

The following are some typical quotes from subjects regarding the im-

Table 6

Prebisexual and Current Discomfort Level of Subjects Toward

Multifemale and Multimale Sexual Activity: Compared[a]

(N = 50)

| | Discomfort Concerning | | | | | |
| | Multifemale Sexual Activity | | | Multimale Sexual Activity | | |
	None or Neutral	Slight	Much	None or Neutral	Slight	Much
Prebisexual	34%	20%	46%	32%	20%	48%
Current	82	18	--	62	16	22

[a]Subjectively rated by researcher as result of subjects' answers
to numerous questions throughout interviews.

pact which their emergent bisexuality had on their feelings toward other
women:

> I'm not threatened by other women as before . . . not so posses-
> sive of my husband. Now I compliment other women . . . am less
> competitive with them . . . have an increased sensitivity to people,
> and I'm easier to live and work with.
>
> I feel it is a shame all women can't be bi . . . find I work better
> with women after becoming bi.
>
> My former coolness regarding women changed to warmth and
> closeness. Now I feel less unfeminine because I'm not the ideal
> beauty . . . increased my feeling of femininity.
>
> I believe my previous "sin" training [was] "sick" . . . My
> female lover has added satisfaction to my marriage—she fills needs
> my spouse and other men can't, and I'm now able to expand my per-
> sonality, grow, and evolve as a human being.

I had to destroy old thought patterns . . . if you had told me at 55 I'd be bi I'd have sworn it never would happen . . . have learned more about my sexuality since being bi and "doing" other women.

I have become a real feminist activist since I became bi. I feel great kindred for my fellow females and a need to help them succeed and not be discriminated against. I've learned to appreciate females' physical aspects as well as their heads.

. . . combated my early training to fear other women as predators . . . now see them as allies.

My work relationship is better since—I'm more assertive to other women and men since, and feel now I'm a total person.

Only 4% of these subjects were in any way active in the women's movement prior to their first involvement in multifemale sexual activity, and in those few (2) instances the subjects indicated that that movement involvement was not a motivating factor in their commencement of sexual activity with other females. In comparison, 22% of these subjects became active in the women's movement *subsequent* to their first multifemale sexual experience—a 5.5-fold increase.

Only one (2%) subject was currently inorgasmic both with female and male partners. Three (6%) additional subjects were currently inorgasmic with female partners.

As expected, many subjects waffled on the subject of their preference of a male partner or a female partner in their achieving a partner-stimulated orgasm. Many subjects indicated that their partnered orgasmic satisfaction and enjoyment depended upon a great many variables. Some preferred having cunnilingual orgasms better than coital orgasms, whereas some preferred the reverse. Some preferred orgasms with one type of stimulation from partners of one sex and orgasms from other types of stimulation from partners of the other sex. However, when forced to make an overall choice of preference of sex partner *for partner-stimulated orgasms*, 16% preferred female partners, 37% preferred male partners, and 47% indicated an equal preference. Still, no subject reported that her *overall* preference for males as sex partners had changed.

The impression given by most subjects was that their overall sex lives had become more, as opposed to less, enjoyable subsequent to the development of their bisexuality. No subject reported any negative consequences resulting from their becoming bisexual.

DISCUSSION

This study was undertaken to help develop a better understanding of the nature of human bisexual behavior. A previous report (Dixon, 1984) discussed the study's findings as to the familial, social, and sexual histories of the subjects, with an emphasis upon identifying the factors which may be important in the ontogenetic process of such women commencing voluntary bisexual behavior. The portion of the study on which this report is based was concerned with identifying and examining some of the effects on formerly heterosexual women of their commencing bisexual activity.

In assessing the validity and reliability of the subjects' reports of their sexual histories regarding their multifemale sexual behavior and of the effects that history has had on them, it is useful to consider several factors. The sample was mature in age as compared to most samples used for investigating sexual behavior. Its members had had what is for most such studies an inordinate number of sex partners and amount of other-sex sexual experience, both before and after commencement of multifemale sexual activity. Very few were not currently married, and those marriages appeared by and large to be quite happy and durable. From these factors it appears that the sample had had sufficient experience both before and after the beginning of bisexual activity on which to base the opinions and personal judgments which this study sought to elicit.

Another distinguishing feature of the sample is that in making their forage into bisexuality none of the subjects had to deal with issues of monogamy or with major renegotiations of their marital contract. Swinging couples are, by definition, nonmonogamous and usually recognize the need for specific discussions with their spouse about their sexual activity and their marital relationship. Thus, in commencing sexual activity with other women, these subjects, already swingers, did not have to demand an open relationship with their husbands, nor did they have to acquire new skills in dealing with the emotional/social/psychological issues which may arise in a marriage as it adapts to nonmonogamy.

It is interesting to compare the information in Table 1 concerning the number of female partners with somewhat similar data from two studies of, or involving, female homosexuals. Between 1964 and 1970, Hedblom (1973) studied 65 female homosexuals between the ages of 18 and 55 and found that 82% had had sex with 7 or fewer other females in their entire lives; 58% had had 4 or fewer female sex partners. In a later study of 229 females with multifemale sexual interests or experience, most of whom were homosexual (although one-quarter of the female sample self-identified as "bisexual"), Bell and Weinberg (1978) reported that 81% had had 5 or fewer different sexual affairs with other females; the highest number of partners reported by any subject was 87.

In the main, the sample chose to limit their sexual activities with other females to those occasions in which at least one male (usually the subject's spouse) was also a participant. That was true of current as well as initial sex experiences with other females. The slight increase in the numbers of subjects who were at times engaging in multifemale sex in an all-female environment seemed to be more a function of a momentary unavailability of a male rather than the subjects' desire that no male be present. This response is certainly not what would be expected of homosexually inclined females. Many bisexual women (and probably many homosexual women) believe that a woman's willingness at times to participate in cunnilingus as an "oralist" as well as a "receiver" is symbolic of her greater willingness to participate more fully in the activity, and hence signifies greater personal approval of the activity.

The only other statistic of which the author is aware relative to that type of participation by swinging bisexual women is a statement by Bartell (1971). At swing parties he observed mixed 4-somes where the two women were involved in cunnilingual activity; one of the women remained passive ("receiver" in this study) in some 15% of the cases. That statistic compares to 20% who so far had remained receivers in this study.

The implication that, following their first experience of sex with another female, this sample has generally come to a greater personal acceptance of bisexual activity by more fully participating in cunnilingual activity is reinforced by data in Table 3, which illustrates how the typical subject's feelings about her own bisexuality have progressed with time and experience to an overwhelming general rating of excellent. Those favorable feelings accompanied increased incidences of fantasizing while masturbating, and specifically of fantasizing about females while masturbating. Some subjects even began finding that their fantasies while engaged in sex with males sometimes included females.

It is understandable why, following the commencement of sexual activities with other females, a woman who already had a history of fantasizing might begin fantasizing about females. But this study also raises the unanswered question of why such a late beginning of multifemale sexual activity is associated with a sizeable (over 50%) increase in the *overall* incidence of fantasizing with masturbation.

It is instructive to see how these subjects compare with other groups of somewhat similar females in the frequency of multifemale sexual activity. This sample of bisexual women engaged in sex with other women substantially more often than did the married bisexual women of roughly comparable ages in the sample of the Kinsey group (1953) and the sample of married and single bisexual women in Hunt's (1974) study, but substantially less often than did the combined homosexual and bisexual single and married women in the Bell and Weinberg (1978) sample.

Several possibilities may explain the portion of Table 4 which shows a substantial (2-1/2 times increased median) increase in frequency of multifemale sexual activity by subjects who were currently divorced, widowed, or separated (though each subject was still sexually active with males). One speculation is that bisexual married women who, for whatever reason, lose their spouses may turn to female lovers to help fill that void. That may have increasingly more important implications to such bisexual women as they get older; further research on that specific topic is definitely in order. Other possibilities were that some of those subjects may have found that their sexual needs were being filled better by female lovers, or they were reacting to perceived flaws in their former marriage which they were generalizing to other possible male partners.

However, the amount of multifemale sexual activity the sample engaged in as a whole had not significantly reduced the frequency of marital coitus they otherwise would be expected to report. In fact, the frequency of marital coitus for the currently married portion of the sample is much higher than the national average given by Ramey (1975).

In looking at the increase in frequency of marital coitus in current marriages over its frequency in prior marriages (for subjects about whom those data were collected), and after considering that 80% of that subsample also began multifemale sexual activity during current marriages, one could conclude that for some of those subjects the commencement of sexual activities with other females was somehow connected with the increase in their marital coitus. Further exploration of that possible connection may yield useful information about the cross effects of the two events.

Sexual satisfaction and compatibility with present spouses were clearly the norm in these swinging marriages. In view of that, and the fact that the typical pattern was for the subjects to share not only their extramarital heterosexual and multifemale sexual activities with their spouses but also at least five other (nonsexual) activities, a pattern seems evident that the couples saw the subjects' sexual activities with other females as additional recreational opportunities to be jointly enjoyed. That observation is underscored by the finding that 84% of the subjects concluded that their present or last spouse highly approved of the subjects' sexual activities with other females.

When it came to the question of multimale sexuality, however, a sizeable portion of the subjects and their spouses were uncomfortable with the topic. An interesting turn-about on that matter (see Table 6) had occurred, though, for about 30% of the subjects who either eased or eliminated their discomfort with multimale sexuality subsequent to their own involvement with same-sex sexual activity. By and large the subjects became more accepting of multimale sexuality than did their spouses.

Conversely, it is seen as significant that over one-third of these bisexual women were *not* comfortable with the idea of male bisexuality, a phenomenon which if further studied could yield useful sociological information.

One of the most dramatic changes which can occur in one's life is a change in sexual orientation. Indeed, as mentioned earlier in this report, some authorities doubt that such a change is even possible. It is well accepted that one (or in some cases even more than one) same-sex sexual experience does not necessarily a bisexual make—at least in terms of sexual orientation (SIECUS, 1980).

In studying their more widely based sample of bisexuals, Blumstein and Schwartz (1976d) observed that "no single or small number of patterns seems to predominate among those who call themselves bisexual, or among those whose behavior might be given that label" (p. 7). Further, they said, "One of our most pronounced findings among our female bisexual respondents is the extreme diversity of their lifestyles and sexual histories" (1976a, p. 156). They described (1974, 1976a, 1976c), without giving data, a plethora of variances between their female subjects' amount of overt multifemale sexual behavior and the subjects' actual assumption of a bisexual self-definition. Some of their subjects were said to have had "a great deal of bisexual behavior" prior to labeling themselves bisexual (1976a).

In view of the previously mentioned opinions and findings of other authors that a change of sexual orientation in adulthood is not possible, it seems significant that each of the subjects in this study, all of whom had had such a long and solid history of an exclusively heterosexual orientation, unhesitatingly self-identified as bisexual at the time of their interviews. Accompanying those changes in sexual behavior and self-identification were dramatic changes in subjects' attitudes toward other women and about themselves. In many cases marital relationships, work, family, and personal relationships with other females were altered positively.

One consequence of such fundamental changes in feelings toward oneself as a woman and toward other females in general was the initiation by some of involvement with the women's movement. Blumstein and Schwartz (1976a) indicated that some of the formerly heterosexual female subjects in their study came to bisexuality through the process of their prior involvement in the women's movement. However, this study revealed a different process at work; the experience and enjoyment of having sex with other women led many of these subjects into becoming actively involved in the women's movement.

Significantly, although no subject had changed her overall preference for males as sex partners: (a) fully 92% of the sample was at some time orgasmic with female partners; (b) two-thirds of the sample enjoyed orgasms either more often with female partners or equally often with male and female partners; and (c) the entire sample presently recognized their change in sexual orientation.

CONCLUSION

This study should not be taken to indicate that a change in gender preference does *not* accompany a change in sexual orientation; it simply shows that a change in sexual orientation from heterosexual to bisexual *may* be accomplished *without* a change in gender preference. Indeed, a study of formerly heterosexual women who changed in midlife to a homosexual orientation (Charbonneau & Lander, 1982) has shown that a change in gender preference in midlife *may* also occur. Therefore, the possibility remains that a change in gender preference *may* accompany other orientation changes (such as from heterosexual to bisexual).

Other major conclusions are that for some married women, beginning bisexual activity at or after age 30 with their husband's consent may improve their marriage, their enjoyment of sex in general, their self-esteem, and their nonsexual as well as sexual responses to and relationships with other females. Also, bisexual activity may increase their sexual fantasizing, the incidence of those fantasies including other females, their total number of sex partners, their frequency and total number of sexual contacts, their comfort with the subjects of multifemale *and* multimale sexuality, and their active participation in the women's movement. With all of that it is remarkable that no negative consequences were reported.

REFERENCES

Barkas, J. (1974, January). Two's company, how about three? *Forum*, pp. 34-43.

Bartell, G. D. (1971). *Group sex*. New York: Peter H. Wyden.

Bell, A. (1974). Homosexualities: Their range and character. In J. K. Cole & R. Dienstbier (Eds.), *Nebraska symposium on motivation: 1973* (pp. 1-26). Lincoln, NE: University of Nebraska Press.

Bell, A. (1980, October). Untitled address presented and video taped at The Institute for Advanced Study of Human Sexuality, San Francisco, CA.

Bell, A. P., & Weinberg, M. S. (1978). *Homosexualities: A study of diversity among men and women*. New York: Simon & Schuster.

Bell, A. P., Weinberg, M. S., & Hammersmith, S. F. (1981). *Sexual preference, its development in men and women*. Bloomington, IN: Indiana University Press.

Bieber, I. (1971, April). *Playboy* panel: Homosexuality. *Playboy*, pp. 63, 67.

Blumstein, P. W., & Schwartz, P. (1974). Lesbianism and bisexuality. In E. Goode & R. R. Troiden (Eds.), *Sexual deviance and sexual deviants* (pp. 278-295). New York: William Morrow.

Blumstein, P. W., & Schwartz, P. (1976a). Bisexual women. In J. P. Wiseman (Ed.), *The social psychology of sex* (pp. 154-162). New York: Harper & Row.

Blumstein, P. W., & Schwartz, P. (1976b, October). Bisexuality in men. *Urban Life*, pp. 339-358.

Blumstein, P. W., & Schwartz, P. (1976c). Bisexuality in women. *Archives of Sexual Behavior, 5*, 171-181.

Blumstein, P. W., & Schwartz, P. (1976d, August). *Bisexuality: Some social psychological issues*. Revised version of paper presented at annual meeting of American Sociological Association, New York, NY.

Charbonneau, C., & Lander, P. (1982, December). *Lesbianism as a mid-life choice: Continuities and discontinuities*. Paper presented at the 81st Annual Meeting of the American Anthropological Association, Washington, DC.

Coleman, E. M., Hoon, P. W., & Hoon, E. F. (1983). Arousability and sexual satisfaction in lesbian and heterosexual women. *The Journal of Sex Research, 19*, 58-73.

Dixon, J. K. (1984). The commencement of bisexual activity in swinging married women over age thirty. *The Journal of Sex Research, 20*, 71-90.

Ellis, A. (1962). Are homosexuals really creative? *Sexology, 29*, 88-93.

Freud, S. (1961). Three essays on the theory of sexuality. In J. Strachey (Ed. and Trans.), *The standard edition of the complete psychological works of Sigmund Freud* (Vol. 7, pp. 125-245). London: Hogarth Press. (Original work published 1905)

Gilmartin, B. G. (1978). *The Gilmartin report*. Secaucus, NJ: Citadel.

Harry, J., & Lovely, R. (1979). Gay marriages and communities of sexual orientation. *Alternative Lifestyles, 2*, 177-200.

Hedblom, J. H. (1973). Dimensions of lesbian sexual experience. *Archives of Sexual Behavior, 2*, 329-341.

Hunt, M. (1974). *Sexual behavior in the 1970's*. Chicago: Playboy Press.

Kenyon, F. E. (1968). Studies in female homosexuality, VI: The exclusively homosexual group. *Acta Psychiatrica Scandinavica, 44*, 224-237.

Kinsey, A. C., Pomeroy, W. B., Martin, C. E., & Gebhard, P. H. (1953). *Sexual behavior in the human female*. Philadelphia: W. B. Saunders.

Masters, W. H., & Johnson, V. E. (1979). *Homosexuality in perspective*. Boston: Little, Brown.

O'Neill, G. C., & O'Neill, N. (1970). Patterns in group sexual activity. *The Journal of Sex Research, 6*, 101-112.

Ramey, J. W. (1975). Intimate groups and networks: Frequent consequences of sexually open marriage. *The Family Coordinator, 24*, 515-530.

Ruitenbeck, H. M. (1971). Answers to questions. *Sexual Behavior, 1*, 6.

Saghir, M. (1980). Answers to questions. *Medical Aspects of Human Sexuality, 14*, 4-5.

Saghir, M. T., & Robbins, E. (1968). Lesbian study upsets notion one is dominant, the other passive. *Psychiatric Progress, 4*, 214-221.

Sex Information and Educational Council of the U.S. (1980). Uppsala principles basic to education for sexuality. *SIECUS Report, 8*, 8-9.

Silverstein, C. (1977). Homosexuality and the ethics of behavioral intervention: Paper 2. *Journal of Homosexuality, 2* 205-211.

Socarides, C. W. (1963). The historical development of theoretical and clinical concepts of overt female homosexuality. *Journal of the American Psychoanalytic Association, 21*, 386-414.

Spiers, E. D. (1976). The no-man's-land of the bisexual. *Corrective and Social Psychiatry and Journal of Behavior Technology Methods and Therapy, 22*, 6-11.

Tavris, C., & Sadd, S. (1975). *The Redbook report on female sexuality*. New York: Delacorte.

Weinberg, M. S. (1970). Homosexual samples: Differences and similarities. *The Journal of Sex Research, 6*, 312-325.

Whitam, F. L. (1977). The homosexual role: A reconsideration. *The Journal of Sex Research, 13*, 1-11.

MEN IN MARRIAGES

Marriages of Bisexual Men

Timothy J. Wolf, PhD
San Diego

ABSTRACT. This study examined the marriages of 26 couples in which the husband was bisexual. The subjects were a non-clinical sample married for at least two years and intending to continue their marriages. The sample was, overall, highly educated and earned concomitantly high incomes. Subjects were administered the Klein Sexual Orientation Grid and a research questionnaire to determine successful or problematic aspects of their marriages. Subjects were, for the most part, satisfied with the quality of their marriages, sexually active within the marriages, and open about the husband's homosexual behavior. A high-level of sexual activity within the marriage, open and direct communication, a valued friendship, previous counseling or psychotherapy, cognitive flexibility, and financial independence contributed to the success of these marriages. The husbands reported a great deal of ambiguity about their homosexual behavior, and the couples reported intense conflict dealing with their open marriage styles.

Recently the media and research studies have begun to untangle the myths about bisexual men who continue their heterosexual marriages. The number of these men remains as unknown as the lives they lead. The Kinsey studies (Kinsey, Pomeroy, & Martin, 1948) reported more than 10% of males who were married also participated in some homosexual activities. Kinsey (1948) further reported that 18% of males between the ages of 11 and 55 have demonstrated at least as much homosexual as heterosexual behavior during their lives. Approximately one in five self-identified homosexual men have been married at least once (Bell & Weinberg, 1978; Jay & Young, 1979; Spada, 1979).

Some of the men who choose to begin to accept and be open about their bisexuality are already married. Some self-proclaimed homosexual men choose to marry, while still others are exploring new relationships with women that involve alternative marriage styles. The result of this renewed interest in relationships between homosexual men and heterosexual women has been reflected in recent magazine articles, TV programs, and a major motion picture, *Making Love*. Recent books have focused on the subject: *Barry and Alice: Portrait of a Bisexual Marriage* (Kohn & Matusow, 1980), *Straight Women/Gay Men* (Malone, 1980), *The New Couple: Women and Gay Men* (Nahas & Turley, 1979). *Married and Gay: An Intimate Look at a Different Relationship* (Maddox, 1982), and *The Married Homosexual Man* (M. W. Ross, 1983). Research studies have also explored these relationships (H. L. Ross, 1971, 1972; Gochros, 1978; Latham & White, 1978; M. W. Ross, 1979; Miller, 1979; Coleman, 1982; Wolf, 1982).

A significant number of men and their spouses, families, relatives, and friends are affected by homosexual expression within marriage. Through personal contacts and clinical experience with individuals and couples faced with this phenomenon, this researcher has witnessed their confusion, misinformation, self-doubt, and struggling for validation, identification, and support. These problems have often led to premature flight from the marriages, unsatisfactory communication patterns, or unresolved feelings about those intimate relationships. Research literature has only superficially addressed these concerns. Until recently, what has been written lended itself poorly to generalization because of its anecdotal nature, a small number of case histories, the clinical nature of the population, or biased theoretical approach.

While the process of integrating the husband's homosexual behavior into the marriage is often a difficult one, some studies have reported modes of adjustment. Latham and White (1978), H. L. Ross (1971), and Nahas and Turley (1979) described relationship modes in which the husband's homosexual behavior was integrated into the marriage. The present study focused on couples who appeared to have accomplished, or were working toward, integrating the husband's bisexuality into a working marriage.

Whereas other studies have chosen clinical samples, short-term relationships, or anecdotal data, this study surveyed 26 couples who had been married on an average of 13 years with open disclosure of the husband's homosexual behavior for an average of 5.5 years. The average of five years may be a realistic time-frame for couples to integrate and adjust to the mixed sexual orientation of the spouses (Latham & White, 1978; Kohn & Matusow, 1980; Wolf, 1982). None of the couples was currently in counseling or psychotherapy. By surveying the individual and relationship characteristics of these 52 individuals, this study sought to identify the psychological, sociological, and behavioral variables which allowed these marriages to survive over time.

METHOD

Certain psychological, sociological, and behavioral variables were ascertained for the 52 individuals in these coupled relationships through the use of two instruments, a self-administered questionnaire and the Klein Sexual Orientation Grid (KSOG). The questionnaire contained several sections. The first ascertained demographic information such as age, sex, religion, birth order, income, and number of siblings. The second section contained questions related to history of relationships, initial attraction of partners, and length of present relationship. The third section explored the disclosure of homosexuality within the marriage, the quality of the marriage, social participation, and communication styles. And the final section explored sexual behavior within and outside of the marriage. (For research validity and reliability studies of the research questionnaire refer to Wolf, 1982, pp. 47-49. Statistical confidence levels for correlations are further documented in this research.)

The Klein Sexual Orientation Grid (1980) was patterned after the original Kinsey scale. The KSOG expanded the scope of the original scale to include all the factors of sexual attraction, behavior, fantasy, emotional preference, social preference, self-identification, and lifestyle. These factors are separately rated for the present, past and ideal. The rating scale is an equal-appearing interval scale from one to seven, one for exclusively heterosexual and seven for exclusively homosexual in sexual orientation.

The 26 married couples were volunteers who agreed to fill out the questionnaire, as well as the KSOG. Subjects were solicited locally as well as nationally through homosexual and bisexual organizations, advertisements in homosexual and bisexual publications, referrals through professional contacts, and referrals from couples in the present study.

Subjects in the present study were a non-random sample selected on an availability basis; generalization of results is limited to this same population. An attempt was made to select couples representing a wide variety of geographical settings: subjects responding were from California, Arizona, Colorado, South Carolina, Illinois, and New York.

Subjects in the study met the following initial requirements. They were married for at least two years, and had for at least two years had some form of open disclosure about the husband's homosexual behavior outside of the marriage. The couples must have been living together and not in the process of dissolution of the marriage. And finally, the couples were not currently involved in counseling or psychotherapy.

RESULTS

The sample population of the 26 couples had a mean age of 39 with a range from 24 to 59. Females ranged in age from 24 to 54 (mean age, 36), and males ranged in age from 29 to 59 (mean age, 42). The 26 couples were married an average of 13 years, with a range of 2 to 31 years. All of the wives in the sample were aware of the homosexual nature of the male's relationships outside of the marriage. The average length of time during which open disclosure of homosexuality had existed in the marriage was 5.5 years. The length of time these couples had been involved in an open marriage in which the husbands were having homosexual contacts varied from 2 to 16 years.

Descriptive Characteristics

Sixty-nine percent of males were aware of their homosexuality upon entering the marriage. Fifteen percent reported they were unaware, 12% reported a conscious desire to escape attraction to the same sex, and one male responded that he chose this relationship because of social and family pressures.

When females were asked why they married a bisexual man, 23% reported they were unaware because their husbands were unaware, 35% said the partner withheld the information, and 38% chose the marriage initially with awareness of homosexuality (Table 1).

When asked at what point in their marriage the husband's bisexuality became an open issue, ten couples (40%) replied that the husband's homosexual behavior was known initially in the marriage. One couple indicated it became known during the first year of marriage, two couples between the first and third years, two couples between the third and fifth years, and two couples between the fifth and eighth years. Eight couples (32%) reported this disclosure was made after eight years of marriage.

Eight percent reported not having religious upbringing as a child. Of the remaining 92%, 29% reported Catholic unbringing, 42% Protestant, 11% Jewish, and 10% other religions. These figures showed a dramatic shift when the response was to current religious participation. Ten percent remained actively Catholic, 5% Jewish, and 10% Protestant. Seventeen percent currently participated in other religious organizations, the frequently listed ones being the Unitarian and Metropolitan Community Churches. Fifty-eight percent of the sample no longer participated in any organized religion.

The sample was highly educated and earned high incomes. The educational levels of the subjects included 10% with a high school education, 42% college educated, 25% master's degrees, 17% doctorates of phi-

Table 1

Description of Male and Female Subjects Regarding
Reasons for Marriage

Female: Reason for marriage to bisexual or homosexual male.	Females (%)
Spouse unaware of homosexuality/bisexuality	23
Spouse withheld information	35
Chose relationship for limited time	4
Aware of spouse's bisexuality/homosexuality	38

Male: Reason for marriage	Males (%)
Unaware of homosexuality/bisexuality	16
Conscious desire to excape attraction to same sex	
Awareness of homosexuality/bisexuality as rational choice for love, children,etc.	68
Social/family pressures	4

losophy, one medical doctor, and two lawyers. Males comprised a greater proportion of the higher educational slots (See Table 2).

In line with educational levels, 42% of the sample had individual incomes over $30,000 annually. Only one male had an income of under $10,000 annually, 31% of the males reported $20,000 to $30,000, and 65% of the males listed annual incomes of over $30,000 a year. The average combined income for couples in the study was over $50,000 annually.

Thirty-one percent of the males had experienced committed sexual relationships with females prior to their present marriage. Forty-two percent of the females reported committed sexual relationships with males prior to this marriage. Twenty-seven percent of the males, and none of

Table 2

Description of Sample According to Educational Levels

Educational Level	Males (%)	Females (%)	Males and Females (%)
Grades 1-12	8	12	10
College	30	52	40
Master's Degree	27	24	25
Doctorate Degree	23	12	17
Medical Doctor	4	0	2
Lawyer	8	0	4

the females, reported committed sexual relationships with members of the same sex prior to their present marriage. Fifteen percent of the males and 23% of the females were previously married. Only one male and one female reported that homosexuality had been an issue in their previous marriages. Thirty-five percent of the males and 8% of the females reported that they had serious reservations about entering into their present marriages. Some of the reservations voiced by the males were "concern for success," "concern about heterosexual performance," "afraid my homosexuality would be an issue," and "would marriage 'cure me'," "could I go straight?"

Subjects were asked to rate the quality of their marriages. Forty-two percent of males and 32% of females described their relationships as "outstanding," 34% of males and 46% of females described it as "better than average," and 8% of males and 12% of females described theirs as "average." Sixteen percent of the males described their marriages as "below average," and 12% of females and none of the males listed theirs as "poor" (Table 3).

When the 52 subjects were asked to list, in order of importance, the significant reasons for staying in their marriages (religious, personal freedom, sexual, children, financial, social, friendship, family), 62% of males and 77% of females chose friendship of partner as their first choice (Table 4).

When questioned about with whom they spend their social life, 17% of

Table 3

Description of Subjects According to Quality of Marriage

Quality of Marriage	Males (%)	Females (%)	Males and Females (%)
Outstanding	42	32	36
Better than Average	34	46	40
Average	8	12	10
Below Average	16	0	8
Poor	0	12	6

Table 4

Description of Sample According to Reasons for Remaining in Marriage

Reason for remaining in marriage	First Choice		Second Choice	
	Males (%)	Females (%)	Males (%)	Females (%)
Religious reasons	0	0	0	0
Children	24	4	12	28
Financial Security	4	8	20	16
Social Obligation	0	0	0	0
Friendship of Spouse	64	76	28	12
Family Expectations	0	0	0	0

the subjects said exclusively heterosexual persons, 34% mostly heterosexual persons, 27% equally with heterosexual and homosexual persons, and 19% mostly homosexual persons. One male responded that he socialized with homosexual persons exclusively. There was little difference between males and females on this variable.

When asked about the amount of social time spent with their partners, 25% responded that their social life always included their partner, 60% reported it usually included their partner, and 13% minimally included the partner. One male indicated a social life exclusively independent of his partner.

In terms of communication, 62% of the males and 73% of the females responded that they communicated with their partners immediately when irritated. Thirty-eight percent of the males and 27% of the females indicated that they waited to discuss their anger later, gave nonverbal cues, or withdrew and became silent. When asked about their partners' modes of communication, 65% of the males and 58% of the females indicated that their partners communicated immediately when something irritated them. Thirty-five percent of the males and 42% of the females indicated that their partners waited to discuss being irritated later, gave nonverbal cues, or withdrew and became silent when irritated. Females were less likely to perceive that their partners communicated differences to them immediately as compared with the males' perceptions of themselves.

Subjects were also asked whether communication about bisexuality in their marriages had changed during the course of their marriage. Fifty percent of the subjects indicated that communication about this issue was easier and more frequent: "It is easier to discuss it the older we get"; "Becoming more open and comfortable"; "Didn't want to hear it in the beginning"; "He has relaxed somewhat and can talk about it easier"; "It has become more acceptable on my part (wife)"; and, "Went from exploratory to totally open, more honest."

Forty-six percent of the subjects indicated that the level of trust had changed. Commenting on this question, females mentioned breaches of trust in the past: "I feel more suspicious and jealous at times since he lied in the past"; or "It became difficult to trust him when he said he was working and I felt he might be with someone else." Other females commented that "our trust has deepened." "I am far surer of his love for me and my love for him." Males were likely to comment upon the conflict of trust associated with outside relationships: "I am less trusted because of possible important outside relationships"; "She has become more suspicious"; or "She doesn't trust me about what I say about my other life." Other males indicated trust had increased: "I have more freedom to be gay without guilt feelings"; "She is more trusting of men and I am more comfortable being open with her"; or "We trust each other more since there are no secrets."

When responding to questions about time spent apart, 27% of subjects indicated they had been separated for more than a month for other than business or family reasons. All of these subjects stated that the separation was useful in maintaining their relationship.

Fifty-eight percent of the sample had at least one child. Fifty percent of the parents of school-age children replied their children were aware of their father's homosexuality. Of the 42% who did not have children, 12% reported they planned to have children, and 30% reported they had no plans for children. Only one person indicated his homosexual behavior would preclude the option of having children.

Eighty-five percent of the males and 76% of the females indicated they expected their marriage would be sexually open in the future. Eight percent of females indicated that they saw their sexual relationships as monogamous in the future. Fifteen percent of the males and females were undecided on this issue. Sixty-two percent of the males and 42% of the females reported they would choose this kind of marriage again. When questioned further about the beliefs in their marriage, 30% of the males and females indicated that they believed their marriage would last forever. Thirty-five percent of the males and 46% of the females indicated that their marriages would last a very long time, and 35% of the males and 23% of the females indicated that their marriages would last only for awhile.

Seventy-eight percent of the males and females indicated that they would have benefited from having a couple like themselves with whom to discuss the adjustment issues of their relationships, and indicated their willingness to participate in support groups. Thirty-one percent of the males and 38% of the females indicated that they had received counseling or psychotherapy prior to their present marriage. During their present marriages, 42% of the males and 38% of the females received therapy concerning their own or their spouse's bisexuality. Thirty-two percent of the sample spent from 1 to 12 months in therapy as a couple dealing with issues of the husband's orientation.

Of the 26 females, nine (35%) reported having homosexual boyfriends or close friends. Two females had committed sexual relationships with bisexual men prior to their present marriages. Fifty-four percent of the women reported sexual relationships with men other than their husbands during their marriage and 23% of women maintained such relationships. Three women had sexual relationships with other women during their present marriages and all three currently maintained these liaisons. Seventy-eight percent of women reported having sexual intercourse with their husbands from once a month to 24 times a month, while 22% did not have sexual relations with their husbands. Fifty-eight percent of the women reported being satisfied or fulfilled by the sexual relationships with their spouses.

Sixty-eight percent of the husbands reported having sexual intercourse with their wives from once a month to 24 times a month, with an average of five times a month. Males reported having outside homosexual encounters from once a month to 16 times a month. Only one husband was having sexual contacts with women other than his wife, which had caused a considerable amount of conflict within the marriage since his wife perceived this as more threatening than his homosexual contacts.

Correlations Among Questionnaire Data

Since this research was intended only to be exploratory and descriptive, and generalizing these results is limited due to sample size and selection, identified trends are tentative and will require replication in future research before any broad conclusions can be drawn.

Several Spearman rank-order correlations were significant. Couples who spent more time in counseling or psychotherapy tended to be older, have higher incomes, and to disclose the issues of the husband's bisexuality later in the marriage. Couples who spent a longer time in therapy were more likely to rate the quality of their marriages as positive and spent a greater amount of time socializing with heterosexuals rather than homosexuals.

Persons who self-rated the quality of their marriages more positively were also more likely to indicate that their relationship would last "forever," spent more time socializing with heterosexual rather than homosexual persons, and had known about the husband's bisexuality previous to, or earlier in, the marriage.

The time at which the homosexual behavior became an open issue in the marriage significantly correlated with variables of social time, age, and whether the marriage would continue. Partners for whom the issue of bisexuality was open from the beginning or near the beginning of the marriage were more likely to socialize with homosexuals, describe their marriage as lasting "forever," and tended to be younger in age.

The presence and frequency of sexual intercourse were positively correlated with self-ratings of marital satisfaction. Of the 40 subjects who maintained sexual relationships with their spouses at least once a month, only 1 person indicated the quality of the marriage as below average. On the other hand, of the 12 subjects who indicated they did not have ongoing sexual intercourse, 6 described their marriages as poor or below average, 2 as average, and 4 better than average. Both maintaining a sexual relationship and the frequency of sexual intercourse were significant indicators of the self-rated quality of the marriages. In addition, couples with higher frequencies of sexual intercourse were more likely to say their marriage would last "forever," had higher incomes, shared and discussed the husband's homosexuality earlier in the marriage, and spent more social time exclusively with their partners.

Responses to the Klein Sexual Orientation Grid

Subjects were asked to label themselves as heterosexual, homosexual, or bisexual. Twenty-four of the 26 females replied that they considered themselves heterosexual, 2 bisexual. Of the males, 19 (73%) self-labeled as bisexual, 7 (27%) homosexual. Overall, the men in this sample scored in the four, five, and six areas of the seven-point hetero-homosexual continuum of the KSOG. Although these men were sexually active with their wives, their primary erotic behavior, attraction, and fantasy were homosexual. In terms of emotional and social preference, lifestyle, and self-identification, they approximated a bisexual norm which was illustrated by a four on the continuum.

DISCUSSION

This study examined the individuals in 26 marriages in which male homosexual behavior existed. Despite this aspect of commonality, they cannot be described as a homogeneous group. Each of the couples seemed to have a unique style of adjustment. They may be more precisely described as a cross-section of American couples with few differences overall in income and educational brackets. Although the husbands may have had other significant erotic attractions (which again may not distinguish them from other husbands), the majority of these couples maintained sexual activities, reported sexual satisfaction, and reported on-going marriage commitments. They became lovers and married for many of the same reasons exclusively heterosexual couples do: friendship, physical attraction, intellectual compatibility, emotional attachment, desire for children, economic benefits, and family and social pressures.

This study described those variables which may have fostered the acceptance of the male's homosexual behavior and created the stability found in most of these marriages. One of the important variables within this sample was the communication in marriage, everyday communication and communication about the husband's homosexual behavior. Couples expressed more satisfaction in their marriages when they had more direct styles of communication and when they had communicated the issues of the husband's homosexual behavior early or initially in the marriage. It may be suggested that couples with more immediate modes of communication would be more likely to disclose issues like the husband's homosexual behavior, and that couples with good communication skills may be successful in many types of relationships as long as certain other basic elements of relationship are satisfied.

That younger couples had more open disclosure of bisexuality may also reflect recent more open social attitudes toward homosexuality. Younger men may be more willing to risk this disclosure and women may be more willing to accept that behavior. Perhaps the gay liberation movement is providing more choices to younger homosexual men who would like to marry and have children. This marital option may fulfill the unique needs of the individual, independent of social or familial pressures for marriage and against homosexuality.

In light of the more relaxed attitudes toward homosexual behavior, younger couples with open disclosure of the husband's bisexuality were more likely to have socialized with homosexuals. Older couples tended to socialize more with heterosexuals. Socializing with homosexuals is part of the "coming out" process and an important part of the life of the younger bisexual partner, whereas older couples appeared to be more assimilated in the mainstream of heterosexual society.

Satisfaction in the marriage was positively correlated to increased frequency of sexual intercourse. This was consistent with the conclusions of Latham and White (1978) and has been validated for many types of American couples (Blumstein & Schwartz, 1983).

Their level of prosperity may have afforded these couples advantages that helped them come to terms with the husband's sexuality and still remain married. Higher income couples were more educated, more likely to have benefited from reading bisexual or homosexual literature, more able to afford psychotherapy, able to take separate vacations, and able to have flexible schedules and even maintain two apartments which gave the husband the space for same-sex liaisons.

Education may also have created a sense of independence and freedom which allowed these marriages to remain intact, as well as fostered more tolerant attitudes toward homosexuality, bisexuality, and open lifestyles. More highly educated persons may have had a greater ability to deal with the dissonance basic to the inherent complications in these marriages. Also, one of the primary qualities of the marriages of these men and women was their intellectual compatibility.

Couples overwhelmingly stressed the friendship of their spouse as the reason for staying in the marriage. Couples who cited this reason were more satisfied with their marriages than couples who cited more externally motivated reasons like children or financial security. Perhaps the bond of friendship was forged through the often agonizing process of integrating the husband's homosexual behavior into the marriage. Kleinberg (1980) wrote that "gay men and straight women share the richest, most adult, and most moral of friendships" (p. 105) because both find a genuineness which is outside the oppressive internalized restrictions society generally imposes on men's and women's roles or on their marriages or relationships.

Many of the personal difficulties of the husbands in this study focused around the inherent contradictions of their identification as a bisexual male. They had chosen marriage partly out of an aversion to being labeled a homosexual, and thus had formed a primary and sexual relationship with a woman. For a variety of reasons which may have included a close emotional or friendship attachment to a woman, desire for children, social or family pressure, or an aversion to an exclusively homosexual identity, these men had chosen a primarily heterosexual lifestyle. In their struggle to integrate their marriage and heterosexuality with their homosexual feelings and behavior, the bipolar labeling process which society imposed reinforced confusion and contradiction.

The ambiguity of the bisexual self-label was also apparent from the KSOG. Some of the males' comments about self-labeling as bisexual included: "I'm not sure this is a true choice. I almost feel it is a cop-out"; "It is really more than I can handle so I lean toward men"; and "I have found no sexual label with which I can identify." It was also apparent from the KSOG that self-labeled homosexual men, as differentiated from the bisexual men, showed congruence with their present and ideal attraction, behavior, and fantasy. The bisexual men, on the other hand, consistently chose to move away from a more exclusive homosexual orientation toward "both sexes equally" in their present and ideal sexual attraction, behavior, and fantasy. These men may have been attempting to adjust their feelings and behaviors to accord with the realities of being married.

The wives in this study were, like the husbands, a heterogeneous group with few obvious characteristics in common. Their histories showed no tendency toward emotional or sexual problems or pathology which would lead them defensively to choose to marry a bisexual man as might be predicted. They were often the crucial compromisers and communicators who weighed the negative aspects of the husband's homosexual behavior against the more positive aspects of their marriages. Their initial dependence in the marriage often blossomed into new independence as they struggled to maintain the marriage.

While the marriages of bisexual men and their wives are extremely complex, this study presented an overview of the characteristics and struggles of 26 couples. More research is needed to gain a more complete picture of their families, sexual behaviors, and childhood dynamics. Research is also needed regarding bisexual women in marriages. Such research would help provide encouragement, information, and models for those struggling with similar crises in their marriages.

REFERENCES

Bell, A. P., & Weinberg, M. S. (1978). *Homosexualities: A study of diversity among men and women.* New York: Simon & Schuster.

Blumstein, P. W., & Schwartz, P. (1983). *American couples.* New York: William Morrow.

Coleman, E. (1982). Bisexual and gay men in heterosexual marriage. Conflicts and resolutions in therapy. *Journal of Homosexuality, 7*(2/3), 93-103.

Gochros, H. (1978). Counseling gay husbands. *Journal of Sex and Marital Therapy, 5*, 142-151.

Jay, K., & Young, A. (1979). *The gay report: Lesbians and gay men speak out about sexual experiences and lifestyles*. New York: Summit.

Kinsey, A. C., Pomeroy, W. B., & Martin, C. E. (1948). *Sexual behavior in the human male*. Philadelphia: W. B. Saunders.

Klein, F. (1980, December). Are you sure you're heterosexual? or homosexual? or even bisexual? *Forum Magazine*, pp. 41-45.

Kleinberg, S. (1980). *Alienated affections: Being gay in America*. New York: St. Martin's Press.

Kohn, B., & Matusow, A. (1980). *Barry and Alice: Portrait of a bisexual marriage*. Englewood Cliffs, NJ: Prentice-Hall.

Latham, J. D., & White, G. (1978). Coping with homosexual expression within heterosexual marriages: Five case studies. *Journal of Sex and Marital Therapy, 4*, 198-212.

Maddox, B. (1982). *Married and gay: An intimate look at a different relationship*. New York: Harcourt Brace Jovanovich.

Malone, J. (1980). *Straight women/gay men: A special relationship*. New York: Dial Press.

Miller, B. (1979). Unpromised paternity: The lifestyles of gay fathers. In M. Levine (Ed.), *Gay men: The sociology of male homosexuality* (pp. 239-252). New York: Harper & Row.

Nahas, R., & Turley, M. (1979). *The new couple: Women and gay men*. New York: Seaview Books.

Ross, H. L. (1971). Modes of adjustment of married homosexuals. *Social Problems, 18*, 385-393.

Ross, H. L. (1972). Odd couples: Homosexuals in heterosexual marriage. *Social Problems, 2*, 42-49.

Ross, M. W. (1979). Heterosexual marriage of homosexual men: Some associated factors. *Journal of Sex and Marital Therapy, 5*, 142-151.

Ross, M.W. (1983). *The married homosexual man*. London: Routledge & Kegan Paul.

Spada, J. (1979). *The Spada Report*. New York: New American Library.

Wolf, T. J. (1982). *Selected psychological and sociological aspects of male homosexual behavior in marriage*. Unpublished doctoral dissertation, United States International University, San Diego, CA.

Bisexual Men in Marriage:
Is a Positive Homosexual Identity
and Stable Marriage Possible?

David R. Matteson, PhD
Governors State University

ABSTRACT. The negative picture of mixed-orientation marriages portrayed in previous research is challenged by results from a study and two-year follow-up of a non-clinical sample of 41 spouses representing 30 marriages. Evidence suggests that more recent marriages involving a bisexual are made for positive reasons, rather than as an escape from homosexuality. A comparison of couples in which the homosexual behavior is acknowledged to those in which it is secretive suggests a positive homosexual identity can be developed in the acknowledged situation. Data from a two-year follow-up provide information on the factors which led to the stabilization of such marriages. A schema of developmental crises, decisions, and consequences is presented.

The study of homosexuality and other alternative lifestyles has moved through a number of stages in the last decade. Most early studies treated as deviant the homosexuality of partners in heterosexual marriages. The samples in these studies were usually drawn from clinical or institutionalized populations, providing data which reinforced the supposition of pathology. Later, researchers began to view alternative lifestyles as of interest in their own right. Attempts were made to find non-clinical samples who were self-identified (e.g., as homosexual), and compare these to the majority population. A third type of research is emerging which affirms the bisexual lifestyle being studied and attempts to discover patterns of coping which are functional within that lifestyle. Where comparison groups are used, they are between subsamples within the alternative lifestyle.

Three research studies of the last type will be reviewed here as background for this study of bisexuality. (For a more comprehensive review of literature, see Matteson, 1983.) One study in Belgium (H. L. Ross,

Dr. Matteson is Professor of Psychology and Counseling at Governors State University. Requests for reprints or further information may be sent to the author at Governors State University, University Park, IL 60466.

149

1971) focused on how these couples cope. The sample's eleven couples were contacted through an organization of self-identified homosexuals. Three modes of coping were described: platonic marriage, a double standard, and open marriage. In the platonic couples, sexual conflict was handled by abandoning sexual activities within the marriage and focusing on the non-sexual satisfactions of coupledom and family life. Homosexual activities were usually impersonal and infrequent, in some cases without the spouse's knowledge.

In the double-standard marriages the husband established an acknowledged homosexual liaison outside the marriage, but retained a fundamental allegiance to his wife, who permitted the outside liaison as a means of maintaining the marriage. The wife usually resented this arrangement and doubted that her husband would be able to maintain the dual commitment.

The most successful marriage reported was that in which both husband and wife gave priority to their relationship, but accepted extramarital sexual relationships for either of them. Ross attributed this "innovative marriage" to "unusual circumstances: the sexual versatility of the husband (who defined himself as bisexual) and the broadmindedness of the wife" (p. 392).

A second study (Miller, 1979) described four lifestyles of married and formerly married bisexual men, and clarified some factors necessary for self-acceptance of homosexual behavior. These included integrating their homosexuality into the fabric of everyday life (in contrast to pursuing depersonalized and furtive sex) and developing reference groups which support homosexual identity. In Miller's sample, the move to a positive homosexual identity occurred only for those husbands who separated from their wives. The major event which aided the transition from a covert, highly compartmentalized lifestyle to an openly homosexual stance was the initiation of a homosexual love relationship.

Most previous researchers have seen the bisexual husband as caught in a dilemma. If he conceals his homosexual activities he in unlikely either to feel positive about his place in the gay world or congruent about his marriage. His secrecy perpetuates a cycle of negative expectations (M. W. Ross, 1979) and a negative view of self. Conversely, disclosing his homosexual behavior, while it may lead to personal integration, usually results in separation and divorce (Coleman, 1981/1982; Bozett, 1982).

Regarding Bozett's (1982) study, the high rate of marital failure in his sample may have been due to the fact that his sample was drawn from homosexual groups in which currently married homosexuals were likely to be under-represented. Note that the majority of Bozett's subjects were already separated from their wives at the beginning of the study. The high rate of marital failure reported by Coleman (1981/1982) also may be due to the use of a clinical sample, or to Coleman's treatment approach, which by not involving the wives on the very first interview, inadvertently communicated that the man's sexual identity issues were a higher priority than the resolution of the marriage. As is widely recognized in family and couple therapy, the therapist's decisions regarding who to see together in treatment have consequences for the outcome of treatment (see Gurman & Kniskern, 1978).

The third study, Latham and White (1978), described a sequence of phases of adjustment. The first phase of the marriage, prior to disclosure, was a withdrawal from and avoidance of homosexual activity on the part of the husband. This stage lasted from 1 to 5 years, and any homosexual activity which did occur was clandestine and guilt-producing. Most of the wives who knew of their husbands' past homosexual interests had assumed such an activity would not reoccur. When the husbands resumed their homosexual activities and such were disclosed or discovered, the wives at first responded very negatively. Often the homosexual "problem" became the scapegoat for other difficulties experienced in the marriage. The stress, however, often prompted some cognitive reorientations.

In the "disclosure-acceptance stage" (Stage II) the partners began to establish effective coping patterns in order to continue the marriage. Typically, the husband no longer felt anxious or guilty about his homosexual interests per se (though guilt about marital "infidelity" often continued). Very different patterns and degrees of trauma were experienced by different couples, but the outcome was well described by one of the wives:

> I've learned . . . that I have no control over anyone but myself . . . I can't change him. I no longer want to . . . What he wants, it's something I really can't give him, and so it's no reflection on our own relationship. (p. 205)

The process of attitude change continues to Phase III, the "adjustment-coping stage," in which greater degree of sexual expression is allowed for both partners, often with the encouragement of the husband, but clear rules are negotiated to govern the boundaries of the outside sexual contacts. However, not all of the wives continued to have extramarital sex; those who did had it less frequently than their husbands. The foci of conflicts, when they occurred, shifted away from the issue of homosexuality to problems common to most marriages.

The research literature presents a striking contrast between successfully innovative marriages and those in which concealed homosexual behavior prevents a positive identity and destroys a marriage. In order to assess the stability of innovative marriages and their relationship to a positive sexual identity, this study followed over time a non-clinical sample of couples who were living together at the beginning of the study. Both "acknowledged'' and ''secretive'' marriages in the same sample were studied.

Though the present study was exploratory and included a broad range of data, it focused on three questions.

1. Are the motivations for entering these marriages changing, given changes in attitudes toward homosexuality?
2. Can marriages in which the husband is actively homosexual become stable marriages? (''Actively homosexual'' is used here to mean actually engaging in sexual relationships with other men.)
3. Can men who engage in homosexuality develop positive sexual identities while remaining in heterosexual marriages?

METHOD

Procedures

The men in this study are bisexual in behavior and 86% of the men refer to themselves as bisexual. But there are also 86% who refer to themselves as gay or homosexual (obviously the great majority are comfortable with either term), and a slight majority (55%) who prefer the descriptors ''gay'' or ''homosexual'' to ''bisexual.''

Thirty men were interviewed for 1-1/2 to 5 hours each. Those husbands whose wives were aware of their husband's homosexuality were asked for permission to contact their wives. Eleven wives were interviewed. Approximately two years later, the men were recontacted to learn the current status of the marriage.

The interviews were audio-recorded, and were coded for computer analysis by the author. After removing identifying information, the wives' interviews were independently assessed on the personality variables discussed in the comparison of together and separating wives. Except for the Kinsey Scale of sexual orientation (Kinsey, 1948) and two measures of homosexual identity adapted from Miller (1978) and Berzon and Leighton (1979), all ratings were based on impressions from the interviews. (For further information on coding, contact the author.)

Description of Total Sample

The majority of the thirty husbands in the study had answered an advertisement in Chicago's gay newspaper regarding the formation of a support group for homosexuals in marriages; other men were referred to the author by a gay hotline or by previous subjects. It is generally recognized by researchers of alternative lifestyles that representative samples cannot be obtained. Although the present study did not use a clinical sample, it is likely that many of the marriages were at a crisis point; certainly many of the husbands were at a decisive point in forming their sexual identity.

At the time of the interviews, the husbands had an average age of 41 years; their mean age when married had been 25. All but two of the men were Caucasian. All except six of the married couples had children. The educational level of the sample was considerably above average; only five husbands had not completed college, and over two-thirds had graduate degrees. The husbands' occupations ranged from blue collar work to executive, but social service and academic professions were clearly overrepresented. Over a third were teachers, counselors, or ministers.

In the first analysis, material from the initial interviews is summarized to discern the spouses' reasons for entering such marriages, and a comparison is made between couples who had married prior to the emergence of gay liberation and couples who married after its emergence. Analyses II and III address the issue of the stability of these marriages. In Analysis IV, comparisons are made between those marriages in which the homosexual activity was acknowledged and those in which it was secretive, and between those couples still together at the time of follow-up and those who had separated.

Analysis I: Motivations for Entering Mixed Orientation Marriages

Members of hidden minority groups undergo a different socialization process than do members of visible minorities such as ethnic or racial groups (Miller, 1978; Weinberg, 1978). Homosexuals are generally reared in heterosexual homes by heterosexual parents, and learn of their minority status only through their private fantasies and experiences. For some it is a slow and sometimes painful process of discovery. The question, ''Why do homosexual men want to marry women?'' begins with the false assumption that most of these men, at the time of the marriage, identify themselves as homosexual.

In our sample, less than one-third of the husbands thought of themselves as homosexual before they met their wives, and only seven of those were clearly involved in a homosexual peer group. Two of these men contracted for open marriages from the start, stating that because of their homosexuality they could not promise monogamy.

The majority of the husbands presumed that their heterosexuality would make monogamous marriage possible. In total, 83% of the men expected to remain monogamous when they married. And most did remain monogamous for a number of years. As suggested in Table 1, the vast majority of husbands were predominantly heterosexual in behavior at the time of marriage. However, some years into the marriage, homosexual desires were again gratified (or, in three cases, emerged for the

TABLE 1

HUSBAND'S[1] SEXUAL ORIENTATION ON KINSEY'S SCALE[2]

	Behavior	Fantasy
At time of marriage	2.8	3.5
Estimate over lifetime	3.0	4.6
At time of interview	3.5	5.4

1. N = 30. See sample description, Analysis I.
2. Kinsey Scale (1948)

    0 = Exclusively heterosexual.

    1 = Predominately heterosexual, only incidental homosexual.

    2 = Predominately hetero, but more than incidental homo.

    3 = Equally hetro and homo.

    4 = Predominately homo, but more than incidental hetero.

    5 = Predominately homo, only incidental hetero.

    6 = Exclusively homosexual.

first time and were acted on). Usually a year or two of sporadic activity occurred before the man experienced a crisis in sexual identity which often led to disclosure of a homosexual incident to the wife. Only one of our thirty husbands reported consistent monogamy throughout his marriage. (Coleman [1981/1982] mentions that 5 of the 20 men remaining in marriages at the time of his follow-up were committed to monogamy. Research is needed on men who are consciously bisexual but choose monogamy. The low success of that lifestyle in the present study may be partially due to the way in which our sample was obtained.)

Attitudes Toward the "Gay Life"

Previous research, largely based on clinical samples, has suggested that a major motive for homosexuals to marry is their negative feelings toward gay lifestyles (Hatterer, 1974; Imielinski, 1969; Dannecker & Reiche, 1974; M. W. Ross, 1979). Though one should not underestimate the negative effect society's suppression and denigration of homosexuality has had on our subjects, escape from homosexuality does not appear to have been a major motivation for their marrying.

Twenty-three of the 25 men who had adult homosexual experiences prior to marriage discussed their feelings about these experiences; almost half of them felt positive about them before marriage. A slim majority (12) felt negative, and hoped their homosexuality could be overcome. This percentage (52%) is strikingly lower than that found in clinical studies. Only 20% of our subjects ever sought therapy with the hope of overcoming their homosexual tendencies, in contrast to 36% in a recent clinical sample by Coleman (1981/1982). Others were negative because of religious teachings, loneliness, and worries that their homosexuality would interfere with their marriage.

Only 20% implied that negative attitudes toward being homosexual influenced their decision to marry. Six of the 23 husbands appear to have felt strong social pressure to marry. This, along with the belief that their bisexuality made marriage possible, were the only reasons they stated for marrying.

Historical Effects on Reasons for Marrying

One possible reason for the subjects' more positive attitude toward marriage may be the changes in sexual attitudes which have occurred in society recently. Maddox (1982) has suggested that reasons homosexuals have married in the past may not be those of the present.

Regarding whether motivations for bisexuals to enter marriages are changing, men who had married before and after the beginnings of gay liberation were compared (using 1970, just after the Stonewall incident, as our dividing point; see Table 2, columns 2 and 3). Thirty-six percent of the first group, compared to only 9% of the second, had given "one can't settle down with a man" as a reason for marrying. Conversely, 64% of those in the postgay liberation group mentioned attraction to family life as a positive reason compared to only 36% of the pre-liberation group. Similarly, when the two groups were compared on negative views of their own homosexuality, 64% of the men who married prior to 1970 expressed some negative views as compared to only 13% of those who married later.

A further analysis was conducted to discern whether this historical progression continued. The post-gay-liberation husbands were divided evenly into those marrying between 1970-1972 and those marrying in 1973 and after. All subjects who gave "one can't settle down with a man" as a reason for marrying fell into the earlier group. Further, none of the five husbands who married after 1973 made statements suggesting negative feelings about their homosexual activities prior to their marriage; four of the five were "gay identified," having both been a part of a homosexual peer group and accepted their homosexuality prior to marriage.

The pattern seems clear. Homosexual men continue to choose to enter marriages with women, but for more positive reasons than earlier. A final caveat is necessary. As in all cross-sectional data, historical and developmental variables are confounded. The more positive responses may, in fact, be due to the younger age and the greater proximity to time of marrying of the husbands in the later groups.

TABLE 2

HUSBANDS' REASONS FOR MARRYING[1]

	No adult gay exper. pre-marital	Married before 1970	Married after 1970	Total with adult pre-marital gay experience	Grand Total
Attracted to Family Life	**80 (4)**	**38 (5)**	**64 (2)**	**48 (12)**	**73 (16)**
1. Wanted kids	0	43 (6)	36 (4)	40 (10)	33 (10)
2. First special person, settle	20 (1)	29 (4)	27 (3)	28 (7)	27 (8)
3. Looked around, right woman	50 (3)	7 (1)	0	4 (1)	13 (4)
Social Pressure	**29 (1)**	**36 (5)**	**36 (4)**	**36 (9)**	**33 (10)**
4. Outside or parents'	0	14 (2)	9 (1)	12 (3)	10 (3)
5. Period of stress	0	7 (1)	18 (2)	12 (3)	10 (3)
6. Woman pushed for marriage	0	14 (2)	9 (1)	12 (3)	10 (3)
7. High school girlfriend	20 (1)	14 (2)	0	8 (2)	10 (3)
No Model for Gay Family					
8. Can't settle with a man	**0**	**36 (5)**	**9 (1)**	**24 (6)**	**20 (6)**
Others	**20 (1)**	**36 (5)**	**18 (2)**	**28 (7)**	**27 (8)**
9. Realized bisexual	0	21 (3)	18 (2)	20 (5)	17 (5)
10. First woman not afraid of	20 (1)	0	0	0	3 (1)
11. None clearly stated	0	14 (2)	0	8 (2)	3 (2)
Total number of responses	(6)	(27)	(14)	(41)	(47)
Total number of persons responding	5	14	11	25	30

1. Numbers in parenthesis indicate numbers of subjects giving that response. Numbers outside parenthesis indicate percentage of men in that column giving that response. Percentages total more than 100 since subjects averaged more than one response each. **Bold print** figures are sum for that broader category, itemized immediately below.

Wives Who Marry Knowingly

As noted, the majority of husbands in this study did not identify themselves as homosexuals at the time of their marriages. However, about a third of the wives had received at least partial disclosures of their husband's homosexual experiences or inclinations. (This finding is consistent with data from previous studies with non-clinical samples: Bell & Weinberg [1978], Bozett [1982]. It contrasts with the 15% of premarital disclosure in a clinical sample: Coleman [1981/1982].)

Data indicated a range of reasons why these women married. Most of the women expected marital fidelity despite knowledge of the husband's prior homosexual behavior. As noted, their expectation was met in the early years of marriage. Two wives agreed to "open marriages" from the start, but only their husbands became involved outside the marriages. One couple was drawn together chiefly because of a mutual desire for children. That marriage lasted eight years.

Analysis II: Marital Stability

The question addressed in this analysis concerns whether bisexual husbands can have stable marriages. Approximately two years after the interview an attempt was made to contact the husbands who had been homosexually active and living with their wives at the time of the interview. Twenty-four of the subjects could be clearly categorized as in acknowledged bisexual marriages (hereafter, ABMs) or secret bisexual marriages (SBMs, in which the husbands' homosexual activities were not discussed), and constituted the sample for this analysis. The distinction between ABMs and SBMs is based on whether the husband had disclosed his homosexual desires and activities to his wife *and* whether she had acknowledged this as a fact of their marriage. The phrase "secret bisexual" may mean that the husband had never disclosed his homosexual activity to his wife, or that such disclosure had occurred and been clearly rejected by the wife, leading to a mutual conspiracy of silence. That is, the "secret" was sometimes maintained by the wife as well as the husband. (The phrase "acknowledged bisexual" is preferable to the term "open marriage," because open marriage is usually taken to imply extramarital sexual activity on the part of both spouses. This was not the pattern in our acknowledged marriages. Six of the 13 wives experimented with extramarital sex with men, but three of them decided it was not right for them, though in some cases it decreased their fear of their husbands' extramarital involvements. The three women who opened their side of the marriage had separated from their husbands by the time of the follow-up.)

As shown on Table 3, despite the fact that many of our sample were at a turning point in their marriages when interviewed, 67% of the mar-

TABLE 3

CLASSIFICATIONS OF BISEXUAL MARRIAGES AT TWO-YEAR FOLLOWUP

	Together	Separated	Total
Acknowledged	9 (69%)	4 (31%)	13 (100%)
Secret	6 (67%)	3 (33%)	9 (100%)
Shifted	1 (50%)	1 (50%)	2 (100%)
Total	16 (67%)	8 (33%)	24 (100%)[1]

1. These couples had been Secretly Bisexual Marriages (SBM) at the time of the interview, but by the followup the husbands had disclosed their homosexuality to the wives, so they had shifted to the ABM category.

2. Our total sample of husbands in Analysis I (n = 30) was reduced to 24 in Analysis II as follows: Two husbands had already separated from their wives at the time of the first interview (it would be inappropriate to include them in calculations of marital stability over time, which should start with intact marriages). Another subject had never been homosexually active since marrying.

   Of the 27 subjects who were homosexually active and living with their wives at interview time, 25 were successfully recontacted at followup. One of these was dropped from analysis; his pattern of sequential monogamy, moving back and forth between gay lover and wife to the despair of both, did not fit our categories. This left a sample of 24 for Analysis II. Those in the "Shifted" category were not included in Analysis IV, leaving N = 22.

riages were still intact after two years. Though a rate of one-third separating within a two-year period is no doubt higher than the norm, it is strikingly low given the negative predictions of previous researchers. It is noteworthy that the data in Table 3 show no difference in the rate of marital failure between the two types of marriages (ABMs and SBMs). This is discussed more fully in the next analysis.

Analysis III: Marital Stability and Disclosure

Previous researchers have suggested that it is the disclosure of the husband's homosexual activities and desires which leads to the dissolution of these marriages (Miller, 1978; Bozett, 1982). Though the husband's disclosure of homosexuality clearly precipitates a crisis in the marriage, our data and the Latham and White (1978) study showed that many of these marriages survived. If the husband tells his wife that his homosexual desire and fantasies are re-emerging, that he is struggling with how to handle them, it has a different impact than if he lets her know that he has been "cheating" for years.

In the present analysis, the sample is limited to twelve couples for whom disclosure had occurred by the time of the follow-up study. These couples had either broken up, or had continued in the marriage for at least four years since the disclosure. (A more stringent criterion of four years for defining stability was used in this analysis.) As shown in Table 4, the twelve husbands can be grouped as those who disclosed their homosexual activities within a year of resuming them (N = 8) and those who waited from five to thirteen years to disclose the behavior to their wives (N = 4). For the total group, 42% were still together four years after the disclosure. However, the distribution of stable versus broken marriages for these two groups was quite different. Only 25% of those husbands

TABLE 4

DISTRIBUTION OF STABLE vs. BROKEN MARRIAGES

Related to Disclosure & Deceit

	Stable couples	Separated couples
Early disclosure (N = 8)	4 (50%)	4 (50%)
Disclosure after deceit (N = 4)	1 (25%)	3 (75%)
T =	5 (42%)	7 (58%)

N = 12. See Analysis III for description of sample, and interpretation.

who disclosed after five or more years of secretive activity were still in the marriage; the others had separated. However, of the husbands who promptly disclosed the resumption of homosexual activities, 50% were in stable marriages four years after disclosure.

It seems safe to assume that the honesty of those husbands who disclosed early is correlated with their greater expressiveness and communication skills (see the next Analysis). The present analysis suggests that it was extremely difficult for couples to move to that quality of communication where the wife's trust had been breached by the husband's deception.

These data suggest that over a period of two years following the husband's contacting us, approximately two-thirds of the marriages were still intact. However, the separation rate was much higher for late disclosure couples than for those with early disclosure.

Analysis IV: Four Classifications of Bisexual Marriages

The chief question addressed in this section is whether men who engage in homosexual activity can develop positive sexual identities while remaining in heterosexual marriages.

In this analysis, the husbands were divided on one dimension into those in secret (SMB) and acknowledged (ABM) lifestyles. Only subjects who were in the same category at both interview and follow-up time were included in the sample. On the second dimension, subjects were classified in terms of whether or not the marriage was still intact at the time of follow-up (together vs. separated). Table 3 shows the interaction of these two dimensions and explains the dropping of some subjects from further analyses. Numbers in each of the four cells ranged from nine to three; because of these low numbers, description of the four types must be taken as tentative.

Socio-Sexual Development of the Four Types

The sequence of the critical socio-sexual events in the lives of these husbands and the ages at which each occurred were different in each of the four groups. The descriptions which follow are composites for each group.

ABM/TOGETHER: Husbands in the ABMs who were still living with their wives averaged age 40 at the first interview. Their first sexual experience with a male occurred in early adolescence, about age 13, with a friend or relative with whom they were already close. Having once had a homosexual experience, they continued to have others until meeting their future wives. Furtive sex dominated mid-adolescence; relationships with lovers or close homosexual friends were more common in the college years. Though many of these men dated women in high school, their first genital experience occurred at 22 and first coitus at 24, usually with their fiances or wives. The wife was seen as a very special person, for whom the husband decided to give up homosexual activities. The first years of the marriage were usually monogamous (range = 3 to 11 years). Homosexual activity was then resumed and disclosed to the wife. In some cases, the wife consented to the husband's homosexual involvement in what the husband now considered "a part of myself I've got to integrate." Few of the men were surprised when their homosexual impulses re-emerged. Most had always seen these desires as a part of themselves. Though they had believed, for a period, they could suppress them, they now wanted to end the suppression and affirm their homosexual identity.

ABM/SEPARATING: These men tended to be much younger than the previous group, averaging 33 years old at the first interview. Their first genital experiences, either homosexual or heterosexual, occurred at the age of 17 (four years later than the first homosexual experiences of the previous group). They married the year in which their first heterosexual coitus occurred, at the age of 22. Usually they had met a very special woman, and married out of a longing for a family life. With one exception, they had disclosed their homosexual inclinations to the wives before the marriage, and waited less than a year to resume homosexual activities.

SBM/TOGETHER: This was the oldest group, the men averaged 44 years of age at the time of interview. Like the other group whose marriages are intact, these husbands began homosexual experiences early (age 13) and explored homosexuality for years before marrying at 27. The premarital homosexual experiences of this group fit no common pattern, but their negative homosexual attitudes and expressions of guilt were higher than in the ABM groups. One man avoided all sex until age 25, while another had been a hustler, who recoiled from the "viciousness" of the gay circuit. Most of their homosexual experiences were anonymous and impersonal. Heterosexual experience was limited; half had never experienced coitus with any women except their wives. One-half resumed their homosexual activity secretively soon after the marriage, but half abstained, in one case for 10 years.

An exception to the negative pattern, one husband, a top-level executive, seemed happily married, talked enthusiastically about his kids, and was consistently open and emotionally sensitive while participating in a personal growth group. This man's only regret was that he had to limit his homosexual experience to impersonal contacts in other cities to avoid risks of exposure.

SBM/SEPARATING: These men averaged 41 at the time of the interview. Like those men whose marriages remained intact, they had had early adolescent homosexual experiences (beginning at age 14).

However, they discontinued them from mid-adolescence to age 25, after they had married. They began genital contact with women at 21, coitus at 22, and married at 24 (slightly earlier than either of the marriage-intact groups). Strong negative attitudes or denial of homosexual tendencies characterized this group until 6 to 14 years into the marriage. In one case, the first adult homosexual experience was delayed until 16 years after the marriage. Two of the three men married young; all were sexually faithful in the first 3 to 16 years after the marriage. They turned to secretive homosexuality, gradually grew distant from their wives, and broke up a year or two after disclosure. In one instance, divorce occurred because of emotional distance and other problems; no sexual disclosure occurred.

COMPARISONS BETWEEN INTACT MARRIAGES AND SEPARATING COUPLES

What personality characteristics differentiate the bisexual men who remain in marriages and those who separate?

In the following comparisons, data are pooled from the ABM/together and SBM/together groups (Together n = 15) and the ABM/separating and the SBM/separating (Separating n = 7). Because of the small n's, trends are reported. (Except where noted, all data in this analysis are based on the husband's interviews, which were coded and analyzed using SPSS Crosstabs and SPSS Breakdown programs. All levels of significance are two-tailed F probabilities, since no directional hypotheses were proposed.)

Sexual Attitudes and Behavior

Miller (1978) suggested that it is necessary for husbands to leave the marriage to develop a positive homosexual identity. However, none of our measures of homosexual identity at interview time revealed any differences between the husbands who were separated two years later and those still married. Neither did the group differ on measures of sexual orientation over their lifetimes. The two groups differed markedly in present sexual behavior. It appeared that the together group, having already experienced considerable homosexual activity prior to marriage, felt less need for more. In contrast, the husbands who later separated appeared to be in the thralls of a "second adolescence," a homosexual rebirth. They were significantly more active in the homosexual community, both socially and sexually, than the husbands whose marriages survived (p = .03 and .19 respectively). The fact that the husbands whose

TABLE 5

**SEXUAL ORIENTATIONS OF TOGETHER & SEPARATING HUSBANDS [1]
ON KINSEY'S SCALE [2]**

	Together	Separating
Behavior at time of marriage	2.3	.8
Fantasy at time of marriage	4.0	2.4
Behavior over lifetime	2.7	2.9
Fantasy over lifetime	4.8	4.1
Behavior at time of interview	2.7	5.9
Fantasy, time of interview	5.2	5.6

1. Together N = 15; Separating N = 7. See sample description Analysis IV.

2. Kinsey Scale (1948)

    0 = Exclusively heterosexual.

    1 = Predominately heterosexual, only incidental homosexual.

    2 = Predominately hetero, but more than incidental homo.

    3 = Equally hetro and homo.

    4 = Predominately homo, but more than incidental hetero.

    5 = Predominately homo, only incidental hetero.

    6 = Exclusively homosexual.

marriages remained intact were older when they married than the others (mean age 26.5 compared to 23, p = .01) and had begun homosexual experience earlier further supports the impression that these husbands had partially resolved the crisis of combining two sexual identities, being homosexual and married, before deciding to marry. The pattern suggests that acceptance of homosexual experiences prior to marriage increased the probability of the marriage working. Again, individual differences should be noted. One husband who first discovered his homosexual desires years into the marriage had developed a very positive homosexual identity and remained in an acknowledged marriage.

Personality Differences Between Together and Separating Husbands

Those husbands who remained married at follow-up had been rated (from the interview tapes) as more empathic and able to listen to their wives (p = .03), and more invested in personal growth and therapy (p = .08). They were classified in the higher categories of intimacy, and appeared more dedicated to their wives (p = .05).

Perceived Personality Differences
Between Together and Separating Wives

Husbands who later separated described their wives as more likely to think in black and white terms, as compared to the more complex cognitive patterns of wives in the together couples. The latter were also described more positively in regard to dedication to the marriage and to husband (p = .05), more intimacy with spouse (p = .08) and with other women (p = .19). The husbands' perceptions of the wives did not differ in regard to attitudes about homosexuality, or jealousy regarding extramarital involvements. Both groups of couples were seen as having friends who supported the marriage, but the wives who later split appeared to have more friends who supported them as individuals (p = .23), and seemed less dependent on their husbands socially, emotionally, and financially.

Both categories of couples experienced serious value conflicts. But the wives' interviews suggested (consistent with husbands' perceptions) that the wives who stuck to the marriages were not only more committed, but also more dependent on their husbands for support. Acceptance of the husbands' homosexuality was as high for wives who separated, but complaints about infrequent sex with their husbands were unanimous in this group of wives. A rater, blind to the wives' future marital status, found the separating wives to be more enterprising, inventive, ingenious and opportunistic, and more cooperative and sincere; clearly these women had a high level of self-confidence and social skills.

Though the two groups of wives had about the same mean ratings of attitudes toward open marriages as their husbands, the interviews with the wives showed that those who later left the marriages fell into one of two extremes. Some were disgusted by the idea of open marriages; others affirmed open marriage, became involved with another man, and then left the bisexual for a heterosexual marriage. ABM wives who remained with their husbands consistently placed a high value on marital fidelity, even after exploring extra-marital sex. In this respect, our stable ABMs resemble the "double-standard marriages" (H. L. Ross, 1971) behaviorally, if not in attitudinally.

Quality of Marriage

In most of the couples, including the SBMs, some partial disclosure of homosexual activities had occurred. When the husband moved from concealed homosexuality to the disclosure stage, some couples entered into a conspiracy of silence, while others quickly moved to a cycle of mutual rejection. Those couples who later broke up began to threaten to divorce immediately after the disclosure. In contrast, the majority of together couples had found some way to handle difficulties, and were further along in problem solving at the time of the interviews (p = .29). Only two of the seven couples who split had entered a stage of adjustment and coping.

In the couples who split, the disclosure was often followed by abstinence from marital sex. In contrast, a slight majority of together couples experienced an *increase* in sex after the disclosure, fitting the pattern noted: the husband moving toward a balanced bisexual lifestyle without repression of either homosexual or heterosexual expression. There is considerable evidence in our interviews that suppression of homosexual expression may lead to impoverishment of the total sexual life of the husbands. Conversely, homosexual expression frequently leads to an enrichment of sex in the marriage. Again it must be stressed that there are individual variations within this general pattern.

When separation occurred it reflected the couple's general pattern of disengagement. The initiative for time spent together usually came from the wife, even though husbands viewed themselves as more needy (p = .03). Husbands of the couples still together were more likely to take this initiative, though this tendency did not approach significance (p = .40).

Summary

Numerous variables from the initial interviews with the couples were successful in differentiating between those couples who remained together and those who separated two years later. There was no evidence that the level of homosexuality at the time of the interviews was a factor in separation. A key factor seems to have been the amount of prior exploration of homosexual behavior. Those husbands who had not had much premarital experience had a tendency to move so fully into a homosexual lifestyle that they withdrew both sexually and emotionally from their wives and families. There was also real excitement and involvement in the homosexual life on the part of the other husbands, but that was balanced with an improvement in marital sex (in half the intact marriages), and a willingness to take initiative to ensure that the married couple spent time together. The husband's dedication to their marriage, and the couple's ability to listen and willingness to seek counseling for themselves seem to be positive factors.

It is possible that rigidity on the wife's part was a factor in preventing the marriage from moving through the disclosure stage into a period of negotiation and reconciliation. On the other hand, some of the women who left the marriages were clearly very healthy and independent persons, women who had the support and self-confidence to get out of a situation that they did not find as satisfying as a monogamous relationship.

COMPARISONS BETWEEN
ACKNOWLEDGED AND SECRET BISEXUAL MARRIAGES

No differences were found between the ABM and SBM couples in economic status, or in the percentage who were childfree. The mean number of children was higher for SBM couples, but this was probably due to their being older (husbands' mean age 43 compared to 38).

Sexual Attitudes and Behavior

Though little difference was noted in the sexual fantasies of the two groups of husbands (Table 6), the ABM husbands appeared to have centered more of their sexual attention on their wives at both the time of marriage and the interview. There were no significant differences in the frequency of homosexual activities of the two groups; the higher ratio of heterosexual activity in the ABM husbands reflected their more frequent marital sex. It is interesting that the husbands whose homosexuality was acknowledged in the marriages did not have more frequent homosexual experiences; apparently they imposed limitations on such activities on themselves. The SBM husbands, on the other hand, may have participated less frequently in marital sex because of guilt over their secret homosexual activity.

TABLE 6

SEXUAL ORIENTATIONS OF ACKNOWLEDGED & SECRETLY BISEXUAL HUSBANDS [1] ON KINSEY'S SCALE [2]

	Acknowledged	Secret
Behavior at time of marriage	1.0	2.9
Fantasy at time of marriage	3.7	3.0
Behavior over lifetime	2.4	3.1
Fantasy over lifetime	4.6	4.6
Behavior at time of interview	3.5	4.1
Fantasy, time of interview	5.5	5.1

1.   Acknowledged N = 13; Secret N = 9. See sample description Analysis III.

2.   Kinsey Scale (1948)

   0 = Exclusively heterosexual.

   1 = Predominately heterosexual, only incidental homosexual.

   2 = Predominately hetero, but more than incidental homo.

   3 = Equally hetro and homo.

   4 = Predominately homo, but more than incidental hetero.

   5 = Predominately homo, only incidental hetero.

   6 = Exclusively homosexual.

The differences in the earlier homosexual histories of these two groups undoubtedly influenced their attitudes. The ABM men started adult homosexual relationships earlier (age 22-1/2 compared to 26-1/2), and sexual experiences with a homosexual partner earlier (25 compared to 31-1/2), than did the secretive husbands. This reflected the greater involvement of ABM men in the gay culture rather than anonymous "tea room" sex (Humphreys, 1969). Thus their homosexual experiences prior to marriage were markedly different, though the two groups were similar in their heterosexual experience levels.

The SBM husbands' recollections showed that they held more negative stereotypes of homosexuals than did the acknowledged husbands. Sixty percent of the secretive husbands believed the myth that homosexual men are usually effeminate, while only 18% of the acknowledged husbands did. All of these inhibitions and fears may have discouraged the SBM husbands from earlier homosexual exploration, even if their urges and fantasies were as strong as those of the ABM husbands.

Self Acceptance and Positive Homosexual Identity

The most striking difference between the acknowledged husbands and secretive bisexual husbands was in their level of affirming a homosexual identity. Though SBM husbands no longer denied their homosexual behavior, in contrast, the ABM husbands not only accepted their homosexual experience but also affirmed and felt positive about their being homosexual. The differences were significant for three separate measures. While SBM husbands maintained a heterosexual public identity, ABM husbands were publicly homosexual in some areas. One-fourth of the acknoweldged husbands had "come out" to their wives and others. ABM husbands had experienced significantly more of the events which contributed to a positive homosexual identity (Berzon & Leighton, 1979) than had the secretive husbands (p = .001). The men in the ABMs were more comfortable about the possibility of their children being homosexual and believed their wives shared these views. SBM husbands, however, believed their wives' attitude would fall between neutrality and disgust. These more negative perceptions may have reflected the SBM men's homophobia as well as their wives' attitudes.

PERSONALITY DIFFERENCES BETWEEN
ABM AND SBM HUSBANDS

The ABM husbands were rated as more empathic, more open in sharing with spouse, more open about their emotions, more positive in terms of mental health, clearer in using "I statements" to communicate their needs (p < .05), and more complex in their perceptual style.

Perceived Personality Differences Between ABM and SBM Wives

From the husbands' descriptions, the ABM wives were rated more positively (at $p < .05$) for empathy, openness in sharing with husband, emotional openness, mental health, and clarity in expressing own desires. Complexity of perception was higher for ABM spouses, but did not reach significance.

Those wives who openly dealt with their husband's homosexuality appeared to have developed stronger support systems for themselves, both in terms of individual friends and friends of the couple who understood and supported the marriage. Jealousy was a difficult issue since the wives knew of their husband's extramarital involvements; typically, they set firm limits on the information they listened to. However, the ABM husbands rated them lower on jealousy than the SBM husbands rated their wives, when these husbands fantasized their wives' reactions to disclosure. ABM wives were seen as more capable of intimacy in relation to their husbands, other men, and other women ($p < .05$ in all cases), as well as more dedicated to the marriage than the SBM wives. ABM wives were also seen as more aware of the limits they needed, and more likely consciously to contract for them with their husbands.

Quality of Marriage

Although the two groups of couples seemed similar in the amount of time they spent together as a couple, the quality of relationship appeared higher for the ABM couples in terms of communication, problem solving, and marital sex. SBM couples typically handled differences by going their separate ways, which sped up the disengagement which occurred if the bisexual issue surfaced. The emotional and sexual closeness of the ABM couples appeared to have been fairly continuous throughout their marriages. The SBM husbands seemed somewhat socially dependent on their wives, though they did not view themselves as emotionally or financially dependent.

Despite their advantages, the ABM marriages had their share of struggle, conflict, and pain. In most cases, the husbands homosexuality conflicted with the wife's desire for monogamy. Thus, it is not surprising that these couples developed support systems, and that the wives more frequently sought counseling in coping with their marriages.

Summary

It did not appear that acknowledgement of homosexual activity in the marriage increased its frequency, as compared to the frequency in secretive husbands. The conspiracy of silence, however, appeared to increase the emotional distance between partners (as is well described in Bozett, 1982). Striking differences occurred between the ABM and SBM groups. Both ABM husbands and wives appeared to have had higher levels of mental health, communicativeness, and intimacy. The ABM husbands were much higher in level of self-acceptance, many of them affirming a homosexual identity. These advantages appeared to precede the marriages; the style of marriage reinforced and amplified the difference.

CONCLUSIONS

It is hoped that this study will challenge assumptions perpetuated in previous studies. It is further hoped that the conclusions will inspire new investigations which may, in turn, reveal the limits of the present data.

The data suggest the following answers to the initial questions:

(1) Are motivations for entering bisexual marriages changing? Motivations were largely positive for this sample, and appeared to be increasingly positive; the younger couples entered marriages with greater awareness and acceptance of the husband's sexual identity and orientation.

(2) Can marriages in which the husband is actively homosexual become stable marriages? Judging from a two-year follow-up, about 67% of the marriages remained intact. Since the sample may have included a disproportionately high ratio of marriages in crisis, it is probable that an even higher percentage of these marriages remained ''stable'' for at least two years. However, it is also likely that the increased openness of the gay communities will make it harder for the SBM husbands to feel comfortable with a conspiracy of silence. When disclosure followed years of hidden extramarital sex, the mistrust engendered made it difficult to keep the marriage stable. The acknowledged bisexual marriages proved to be the more stable.

(3) Can a homosexual man develop a congruent sexual identity while remaining in a heterosexual marriage? Not only did the ABM husbands accept their homosexuality, but also they affirmed it. And this affirmation held for those husbands who, prior to marriage, had very negative views of homosexuality. Clearly, a positive homosexual identity was possible to this form of marriage. And, it was equally clear that such a positive identity was far more difficult to achieve in a traditional marriage in which the homosexuality was not acknowledged by the wife.

It seems useful to sketch a hypothetical model of the decision points and their consequences in the development of bisexual marriages. The developmental model portrays a sequence of seven critical events in bisexual marriages.

(1) *Premarital Sexual Experience*. Sexual exploration by a man prior to marital commitments seemed to be associated with a firmer and more

positive sense of his own sexual identity. We have hypothesized that it is also associated with the choice of a more tolerant and flexible wife. Conversely, a man whose marriage is partially an evasion of his homosexuality is likely to choose a woman who is also less comfortable with it.

(2) *Age of Marriage.* Early marriage was negatively associated with stability. It may also be negatively associated with a mature decision regarding choice of a compatible, self-affirming woman.

(3) *Developing the Primacy of the Marital Relationship.* The beginning phase of the marriage seemed to be more important to developing primacy. In most of the ABMs which broke up, the husbands had resumed homosexual activity within four years after marriage. In the five stable, acknowledged bisexual marriages (Analysis IV), three of the husbands were monogamous for 5 to 11 years. The other two had disclosed their homosexual activity before their marriages, continued homosexual activities from the onset of the marriage, and set very firm limits on their extramarital involvements.

(4) *Resumption of Homosexual Activities.* Resumption produced less of an identity crisis for those husbands who had acknowledged their homosexuality prior to marriage. These men were more likely to disclose their revived homosexual desires to their wives early in the process. Those husbands who had not accepted their homosexual desires yet resumed sexual acts with other men were faced with double guilt, feeling bad for being ''queer'' and for ''cheating.'' Because they perceived their wives as more dependent and more rigid, they delayed disclosure. The wives who eventually found out reacted to three emotionally charged issues: the husbands' sexual identity, infidelity, and deceit. Thus, husbands who do not disclose their homosexuality early are frequently caught in a spiral of mistrust and distance which often destroys their marriages.

(5) *Wives' Responses to Disclosure.* It may be an immediate rejection of ''negative'' characteristics discovered in their husbands, which leads to the end of the marriage. There may be a difficult period of ambivalence. The wives who can acknowledge and accept the husband's bisexuality may move into a renegotiation of the relationship—either an acknowledged bisexual marriage or an amicable divorce. The development of mutually acceptable guidelines, followed by stabilization and secure intimacy, appears to take four or more years. The wife learns she cannot control her husband; however, she can clearly express her needs and limits of tolerance. She is capable of taking care of herself when her husband is not available.

(6) *Nurturance of the Marriage.* In marriages which survived the husbands took more initiative to spend time with their wives, rather than relying on the wives to initiate contact. The husbands were also more empathic. The clearer the wife became about not depriving him of his homo-

sexuality, the more likely the husband was to stop being defensive and start tuning into her feelings and needs.

(7) *A Responsive Pattern.* A pattern of negotiations, compromises, and most importantly, *a deep appreciation of differences* may develop. Marital stability may gradually be restored, with each spouse understanding and respecting the other more fully, and each desiring to remain intimate and committed to the other.

REFERENCES

Bell, A. P., & Weinberg, M. S. (1978). *Homosexualities: A study of diversity among men and women.* New York: Simon & Schuster.

Berzon, B., & Leighton, R. (Eds.). (1979). *Positively gay.* Millbrae, CA: Celestial Arts.

Bozett, F. W. (1982). Heterogeneous couples in heterosexual marriages: Gay men and straight women. *Journal of Marital and Family Therapy, 8,* 81-89.

Coleman, E. (1981/1982). Bisexual and gay men in heterosexual marriage: Conflicts and resolution in therapy. *Journal of Homosexuality, 7*(2/3), 93-103.

Dannecker, M., & Reiche, R. (1974). Der gewöhnlich homosexuall; Eine sociologische Untersuchung über männliche homosexuelle in der Bundesrepublik. Frankfurt am Main: Fischer Verlag.

Gurman, A. S., & Kniskern, D. P. (1978). Research on marital and family therapy: Progress perspective and prospect. In S. L. Garfield & A. E. Gergin (Eds.), *Handbook of psychotherapy and behavior change: An empirical analysis* (2nd Ed.) (pp. 817-903). New York: John Wiley & Sons.

Hatterer, M. S. (1974). The problems of women married to homosexual men. *American Psychiatry, 131,* 275-277.

Humphreys, L. (1969). *Tearoom trade: Impersonal sex in public places.* Chiacgo: Aldine.

Kinsey, A.C., Pomeroy, W.B., & Martin, C.E. (1948). Sexual behavior in the human male. Philadelphia: W.B. Saunders.

Imielinski, R. (1969). Homosexuality in males with particular reference to marriage. *Psychotherapy Psychosom, 17,* 126-132.

Latham, J. D., & White, G. D. (1978). Coping with homosexual expression within heterosexual marriages: Five case studies. *Journal of Sex and Marital Therapy, 3,* 198-212.

Maddox, B. (1982). *Married and gay: An intimate look at a different relationship.* New York: Harcourt Brace Jovanovich.

Matteson, D. R. (1983). *Report on bisexual men in marriage: Interviews and two-year follow-up.* Unpublished manuscript.

Miller, B. (1978). Adult sexual resocialization: Adjustments toward a stigmatized identity. *Alternative Lifestyles, 1,* 207-234.

Miller, B. (1979). Unpromised paternity: The life styles of gay fathers. In Martin Levine (Ed.), *Gay men: The sociology of male homosexuality* (pp. 239-252). New York: Harper & Row.

Ross, H. L. (1971). Modes of adjustment of married homosexuals. *Social Problems, 18,* 385-393.

Ross, M. W. (1979). Heterosexual marriage of homosexual males: Some associated factors. *Journal of Sex and Marital Therapy, 5,* 142-150.

Weinberg, T. S. (1978). On "doing" and "being" gay. *Journal of Homosexuality, 4,* 143-156.

A Study of
the Married Bisexual Male:
Paradox and Resolution

John J. Brownfain, PhD

University of Michigan-Dearborn

ABSTRACT. Men who live in conventional marriages and at the same time have significant love-sex relationships with members of their own sex are largely an invisible group in our society. However, there is evidence to suggest that they are not rare, only rarely identified. How these men perceive themselves, reconcile the ordinary aspects of their lives with their atypical sexuality, and conduct themselves in marriage and family life are the focus of this study. Particular attention is paid to two major paradoxes in their lives: (1) the contradiction between their heterosexual public identity which places them comfortably in the mainstream of society and their stigmatized and forbidden homosexual desires and behavior; and (2) the ethical issue of deceiving their wives as well as others to whom they are intimately related.

Sixty men drawn from a non-clinical population presented their life stories in extended tape-recorded interviews. These men show great variations in their patterns of psychosexual development as well as in their accommodations to marriage and do not fit readily into simple categories. Most of them have found fulfillment and have no wish to change the pattern of their lives. In part, the study contrasts the more successful with the less successful marriages. A major conclusion is that some men are able to express with minimal conflict their homosexual and heterosexual impulses within the framework of a conventional marriage.

In the literature about the myriad aspects of sexuality, little has been said about the phenomenon of bisexuality, and even less about individuals who choose to live within a conventional marriage while simultaneously having significant love-sex relations with members of their own sex. Men and women who behave this way are largely an invisible group in our society, but there is evidence to suggest that they are not rare, only rarely identified. In this study, focus is upon the life experience of bisexual men, not bisexual women. Attention is also paid to the men's wives when possi-

Dr. Brownfain is Professor of Psychology at the University of Michigan, Dearborn. He is a Diplomate of the American Board of Professional Psychology and an AASECT Certified Sex Therapist. Reprint requests should be addressed to the author, Department of Behavioral Sciences, University of Michigan, Dearborn, 4901 Evergreen Road, Dearborn, MI 48128.

ble but this is of secondary interest. Men who live largely in the prosaic "straight" world while simultaneously participating in the marginal, secretive, and stigmatized world of homosexuality, engage in a precarious balancing act. They live a "split level" kind of existence which requires them to resolve cognitive and behavioral dissonances of the most challenging kind. Herein lies the most striking paradox of their lives: the contradiction between their heterosexual public identity which places them comfortably in the mainstream of society, and the stigmatized and forbidden homosexual desire and behavior which places them beyond the pale. The second great paradox, inextricably linked to the first, grows out of the ethical issue of concealing a fundamental fact of their existence from their wives as well as from others to whom they are intimately related. It is our purpose to study these paradoxes and their resolutions and, further, to explore how married bisexual men experience and identify themselves, conduct themselves in marriage, family life, and in their secret lives, understand their past and perceive their future.

THE CONCEPT OF BISEXUALITY

Bisexuality does not lend itself to easy definition. Its ambiguity has generated a host of meanings. Both Freud (1961) and Jung (1951) used the term to refer to the biological substratum out of which masculinity and femininity emerge, but neither ever regarded it in its behavioral manifestations as a viable form of adjustment. For Freud, bisexuality expressed was homosexuality revealed, a condition explicable in terms of infantile oedipal fixations. Jung explained it as the waywardness of the anima and the animus, the archetypical expressions of the eternal feminine and masculine in our collective unconscious. The psychiatrists, psychologists, and sexologists of today, the theorists of sexuality and the therapists of its disorders, are mostly inclined to view bisexuality as a disguised form of homosexuality, all the more pathological for its disguise. The study of male and female homosexuality by Saghir and Robbins (1973) is one of many examples of this way of thinking. Within their sample of homosexual males, 53 percent reported having one or more stable heterosexual relationships, 18 percent had been married, and two were still in long-term marriages and combining their heterosexual and homosexual lives with "complete success." Yet none of the men in the homosexual group was identified as bisexual. Bieber and colleagues (1962), Hatterer (1970), and Masters and Johnson (1979) follow the same logic in their influential works. MacDonald (1982) believes that a great deal of research on homosexuality has been contaminated by including male and female research subjects with varying degrees of heterosexual interest and activity in the homosexual sample, and that bisexuals should be studied separately from those who are exclusively homosexual and heterosexual.

In the popular mind, bisexuality is often regarded as a form of gender confusion, as psychic hermaphroditism, or as the state of androgyny. Bisexuals are described with humorous disdain as "switch hitters," as "AC/DC," and as those who "swing both ways." For sophisticated theoreticians who seek to explain the problematic nature of homosexuality, that enterprise becomes enormously complicated by the specter of intermediate states which undo the tidy dichotomy of heterosexuality and homosexuality and play havoc with orderly theories about psychosexual development. Bisexual persons themselves do little to clarify this conceptual perplexity. They are, after all, in the curious position of being condemned by heterosexuals for their heterosexual behavior, and condemned by homosexuals for their heterosexual behavior. Given their varied natures and their invisibility, bisexuals have not yet found justification to unite behind a common cause. To be sure, behind the discomfort with bisexuality is the troubling actuality of homosexuality. If homosexuality has finally and grudgingly been placed in its own exclusive corner where it might be regarded as a natural expression of sexuality for those who stay in that corner, it is disconcerting to find it in its bisexual guise threatening "normal" sexuality. However, if one concludes that it is nature's way that sexual and affectional needs might be expressed in either the homosexual or the heterosexual mode, one might also be able to accept comfortably the expression of both modes in the same person, and then all the difficulties with bisexuality vanish. This is a point of view well expressed in the following quotation from the classic work of Ford and Beach (1951) who approach human sexuality from the perspectives of anthropology and comparative psychology. Though they do not use the word itself, they present bisexuality as the natural condition of humankind.

> Men and women who are totally lacking in any conscious homosexual leanings are as much a product of cultural conditioning as are the exclusive homosexuals who find heterosexual relations distasteful and unsatisfying. Both extremes represent movement away from the original, intermediate condition which includes the capacity for both forms of sexual expression.

To recognize the existence of bisexuality is to extend enormously our awareness of sexual diversity. Bisexuality is not a unitary state, but the connecting link between heterosexuality and homosexuality. It potentially embraces all the variations of those categories and introduces endless variations of its own in all aspects of experience—in sexual behavior, in interpersonal relations, in fantasy, in orientation and preference, and in lifestyle. Finally, we are led to the realization that our varied sexuality is at the very foundation of our individuality.

One cannot speak of bisexuality without referring to an associated term, ambisexuality, used particularly by Masters and Johnson (1979) to describe the behavior of people who enjoy equally homosexual and heterosexual activity without making value judgements about either. Their choice of sexual partners seems to be purely opportunistic and independent of gender. We shall consider them along with all others in our sample simply as bisexual. Despite its many limitations, the term bisexual will be used in this study to describe the sexuality of men who engage in both heterosexual and homosexual acts.

Related Research

There are several works which deal with bisexuality in a general way but do not refer specifically to the bisexuality of married persons. The book *The Bisexual Option*, by the psychiatrist Fred Klein (1978), emphasizes the multi-faceted nature of bisexuality, and presents a number of histories of men and women who regard their bisexuality as a source of happiness and fulfillment. An extensive study of male and female bisexuality is reported by Blumstein and Schwartz (1976). Their relatively large sample (156) emphasized that classical notions about the immutability of sexual preference are often mistaken.

A handful of studies also exist which deal with the adjustment of bisexual men in marriage. The oldest is by H. Laurence Ross (1972), who studied eleven couples (described as "odd couples") in Belgium. Nearly all of these marriages were sexual disasters or otherwise troubled. A study by Latham and White (1978) of five couples discussed the coping mechanisms in marraiges in which the husband shares with his wife some knowledge about his homosexuality. Bozett (1982) studied 18 homosexual men in depth, examined the nature of spousal relationship, and described the conditions which bring about the husband's disclosure of his homosexuality and the wife's response. Of the 18, one man remained married, five separated, and 12 divorced. The controversial book by Masters and Johnson, *Homosexuality in Perspective* (1979), deserves mention here. A notable feature of this work is the authors' claim of having "converted" homosexual husbands who aspired to heterosexuality. The controversy centers about the labeling of these men as homosexual when bisexual or ambisexual might have been more appropriate, and also about the uncertainty of the therapeutic means employed to accomplish this radical change.

Eli Coleman's (1981/1982) study of homosexual men in heterosexual marriages resembles most closely the present study. Coleman studied 31 men who were treated in a "bisexuality group." Following treatment, 11 of the men decided to end their marriage. A follow-up over the next three years showed a further attrition, leaving 14 men continuing in their marriage, men who might be regarded as successfully combining their homosexual activities with their heterosexual marriages.

METHODOLOGY

Sixty men were interviewed in a two year period between 1981 and 1983. These men met the following conditions:

1. They were in marriages of at least eight years duration. The two exceptions to this were men divorced at the time of the interview, after 37 and 28 years of marriage.
2. They were significantly involved in homosexual relationships and activities.
3. They were not in psychotherapy. A total of 17 men had been involved in psychotherapy or counseling (marital or family) at some time in their life.

The sixty men came from the following sources:

1. Eighteen men constituted a chain of referrals (i.e., a "snowball" sample).
2. Seventeen men came from a support group of married bisexual men in the Metropolitan Detroit area.
3. Twelve men attended the author's presentation at various conferences and workshops and volunteered for interviews.
4. Thirteen men were referred by professional and academic colleagues who were acquainted with this study.

Noteworthy, this is essentially a non-clinical group. It is true that a number of these men, particularly those in the Detroit support group and those attending workshops on issues of homosexual identity, were seeking some kind of understanding and sympathy, but were not seeking "treatment."

The study consisted of approximately three-hour long, in-depth interviews emphasizing sexual and social life histories. For most subjects, the interview provided the first opportunity to share their "great secret."

Of the 60, 58 were Caucasian, one was black, and one was Asian. They ranged in age from 30 to 75 with a mean age of 45. The mean age at the time of marriage was 25 (range 19 to 35). The mean length of marriage was 20 years (range 8 to 48). The 60 men had a total of 142 children. Five men were childless. Thirty-six were Protestants, 13 Catholics, 10 Jewish, and one Muslim. Forty-five had college, and 28 graduate degrees. Occupationally, the group was comprised of physicians, dentists, lawyers, academics, clergymen, psychologists, social workers, engineers, teachers, executives, business men, skilled technicians, one assembly line worker, and one farmer. Thus, this sample can be characterized as white, middle class, well educated, and economically successful. It cannot be generalized to the population of bisexual men in long-term marriages.

FINDINGS

Self-Identification of Sexual Orientation

All of these men were assumed to be heterosexual in their communities. Behaviorally, they are bisexual according to the criteria of this study. The Kinsey scale (1948) was used by the author to describe these men in terms of the balance between heterosexual and homosexual behavior. Table 1 presents the distribution of Kinsey scores.

Beyond any objective appraisal of their sexual behavior, these men were asked:

> What do you think deep down about your sexual orientation or preference? Do you think of yourself as straight, heterosexual, homosexual, bisexual, gay, ambisexual?

Table 1

KINSEY RATINGS

Self-identifications:

	Bisexual (N=30)	Gay (N=25)	Heterosexual (N=5)
0 (Exclusively Heterosexual)	0	0	0
1	3	1	3
2	7	2	2
3	10	4	0
4	8	8	0
5	2	9	0
6 (Exclusively Homosexual)	0	1	0
Mean	3	4	1.4

Some men evaded this inquiry by proclaiming that they were neither heterosexual nor homosexual, merely sexual. Some others made it quite clear that they might well choose a different label at another time. Yet, reluctantly or not, each man was pressed to choose a term. A sampling of their responses reflected some of the considerations which influence self-labeling of sexual orientation.

> I've always been gay but I was programmed to marry. That program is just as powerful as my sexual desires. Just say I'm a gay man who is able to have sex with one woman.

> I'm gay on the inside and straight on the outside. But it's on the outside that I live my life. The things I value most are my kids, my marriage, my job and my social life. So let's call me Bi.

> Of course I've been gay as far back as I can remember. I haven't had sex with my wife for 20 years. All my sex is with men, and mostly with one man. Still, I sleep with my wife every night, cuddle with her, care about her and lead the life of a pillar of the community. I'm gay but my life isn't.

> I think I'm really heterosexual. I like the gay thing. It's exciting and great for my ego, but I've done without it for long stretches and I could easily give it up if I had good reasons. It's really a side show for me. My marriage is the main event.

Not unexpectedly, self-labeling of sexual orientation appears to be a powerful discriminator of sexual behavior and marital adjustment. For most men, it sums up both past experience and future expectations. Table 2 indicates that bisexual men, in contrast to self-identified homosexual men, were more content with their marriages, had a more active sexual life with their wives, were more likely to have had significant sexual experiences with females before having had the same with males, and were more likely to have had premarital sex with women other than their wives. Their rating on the Kinsey scale was 3 compared to 4 for men who regarded themselves as homosexual.

Upon follow-up within a year of the interview, six of the self-identified homosexual men (including one who had initially rated his marriage as good) were in the process of getting divorced. The homosexual men were not contemplating remarriage. On the contrary, their intention was to discover the gay world. Notably, they were among the younger men in the sample. Three of the bisexuals, two of whom had rated their marriages as troubled and one as good, had been divorced. Of these three, one had remarried having been divorced by his wife because of his involvement with another woman, another was living with a bisexual girlfriend and a succession of male lovers, and the third seemed intent upon

Table 2

SUMMARY OF FINDINGS

Self-identification:

	Bisexual (N=30)	Gay (N=25)	Heterosexual (N=5)
Age (Mean)	45	43	48
Age at Time of Marriage (Mean)	24	24	23
Years Married (Mean)	20	18	25

– – – – – – – – – – – – – – – –

	N	N	N
Adult Hetero Experience Prior to Homo Experience	22	8	5
Extra-marital Affairs (Hetero)	12	2	3
First Hetero Experience With Wife	12	15	1
Sexually Active With Wive	29	17	5

– – – – – – – – – – – – – – – –

	N	N	N
Marital Adjustment:			
O.K. (Including Ideal - 5)	22	10	4
Wife Knows (In Some Degree) About Husband's Bisexuality	11	7	1
Troubled/Stable	5	7	1
Wife Knows	3	3	0
Troubled/Headed For Divorce	3	6	0
Wife Knows	1	3	0
Divorced	0	2	0
Wife Knows	0	1	0

exploring the gay world. The five men who regarded themselves as essentially heterosexual viewed women romantically and regarded their homosexual experiences as pleasurable, even necessary, but not emotionally significant.

Few of the men had a clear perception of their sexual natures at the time of marriage. Their intimations were subject to a variety of interpretations. More of the homosexual men did express their homosexual needs before marriage, but rarely did this expression result in a significant love relationship. In most instances, the experiences were fragmentary and isolated, and after marriage were abandoned for significant periods. As for bisexual men, those who did not engage in homosexual behavior were in many instances aware of homosexual fantasies. However, any statement about the differences between homosexual and bisexual men is an over-simplification, since for every statement of differences there are important similarities.

Marital Adjustment

The marriages fell into four general categories:

1. O.K. This was the most common description, followed in many instances by the cliché, "We have our ups and downs, but isn't that the way marriage is?" In this group of 36 men, five regarded their marriages as close to ideal, or even (in two instances) as matings of the soul.
2. Troubled but stable. These men reported that they were unhappy with their marriages, but that the marriage bond was still strong. In any event, it seemed convenient to stay in the marriage, often "for the sake of the kids" or because more attractive alternatives did not exist (n = 13).
3. Clearly headed for divorce (n = 9).
4. Divorced at time of the interview (n = 2).

Though it is risky to generalize, these marriages bear a resemblance to those described by the sociologist John Cuber (1972) as "passive-congenial." Such a relationship is stable and predictable, the emotional tone pleasant but flat. The spouses meet role expectations but go about their separate business much of the time. Sex is present but not exhilirating. Facilitating their separate routines is the fact that most of the wives (46 of 58) have full-time jobs outside the household.

Some of the men reported having had an intense level of sexual interaction with their wives in the early years of marriage, which faded with the years. While many of the men continued to initiate sex with their wives, a good number preferred only to respond to the wives' advances.

Whether these men were different from other men their age and class we cannot say. We do not have large-scale, longitudinal studies of marriage which provide normative data on the details of sexual adjustment. To be sure, whether a marriage is happy or not, works well or not, is not a product of sexual interaction alone. Marital success or failure has many ingredients. Sexual attraction and enjoyment is only one and may not in itself be decisive. The less successful marriages revealed incompatibilities having more to do with shared values and sympathies than with the sexual life itself.

To Tell or Not to Tell

In a world of assumptions about exclusive heterosexuality, the decision to marry is most often made before one's sexual identity is fully recognized. It would be naive to suppose that the men who now regard themselves as homosexual had so clear a perception of themselves in their teens and early twenties. At earlier ages, some had been in a state of wavering denial, knowing and not wanting to know, whereas some had been truly ambisexual, responding both to males and females without conflict. A few had explored the gay world and could not find a comfortable place in it. Many had no reason to doubt their heterosexuality, while others who doubted it were reassured to discover that they were capable of heterosexual arousal. Few went into marriage with a sophisticated awareness of their homosexual orientation, although a handful of men told their wives about their sexual ambivalence. In doing so their motives were split between warning the fiancee that she should reconsider her decision to marry and making a disingenuous effort to be completely honest. The young women, convinced that love conquers all, were not to be put off by news they could scarcely comprehend. As the years passed, more of the men became aware of their homosexual desires and as a consequence increasingly engaged in homosexual activities. The great question commonly asked of bisexual men, and by bisexual men of each other is: "Does your wife know?" It is not nearly as important whether anyone else knows. However, before a man can tell his wife, he must know himself. The "coming out" process has been described often enough in other places. It is no different for married bisexual men, though it does involve added complications. The married man guards his secret from the one to whom he is most intimately bound; this secret thus is fraught with meaning on a moral and personal level. The quotations which follow reveal something of the reasons men have whether or not to tell, the manner of the telling, and the ethical considerations involved:

> I told my wife before we married. We were in our last year of college and we both thought we were sophisticated. She said, "It's no big thing, not if you love me." To me trust is part of love. The mar-

riage is working out fine. I get carried away at times. She doesn't say anything, just gets quiet, and I get back on track. (Married 12 years.)

I'm a Christian man. The spiritual is important in my life. So I told her. We were both 19 and she didn't know what the hell it was about. Neither did I. But she never forgot I told her and she's never learned anything since. It was the worst thing I could do. She watches me like a hawk. I put up with it because I know she really loves me. I can't say I love her the same way, but I do care. (Married 29 years.)

We were attending a sex therapy workshop in San Francisco on the week of the gay liberation celebrations. She said, "Let's march with the friends of gays" and I said, "No, let's join the bisexual section." The time seemed right to tell her about my one and only love affair of thirty years ago. She couldn't understand why I didn't tell her sooner. We've always been close and it seems we're closer still, if that is possible. Since then, I've been seeing a gay friend a couple of times a month—nothing heavy. It's fine with her. (Married 37 years.)

She caught me in the act after we were married one year—walked in when she was supposed to be at work. She never let me forget it in spite of all her whoring around. Well, we raised our kids and now we're stuck with each other. When we fight we threaten to split, but it hasn't happened so far. It could be worse. (Married 24 years.)

I follow a principle I learned in medical school. *Primum non nocere*—the first thing is not to hurt. We get along as well as any of the married couples I know, which is to say, so-so. I want to keep it that way. (Married 27 years.)

I love my wife but she's a terrible bigot about everything that doesn't fit her narrow concept of life. I just do what I have to when I'm out of town. It takes nothing away from her and she's got no complaints. She says she'd glad I don't play golf. So this is my hobby. (Married 12 years.)

About Wives

It was possible to go beyond the husbands' perception of their wives reactions by interviewing eight wives who knew about their husbands' homosexual activities. Those wives who already suspected had had time to reflect about the meaning of homosexuality, and thus dealt with the issue with relative calm. For most wives, however, the working through process began with a mingling of shock, disbelief, anger, resentment, and

rage, moving on to gradual understanding, and finally acceptance in varying degrees. Whatever the reaction, the disclosure may be nothing less
than traumatic. Most of the wives who were interviewed appeared
sophisticated and enlightened. For the most part, they could accept intellectually homosexual behavior as appropriate for some men, and
perhaps for their husbands, just so long as certain conditions were observed. For example, their husbands must not fall in love with their male
partners, must not bring home venereal diseases, and must not go to
dangerous places in town, must not stay out too late, and must not neglect
their wives and children. Two wives could not abide their husbands' having casual sex with strangers, but did accept a serious homosexual love
relationship just so long as it did not become more important than the
marriage. Most of the women felt relief that their husbands were not involved with other women. But several women felt otherwise, believing
they knew how to compete with women but not with men. Several of the
eight women professed not to understand the meaning of homosexuality.
They depended upon love and their religious beliefs to see them through.

Brief Histories

The vignettes which follow tell something of the lives of the men involved in this study in terms of their early experience, self-discovery, and
present marital arrangements:

(1) Age 57, two marriages and six children. To his consternation
and pleasure, at age 55 fell instantly in love with a male graduate
student whom he met at a party. The love, obsessive in nature, was
unrequited, but it did reveal to him an aspect of his sexuality he had
never suspected. He regards his wife as the great love of his life.
She is not opposed to his exploration of the gay world.

(2) Age 35, happily married for 12 years, two children. One year
after marriage began a sexual relationship with his best friend. They
are lovers in an exclusive arrangement, meeting one night a week.
Wives know and couples socialize. Stability, regularity, and dis-
cretion characterize the marital and extramarital life.

(3) Age 72, married 37 years, three children, seven grandchildren,
an elder in the church. Retired at 65. At age 68 took a course at a
community college on the anthropology of the city. Teacher took
class to gay bar. He was intrigued and returned on his own. Continues to go to gay dance bars and enjoys an active sex life with partners considerably younger than himself. Wife does not comprehend
his sudden devotion to dancing and concludes that he is in his second
childhood.

(4) Age 47, in second marriage, two children. A frequenter of men's rooms and seeker after glory holes since his adolescence. Highly experienced in homosexual world. His thrill is in the dangers of impersonal sex. Arrested once 15 years ago. Says things are safer now, but dangerous enough to turn him on.

(5) Age 54, married 26 years, two children. Belongs to a loosely organized group of men, all married, who meet once a month or so after work in a motel room for several hours of sexual partying. "It's safe and cheap and there's usually someone new there to make things even more exciting."

(6) Age 56, second marriage, three children. Loves wife (who is beautiful and 20 years younger) romantically and possessively. Does not have such feelings about men. Had his first homosexual experience two years ago. "It bowled me over. I've had a number of experiences since and they all bowl me over. But they don't take anything away from my marriage. I feel about homosexuality the same way I feel about New York City. I love to visit but I wouldn't want to live there."

ADDITIONAL FINDINGS

The following statements are observations and conclusions for which there is considerable support in the life histories. They are stated as brief generalizations because of space limitations.

1. It is best to separate the psychosocial and affectional life from the erotic and the sexual. There are many men who love their wives and children and would not choose to be other than married, yet whose chief sexual pleasure is homosexual.

2. One cannot readily categorize sexual orientation precisely for there are men who in the course of their lives wander from one category to another. A few men seem to be moving away from their homosexuality to a probable exclusive heterosexuality. Still more are moving from a tenuous heterosexuality to an exclusive homosexuality. Some have moved back and forth. Most experience both modes with a variety of emphases.

3. The men in this sample were successful in their work, interpersonal relations, and family life. They were comfortable with themselves and did not seriously wish to change. Some of the men who regarded themselves as essentially homosexual married before the era of gay liberation. If they could do it over again, they might opt for the gay lifestyle, but they accept their lives as they are.

4. Family life is important to them and they love their children. These men had little or no concern about the development of homosexuality in their children. While they had more than the usual sensitivity in such matters, none of the fathers had sure knowledge that any one of their children might be homosexual. Two fathers were concerned about effeminacy in their sons. Only rarely and inadvertently did children learn about their father's homosexual inclinations; when they did, they appeared to assimilate this knowledge with equanimity.

5. Some men never had experienced conflict about their sexuality. Conflict and guilt in some men were most often associated with a fundamentalist religiosity along with strong family pressures to marry. For a good number of men, being a sissy was a greater peril in growing up than being queer or gay.

6. Some men believed that their bisexuality had enriched their lives and enhanced their sensitivity to the human condition. They believed they could know both men and women more intimately. Most men, however, did not regard bisexuality as anything other than a necessary way to be themselves.

7. A handful of these men were conspicuously masculine, another handful somewhat effeminate, but the great majority were in the middle range of unremarkable masculinity.

8. The homosexual experience is not without its hazards. Seven men experienced the humiliation of arrests while cruising public men's rooms, and as many were victims of violence. Seventeen men contracted venereal diseases (most often gonorrhea). Upon follow-up, men expressed anxiety about Acquired Immunity Deficiency Syndrome and were moderating their behavior accordingly. Those who found their main outlets at homosexual baths and bars were more inclined to look at relationships with partners they could trust.

9. Twelve of the 60 men interviewed experienced their first adult homosexual relationship after the age 40, and of this number six had their first experience after 50. Several of these men (and this is true of some of the younger men as well) had not a glimmer of their homosexual potential. They were taken by surprise in situations altogether unpredictable. This, of course, flies in the face of popular wisdom that our sexual destinies are settled once and for all in childhood.

DISCUSSION

Except for those few men for whom homosexual expression had always been as natural as breathing, almost all of the others had already experienced the despair so many men do upon first discovering their homosexuality. For the most part, they had worked through those miseries which turn people into patients. Most did not undertake formal psychotherapy. They found their therapy in living in an ever-changing culture which has allowed them to discover their true sexual natures. Herein lies the resolution of the most challenging paradox in their lives: the reconciliation of the conventional public self with the secret private self. One might easily imagine that men of similar stripe some thirty or so years ago would have had very different fates. Accepting the Ford-Beach thesis that bisexuality is the common human biological potential whose expression is positively reinforced in some societies and inhibited in others, most of these men might well have lived out their lives as conflict-free heterosexuals. Some men with a more powerful disposition toward the homosexual would have found themselves in difficulties best resolved by suppression and denial, or else have become patients in extended psychotherapy. Yet a small number might have been able to choose the homosexual mode without conflict. The changing times have brought to these men the possibility of relationships that go beyond the impersonal transactions in the tea-room trade of a generation ago, and provide environments far more secure and aesthetically pleasing. Clearly, these men are beneficiaries of social changes that have brought about a progressive definition of homosexuality—from sin and perversion to neurosis, to variation, to lifestyle. The opportunity to observe the self from the perspective of coherent theories of personality, the discoveries of Kinsey about what people actually do sexually, the liberation movements of the sixties, all are influences which set these men free to claim their bisexual or homosexual identities without disabling shame and conflict.

Claiming a sexual identity does not mean sharing that identity with others. These men are not hiding from themselves, but in varying degrees they are hiding from others who are important to them. The resolution of the second paradox growing out of the concealment of their true natures from their wives is accomplished in a variety of ways. The pragmatists, the idealists, the guilt-ridden, those who betray themselves, all find their different solutions in accordance with the implicit philosophies of their lives. As to whom they should reveal themselves and what would be the gain, each man must find the answer for himself. The willingness of these men to participate in this study and their gratitude for the opportunity are signs that they wish to share their secret and in some measure be relieved of it. The spontaneous development of self-support groups for married bisexual men is still another sign that those who so obviously fit in the mainstream of society at the level of appearance nevertheless wish to know others like themselves. Whether this is an escape from a sense of fragmentation and separateness and a reaching toward a collective identity based on honest self-disclosure, it is too soon to say.

The concept of bisexuality threatens our hard-won sexual identities.

Human beings think most readily in dichotomies and polarities. The appreciation of ourselves as heterosexual or homosexual implies a denial of the opposite. We not only identify, but also counter-identify. Once we suspect that we are all potential lovers of each other we shall have to ask ourselves who we are and what we are going to do about it.

The discovery in persons of their disposition toward bisexuality ultimately requires the discovery of ways of expressing it which are personally and socially rewarding. The histories of most of the men in this study demontrate that the fulfillment which is part of conventional family is also possible for bisexual men. This is so whether they regard themselves as heterosexual men who need to express their homosexual impulses, or homosexual men who have a capacity to sustain a satisfactory heterosexual relationship. However bisexuality is defined, it would appear that its expression can be life-enhancing for those married men of bisexual disposition who have learned to balance fairly what it is they owe to themselves and to others.

REFERENCES

Bieber, I., Dain, H. J., Dince, P. R., Drellich, M. G., Grand, H. G., Gundlach, R. H., Kremer, M. W., Rifkin, A. H., Wilber, C. B., & Bieber, T. B. (1962). *Homosexuality: A psychoanalytic study*. New York: Basic Books.

Blumstein, P. W., & Schwartz, P. (1976). Bisexuality in men. *Urban Life, 5,* 339-358.

Bozett, F. (1982). Heterogeneous couples in heterosexual marriage: Gay men and straight women. *Journal of Marital and Family Therapy, 8*(1), 81-89.

Coleman, E. (1981/1982). Bisexual and gay men in heterosexual marriage: Conflicts and resolutions in therapy. *Journal of Homosexuality, 7*(2/3), 93-104.

Cuber, John F. (1972). Sex in five types of marriages. *Sexual Behavior, 2,* 74-77.

Ford, C. S., & Beach, F. A. (1951). *Patterns of sexual behavior.* New York: Paul B. Hoeber.

Freud, S. (1961). Some psychological consequences of the anatomical distinction between the sexes. In J. Strachey (Ed. and Trans.), *The standard edition of the complete psychological works of Sigmund Freud* (Vol. 5, pp. 186-198). London: Hogarth Press. (Original work published 1905).

Hatterer, L. R. (1970). *Changing homosexuality in the male.* New York: McGraw-Hill.

Jung, C. G. (1951). *Aion: Researches into the phenomenology of the self* (Vol. 9, pt. 2). Princeton, NJ: Princeton University Press.

Kinsey, A. C., Pomeroy, W. B., & Martin, C. E. (1948). *Sexual behavior in the human male.* Philadelphia: W. B. Saunders.

Klein, F. (1978). *The bisexual option.* New York: Arbor House.

Latham, J. D., & White, G. D. (1978). Coping with homosexual expression within heterosexual marriage: Five case studies. *Journal of Sex and Marital Therapy, 4,* 198-212.

MacDonald, A. P., Jr. (1982). Research on sexual orientation: A bridge that touches both shores but doesn't meet in the middle. *Journal of Sex Education and Therapy, 8*(1), 9-13.

Masters, W. H., & Johnson, V. E. (1979). *Homosexuality in perspective.* Boston: Little, Brown.

Ross, H. L. (1972). Odd couples: Homosexuals in heterosexual marriages. *Sexual Behavior, 2,* 42-49.

Saghir, M. T., & Robbins, E. (1973). *Male and female homosexuality.* Baltimore: Williams & Wilkins.

Integration of Male Bisexuality
and Marriage

Eli Coleman, PhD
University of Minnesota

ABSTRACT. Eighteen couples who had originally entered therapy because of conflicts created by the husband's bisexuality were studied to determine the dynamics and adjustment of their marriages. All the couples, to varying degrees, had been openly dealing with the husband's bisexuality for at least two years. Through questionnaires and psychological instruments, couples indicated that openness and communication helped the relationship. The greatest difficulties they encountered were in their sexual relationships. Marital satisfaction and adjustment was found to be negatively correlated with increasing age, number of children, later onset of homosexual activities, increased emotional involvement with male partners, increased numbers of people who know about the husband's homosexual activities, and increased sexual dissatisfaction and conflict. Basically, this study reinforced the notion that some marriages can survive by way of open communication, acceptance and understanding, dynamics which help compensate for the inherent conflicts these couples face.

Bisexual men who are, or have been, married have received attention in the last 10-15 years (e.g., Ross, 1971; Gochros, 1978; Latham & White, 1978; Coleman, 1981/1982a; Bozett, 1981; Brownfain, 1985; Matteson, 1985; Wolf, 1985; Klein, 1978; Kohn & Matusow, 1980; Nahas & Turley, 1979; Malone, 1980; Miller, 1979a, 1979b). This growing awareness has paralleled a greater openness among marital partners in discussing their outside sexual attractions, including those that are homosexual. Bisexual men have been "coming out" to their wives, it seems, in increasing numbers over the past decade. As a result of their disclosures, these men have been dealing more openly with their bisexuality within their marital relationships. For many, this openness has been the first step in acknowledging their bisexuality, and their intention to end the marriage to pursue exclusively homosexual relationships. For others, this openness has been the first step in ending the lack of intimacy in their marital relationships which had resulted from their lack of honesty. The disclosure can begin a process of integrating the husband's bisexuality into the marriage, rather than terminating the marriage.

This integration process is a difficult one for most couples, but there is some evidence which suggests it is possible. Latham and White (1978) described five couples in which the homosexuality of one or both of the partners was known to the other, and where there was some integration of it in the marriage. These researchers identified three stages of adjustment leading to integration: withdrawal-avoidance, disclosure-acceptance, and adjustment-coping. In the withdrawal-avoidance stage, years one to five were characterized as a time of minimal homosexual activity associated with feelings of guilt. Although the wives usually were aware at the time of their marriage that their husbands had homosexual interests, they assumed that it would not occur during marriage. Once this assumption proved false, anxiety developed in the partners. Such anxiety forced the couple to look for effective coping strategies in order to preserve their marriages. During the disclosure-acceptance stage, the husband felt less guilt about his homosexual interests. The wife developed less of a feeling of failure, and recognized her partner's homosexual interests as something independent of the relationship. During the adjustment-coping stage, a greater sexual expression developed on the part of both husband and wife, the wife was more likely to have outside sexual contacts, and more of an open marriage contract resulted.

The problem with this study, as with others, is that no long-term longitudinal studies of these relationships have been conducted. The data, usually collected at one time, are primarily retrospective. It is unclear whether the rules, guidelines, or new contracts established in the adjustment-coping stage could sustain the relationship and keep it vital.

A model of sexually open relationships has been suggested by some clinicians (e.g., Latham & White, 1978; Coleman, 1981/1982a) as a method of integrating the homosexuality of one or both of the marital partners. This model is based upon research which has indicated a positive correlation between degree of disclosure and openness, and psychological adjustment (e.g., Hammersmith & Weinberg, 1973; Dank, 1973; Weinberg & Williams, 1974). It is unclear whether more disclosure and openness within marriage leads to greater psychological adjustment of both partners and increases marital and sexual satisfaction. The traditional way of coping for a bisexual married man has been to lead a double life. Coleman (1981/1982b) has suggested five developmental stages of homosexuality leading to personality integration, which emphasize personal disclosure, openness, and acceptance of one's homosexuality. Applied to the marital situation, more openness and honesty would be at least necessary for personality integration of the bisexual partner. Yet the question remains whether complete and open disclosure of homosexual feelings and activities leads to psychological adjustment for the couple.

In Coleman's (1981/1982a) study of married men, some couples adjusted through a "double life" strategy where the wife knew very little of the husband's homosexual activity. Other couples found it more effective to establish an open marriage contract. While both strategies seemed to work for the couples, some additional factors which seemed to be important ingredients of successful adjustment were identified as follows: mutual love, and commitment to make the relationship work, a high degree of communication, resolution of feelings of guilt, minimal blame or resentment, a desire for physical contact, the wife having a sense of worth outside the marriage, and the willingness of the partners to acknowledge and accept the husband's same-sex feelings. These factors were tentatively put forth; more research was recommended to test the long-term effects of these coping strategies.

The present study tested the viability of these factors over a longer period of time, and sought correlations of these factors with measures of self-esteem of the individuals in the relationship and of marital and sexual satisfaction. By examining a sample of couples who have dealt with the husbands' bisexuality to varying degrees of openness, and have maintained their marriage for at least two years from the point of disclosure, it is hoped a better understanding of the ingredients of success will be achieved. In addition, this study tested the hypothesis that the degree of openness and communication in the marital relationship, and support from others who know about their situation, would positively correlate with higher self-esteem and marital and sexual satisfaction.

METHOD

Nineteen couples from the author's clinical practice were contacted for participation in this study. They had entered therapy because of conflicts arising from the husband's bisexuality, and they had been developing varying degrees of openness over at least two years. Participation was completely voluntary. This patient population was utilized because of its availability to the author. Most of the husbands in this study were a part of the author's study of bisexuality in heterosexual marriage (Coleman, 1981/1982a). While the limitations of this kind of sample are recognized, the information which can be gained from a longitudinal study nevertheless is considered valuable.

Each of the couples filled out a questionnaire and several psychological instruments, and were interviewed by the author. The questionnaires were designed to gather information about demographics, degree of self-awareness of homosexual feelings and behaviors before and during the marriage, the degree of the wife's awareness of these feelings and behaviors, reasons for getting married, sexual difficulties or problems in marriage, sexual experiences outside the marital relationship, attempts by the husband to eliminate his homosexual feelings, and attempts at counseling or therapy to deal with conflicts in their marriage resulting from the husband's bisexual orientation. Also, information was sought regarding the children's awareness of the father's homosexuality, sources of support for the relationship, degree of openness about the husband's homosexuality outside the marriage, factors which the couple have defined as contributing to the success of their marriage, problems which they have defined in their relationship, the rules for handling the husband's homosexual feelings within the marital relationship, and Kinsey-type ratings of sexual orientation of behavior, fantasy, and emotional attachments for before and during the marriage.

The psychological instruments which were administered included the Tennessee Self-Concept Scale (TSCS) (Fitts, 1965), the Locke-Wallace Marital Adjustment Inventory (LWMAI) (Locke & Wallace, 1959), and the Sexual Interaction Inventory (SII) (LoPiccolo & Steger, 1974). These instruments were utilized to measure self-esteem, personality integration, psychological adjustment, marital adjustment, and sexual satisfaction.

RESULTS

Of the 19 couples contacted for the study, 18 husbands and 14 wives agreed to participate. The average length of time the couples had been dealing openly with the husband's homosexuality varied from 2-19 years, with an average of 5.33 years. The average length of time since first contact with the author was 3.33 years (1-5.5 years).

Demographics

The average age of the 18 males was 44.16, and for the 14 females 43.14 (see Table 1). The majority of the sample was highly educated. Males had more professional and graduate education than the females [$\bar{X}$ = 13.51; df = 3; p < .01; trade/vocational school: males - 0 (0%), females - 1 (7%); some college: males - 2 (11%), females - 3 (22%); college graduate: males - 2 (11%), females - 8 (57%); graduate/professional school: male - 14 (78%), females - 2 (14%)]. Family income was relatively high with males earning significantly more than females [X = 15.28; df = 5; p < .01; financially dependent: males - 0 (0%), females - 2 (14%); less than 5,000: males - 1 (6%), females - 4 (29%); 5001 - 15,000: males - 0 (0%), females - 3 (21.5%); 15,001 - 25,000: males - 4 (22%), females - 3 (21.5%); 25,001 - 50,000: males - 8 (44%), females - 2 (14%); more than 50,001: males - 5 (28%), females - 0 (0%)]. The entire sample was Caucasian. All the subjects had married once, and the average length of their marriage was 18.09 years. Fifteen of the 18 couples had children, and the average number of children for the entire sample was 2.19.

Table 1
SUMMARY OF DATA
18 Couples
Males = 18
Females = 14

		Males		Females	
		X	SD	X	SD
Average Age		44.16	8.36	43.14	8.70
Age at Time of Marriage		27.00	4.34	24.36	2.87
Number of Children		2.19	.96	2.19	.96
Number of Marriages		1.00	.00	1.00	.00
Length of Current Marriage		18.09	8.17	18.09	8.17
Years Since Openly Dealing with Husband's Homo/Bisexuality		5.22		5.22	
Years Since First Contact with Author		3.33		3.33	
		f	%	f	%
**	Awareness of Same-sex feelings prior to marriage	18	100%	3	21%
**	Awareness of Bisexual or homosexual Identity	8	44%	0	0%
**	Acted on Same-sex Feelings prior to Marriage	17	95%	0	0%
**	Marital Partner Knew of Same-Same-sex Feelings Prior to Marriage	4	22%	0	0%
**	Sex with men Outside of Marriage	16	89%	1	7%
**	Marital Partner's Knowledge of Sex with Other Men	12	67%	1	7%
	Marital Partner's Knowledge of Same-sex feelings During Marriage	18	100%	NA	NA
**	Marital Partner's Consent for Sex with Other Men	7	39%	1	7%
	Attempts of Eliminate Same-sex Feelings (other than psychotherapy)	7	39%	NA	NA
	Attempts to Eliminate Same-sex Feelings Through Psychotherapy	7	39%	NA	NA
	Received Therapy to Deal with Conflict of Sexual Orientation and Marriage	15	83%	12	86%
*	Sexual Conflict Within Marriage	16	94%	12	86%

** Using X statistic, p .001
* Using X statistic, p .05

Awareness of Homosexual Feelings Prior to Marriage

All of the males were somewhat aware of their homosexual feelings prior to getting married [yes, definitely: 15 (83%); yes, somewhat: 3 (17%); no: 0 (0%)]. All but one had acted on their same-sex feelings prior to marriage. The majority of the males indicated that their first homosexual experience occurred before the age of 12 [less than 6 years old: 5 (28%); 7 - 12(39%); 13 - 15: 3 (16%); 16 - 19: 1 (6%); 20 - 25: 0 (0%); 26 or older: 2 (11%)]. While they were all aware of their sexual feelings, and had acted upon these feelings, they were less likely to have identified themselves as bisexual [without doubt: 4 (22%); almost certain: 4 (22%); somewhat: 7 (39%); not at all: 3 (17%)]. They were also even more unlikely to have discussed their homosexual feelings with their spouse prior to marriage [yes: 4 (22%)].

The females, on the other hand, were very unlikely to have experienced same-sex feelings before marriage [yes, definitely: 0 (0%); yes, somewhat: 3 (21%); no: 11 (79%)]. None of the women had had any homosexual experience prior to marriage, or had identified themselves as bisexual.

Reasons for Getting Married

When asked about their reasons for getting married, the majority of the males indicated such factors (listed in order of highest to lowest frequency) as the perceived lack of intimacy in the homosexual world, love for their spouses, interest in having or raising children, hope that marriage would overcome their homosexual feelings, and societal pressures to marry. Family pressures to marry were rated as least influential. The females indicated such factors (also reported in order of greatest to lowest frequency) as love for their spouse, and interest in having or raising children. They were least likely to report such factors as societal or family pressures (see Table 2).

Extra-Marital Sexual Activity

Sixteen (89%) of the men had engaged in sexual activity with other men during the course of their marriage (none of the men reported any outside sexual activity with other women). Most of the wives of these men (67%) knew about this activity, and a minority of the wives (39%) had given their consent. All of the wives knew, minimally, about their husband's homosexual feelings. The majority of the men reported that their wives knew they acted on their feelings at certain times, but that their wives did not know, or only knew to some extent, when, where, and with whom: [knew about feelings only: 6 (35%); knew activities take place but no details: 7 (41%); knew activities took place and some details: 3 (18%); knew activities took place and all details: 1 (6%)]. The wives were more likely to report that they were being told, to a greater extent, when, where, and with whom homosexual activities were occurring [knew about feelings only: 6 (43%); knew activities took place but no details: 3 (21%); knew activities took place with some details: 5 (36); knew activities took place with all details: 0 (0%)].

Table 2

REASONS FOR MARRIAGE

	Males		Females	
	N	%	N	%
Societal Pressures to Marry	8	44%	5	36%
Family Pressures to Marry	3	17%	1	7%
Perceived Lack of Intimacy in Homosexual World	18	100%	NA	NA
Love for spouse	15	83%	14	100%
Interest in Having Children	11	61%	10	71%
Hoping Marriage Would Overcome Same-sex Feelings	9	50%	NA	NA

Only one wife reported any outside sexual activity during the course of her marriage. In that case, the outside sexual activity occurred with a male whom her husband later found out about.

Attempts to Eliminate Homosexual Feelings

Some of the men in the study reported they had attempted to eliminate their homosexual feelings and activity. Seven (39%) had received some psychotherapy. Seven (39%) of the men attempted other means such as praying, working hard, keeping active, conditioning fantasies through pornography, and repressing thoughts. None of these methods appeared to have been successful.

Sexual Conflicts Within the Marriage

Almost all of the couples experienced some conflicts within their sexual relationship [men: 16 (94%); women: 12 (86%)]. The sexual difficulties are noted in Table 3. Three significant differences in reported sexual dysfunctions between the men and the women were shown. The women were significantly more likely to report a lack of sexual desire for anyone and to report an inability to achieve orgasm with certain types of stimulation. The men were more likely to report lack of satisfaction with no particular sexual dysfunction.

Table 3

SEXUAL DIFFICULTIES EXPERIENCED IN MARRIAGE

		Males		Females	
		N	%	N	%
	Yes, Definitely	10	59%	2	14%
	Yes, Somewhat	6	35%	10	71%
	No	1	6%	2	14%
*	Lack of Desire for Anyone	2	11%	6	43%
	Lack of Sexual Desire for Spouse	8	44%	8	57%
	Lack of lubrication	NA	NA	3	21%
	Inability to get or sustain erections	2	11%	NA	NA
	Inability to achieve orgasm	1	6%	1	7%
**	Inability to achieve orgasm certain types of stimulation	2	11%	7	50%
	Pain During Intercourse	NA	NA	2	14%
	Inability to have intercourse due to muscular contractions of the vagina	NA	NA	0	0%
	Premature ejaculation	1	6%	NA	NA
***	No sexual dysfunction, but lack of satisfaction	13	72%	0	0%

```
  *   X  = 4.23;  df = 1;  p   .05
 **   X  = 5.89;  df = 1;  p   .05
***   X  = 17.03; df = 1;  p   .001
```

Sexual satisfaction was also measured by the SII. Most mean scores on the SII were in the range of moderate dissatisfaction and difficulties [scaled one to one hundred, higher scaled scores indicate greater dissatisfaction and difficulty]: males - 56.22, females - 61.07; Self-acceptance: males - 70.22, females - 67.23; Perceived pleasure: males - 65.00, females - 66.76; Perceptual accuracy: males - 76.56, females - 67.30; Mate acceptance: males - 63.39, females - 65.59; Total dissatisfaction: Couple - 75.00]. Using statistical t-tests, no significant differences were found between the male and female scores on the SII.

Ingredients of Successful Adjustment

Many of the same factors of successful marital adjustment which had been identified by Coleman (1982a) were mentioned by the couples, such as love, commitment, openness, and acceptance. In additon to these, certain couples identified the following factors: shared values, goals, friends, family ties, and interests; financial interdependence and other economic factors, mutual dependency, a strong commitment to parenting their children, keeping sexual conflicts in perspective with the rest of the relationship, respect, trust, tolerance, patience, honesty, prayer and religious beliefs, therapy support groups, comfort with non-conformity, family pressures, professional pressures, a sense of responsibility to each other and the family, a shared belief in growth and consciousness-raising experiences.

When asked about the problems they encountered in their marriages, the couples listed the following (in no particular order of frequency or significance): adjustment to the husband's sexual orientation, low self-esteem, constant questioning of the viability of the marriage, lack of communication, blaming each other for the difficulties in the marriage, poor conflict resolution, financial problems, depression, lack of a sexual relationship, parenting conflicts, "codependency," lack of respect, jealousy, in-laws, job, "guilt, guilt, guilt," dishonesty, intolerance, defensiveness, and health risks created by outside sexual partners.

The couples developed rules for governing the husband's sexual feelings and activities. They reported the following rules (these rules simply reflect the range of rules couples work out in their relationships, are not those for every relationship, and are not reported in any particular order): there is continual reassurance of commitment and primacy of the marital relationship, the husband always comes home at night, husband is careful about not bringing home sexually transmitted diseases, limiting the number of outside sexual partners, husband will not have anonymous sexual encounters or have sex in public places, nor will become emotionally involved with anyone, couple will not talk about husband's homosexual feelings or activities, couples will talk openly about husband's feelings and activities and acknowledging husband's same-sex feelings, but husband does not act on those feelings, no extra-marital activities will take place in the home, "gay friendships" are "OK," and couples will live apart some of the time.

Sources for Psychological Support

The couples were asked what kind of support they have received for "making their relationship work." They were given a choice of several sources of potential support and allowed to indicate as many as applied. The majority of the men indicated such support sources (listed in order of highest to lowest frequency) as heterosexual, homosexual or bisexual friends, men's support groups, and couples in similar situations. The males were least likely to report support from family members, the religious community, or their own children. Half the females indicated they most likely received support from their heterosexual friends. Half received support from a women's support group. According to Chi-square statistical tests, the differences in sources of support for the husbands and wives were not statistically significant, except for males receiving more support from homosexual or bisexual friends than their wives' heterosexual friends (see Table 4).

TABLE 4

Sources of Psychological Support

	Males		Females	
	f	%	f	%
Heterosexual Friends	14	78%	11	79%
* Bi/Homosexual Friends	14	78%	6	43%
Family Members	4	22%	5	36%
Mens/Womens Support Groups	12	67%	7	50%
Religious Community	3	17%	4	29%
Couples in Similar Situation	9	50%	6	43%
Children	3	17%	5	36%

* $X = 4.10$; $df = 1$; p .05

Degree of Openness About the Husbands' Sexual Orientation

The men in the study were far more likely to have told a number of people about their bisexuality. Six (35%) of the men had told 11 - 20 other individuals. Ten (59%) of the males had told more than 20 individuals. One man (6%) had told 4 - 10 individuals. One of the females had told 1 - 3 people; six (46%) had told 4 - 10 people; three (23%) had told 11 - 20 people; and three (23%) had told more than 20.

Disclosure to Children

Five of the 18 couples who had children had discussed the husband's bisexuality with their children. There were 31 children in this study and 12 (39%) of them had been told. The average age of the children when they were told was 18.08 years.

Self-Esteem, Psychological Adjustment, and Marital Satisfaction

The results of the Tennessee Self-Concept Scale indicated the entire sample was within normal limits for a number of scales (total self-esteem, body, sexuality, family, social, personality integration, and psychological adjustment). Multiple t-tests revealed no statistically significant differences between the males and females on these scales except for psychological adjustment (NDS); there the males had more elevated scores than the females.

Marital satisfaction and adjustment was measured by the Locke-Wallace Marital Adjustment Inventory. The mean score for the males was 83.67 (SD = 23.28), which indicated a moderate level of dissatisfaction in the marital relationship. The mean score for the females was 91.92 (SD = 25.23), indicating a mild level of dissatisfaction. The mean differences between males and females do not represent a statistically significant difference. Quite a range of scores on the LWMAI was indicated by the standard deviations. Only four couples had scores in a range indicating positive levels of marital satisfaction and adjustment (100 or above). Six couples had scores at a mild level of marital dissatisfaction. And, the remaining eight couples had scores reflecting moderate to severe levels of marital dissatisfaction and adjustment.

One particular item on the LWMAI clearly differentiated the males and females. When asked if they had their lives to live over, would they marry the same person, marry a different person, or not marry at all, males were most likely to indicate they would not marry at all (10 of the 18 males), while the females were more likely to indicate they would marry the same person (8 of 14) or marry a different person (6 of 14).

Kinsey-Type Ratings

Each subject was asked to rate themselves on a Kinsey-type scale (0 = exclusively heterosexual; 6 = exclusively homosexual), to rate themselves on the three different dimensions of sexual behavior, sexual fantasy, and emotional attachments, and to rate themselves on those dimensions for the periods of time before their marriage and during the course of their marriage. No significant differences in the males sexual orientation before or during their marriage were apparent. Males were, however, significantly more homosexually oriented than the females. The males were more homosexually oriented in their fantasies than in their behavior (see Table 5).

Correlations

Total self-esteem was found to be positively correlated with having had homosexual experiences before marriage, no sexual problems in marriage, wife's consent for same-sex activities, and marital adjustment and satisfaction (LWMAI). Total self-esteem was negatively correlated with having had marital therapy to deal with husband's bisexual orientation,

TABLE 5

CHANGES IN KINSEY-TYPE RATINGS BEFORE AND DURING MARRIAGE

(0 = exclusive heterosexual; 6 = exclusive homosexual)

		BEFORE	DURING
SEXUAL BEHAVIOR	Males	3.63	2.69
	Females	.00	.07
SEXUAL FANTASIES	Males	5.13	5.00
	Females	.36	.64
EMOTIONAL ATTACHMENT	Males	2.75	3.13
	Females	3.07	3.00

predominant or exclusive homosexual fantasies before and during marriage, and sexual dissatisfaction or conflict (Total SII).

Sexual dissatisfaction and conflict (Total SII) was positively correlated with having had more children, and late onset of homosexual activities. Factors which were found to negatively correlate with sexual dissatisfaction and conflict included not having sexual problems in marriage, increased emotional involvements with same-sex partners, positive self-esteem (Tennessee total), and marital satisfaction and adjustment (LWMAI).

Marital satisfaction and adjustment (LWMAI) was found to be positively correlated with not having sexual problems in the marriage, not having had therapy to deal with conflicts created by the husband's sexual orientation, the wives having a more complete knowledge of husband's homosexual feelings and activities, and postiive self-esteem (Tennessee total). Marital satisfaction and adjustment was found to be negatively correlated with increasing age, having had more children, later onset of same-sex activities, increased emotional involvement with male partners, increased numbers of people who know about the husband's same-sex activities, and increased sexual dissatisfaction and conflict (Total SII) (see Table 6).

Table 6

Correlations of Factors with Self Esteem,

Sexual Conflict, and Marital Adjustment

	Self Esteem	Sexual Conflict	Marital Adjustment
Age	−.17	.20	−.41**
Number of Children	−.16	.36*	−.39*
Duration of Marriage	−.22	.09	−.29*
Education	.04	.06	−.20
Income	−.23	−.05	−.21
Age of 1st Homo-exper.#	−.37	.49*	−.52*
Homo-exper.Before Marr.#	−.43*	.03	−.21
Fiance Aware Before Marr.#	−.28	.36	−.29
Sexual Problems in Marr.	−.32*	−.42**	.43**
Wife's Consent for Husband's Homo activities	−.43*	.27	−.09
Wife's Full Knowledge of Husband's Homo-activities	.17	−.21	.28*
Number of People who Knew About Husband's Sexuality	.04	−.20	−.31*
Therapy for Conflicts in Marriage	−.31*	−.11	.24
Kinsey-Behavior Before Marriage	−.14	−.08	.03
Kinsey-Behavior During Marriage	−.27	.00	−.07
Kinsey-Fantasies Before Marriage	−.34*	.05	.19
Kinsey-Fantasies During Marriage	−.43**	.14	−.28

Table 6 Continued

Kinsey-Emotional Attach. Before Marriage	.18	−.04	−.01
Kinsey-Emotional Attach. During Marriage	.01	.10	−.06
Frequency of Homosexual Activity#	−.27	.21	−.07
Number of Current Sexual Partners#	−.36	.04	.18
Amount of Emotional Involvement with Partners#	.07	−.54**	.19
Total Self Esteem (TSCS)	1.00	−.41**	.40**
Total Sexual Conflict (SII)	.41**	1.00	−.51*
Marital Adjustment (LWMAI)	.40**	−.51***	1.00

Correlations based upon responses from men only.
* p   .05.
** p   .01
*** p   .001

DISCUSSION

This study had described 18 couples who have had to deal with the husband's bisexuality. Many couples were not included in this study because they have since been divorced or separated. A critical period appears to exist following the disclosure of the husbands' homosexuality when the marriages are in great jeopardy of dissolving. The pressure for dissolution may come from the husband or wife. However, for others who continue past this critical period, the threat of separation or divorce is still not eliminated. Even though feelings of commitment and security increase, there still remains an underlying and ongoing conflict in the marriage. If subsequent crises were successfully resolved (and many of these couples had resolved many problem situations), feelings of intimacy and commitment increased, prompting further constructive changes in the relationships. Overall, the fact that these 18 couples are still together confirms Latham and White's postulated stages, since it thus appears that all the couples in this study have gone beyond the withdrawal-avoidance stage, and could be divided into either the disclosure-acceptance or the adjustment-coping stage.

If we look at the demographics of this sample, we might say that long-term success is attributable to having been married for a long time (average length of marriage is 18 years), being in one's mid-forties at the time of the study, having been highly educated, and being financially secure. These factors certainly help offset the stressful effects within a marriage of dealing with the husband's bisexuality. While no correlations were found for length of marriage, education, or income, increasing age and number of children were found to correlate negatively with marital adjustment and satisfaction. It may be that the far-reaching effects of dealing with the husband's bisexuality eventually take their toll on the marriage. Longer follow-up studies are still needed.

All couples in this study indicated that greater openness and communication have helped their relationships. None of the wives expressed doubt or regret knowing of the husband's homosexuality. And while the levels of openness and honesty about the husband's same-sex activities varied among the couples, greater openness did seem to be correlated with greater marital satisfaction, as hypothesized. Unfortunately, no prescription of adjustment was revealed in this study regarding the exact amount of disclosure or communication between the spouses. Each couple had different needs with differing circumstances. Some secrecy seemed to be functional for some of the couples.

While other problems existed in these relationships, the greatest difficulties seem to be in the sexual relationship, the area consistently identified as the problem of disagreement on the LWMAI. Couples' scores on the SII also confirmed this area of difficulty, as their scores were indicative of sexual problems, conflicts, and dissatisfactions. While these couples tended to fall within normative levels of self-esteem and psychological adjustment, they experienced difficulties in their marital and sexual relationship. Apparently, the couples were, for the most part, able to localize these difficulties and not let them adversely effect their self-esteem. While many couples experienced difficulties in their marital and sexual relationship, they still had a basic love and respect for one another.

An important point in understanding these relationships is that problems other than the husbands' bisexual orientation naturally arise. These couples, however, appear to have fewer conflicts created by the husband's bisexuality.

Because these women have had only a few years to deal with their husbands' bisexuality, they are still at early stages of their own coming-out process. It is very difficult for some of them to acknowledge to others that they are married to a bisexual, and many are reluctant to seek out sources of psychological support. It is somewhat ironic that the women are more reluctant to seek out "support groups" than their husbands, given traditional sex-role conditioning. Yet some of that conditioning leads women not to admit to other women their failures in their relationships with men. This reluctance to seek out support might also reflect their own discomfort and sense of shame for being in this situation. Coleman (1981/1982b) indicated that family members go through the same or similar coming-out process as the individual in dealing with homosexuality. Becoming comfortable enough with this orientation to discuss it with others takes time, both for the bisexual husband and his wife.

Many of the wives could be described as dependent. In many ways they have been highly tolerant of their husbands' same-sex activities, the lack of intimacy, and have reacted to his needs. Many of the women have felt dependent economically on their husbands, factors preventing them from being more assertive. At the point of disclosure, many of these women suffered from low self-esteem. This crisis in the relationship forced many to develop more assertiveness, independence, and self-esteem. Their "normal" self-esteem scores on the TSCS attest to the results of their efforts at improved self-esteem. A key factor in achieving successful adjustment appears to have been the development of self-esteem and comfort with independence and separateness.

Most of the men in this study were married in the 1950s and 1960s, a period when the choices afforded homosexual men were restricted. It is no wonder that all of the men, in spite of their awareness of their same-sex feelings, partially based their decision to marry on the lack of intimacy they perceived in the homosexual world, and thus saw marriage as the healthiest adaptation. Many of these men did not even know a "gay world" existed.

The fact that the cultural atmosphere and social acceptance of homosexuality have changed may be a large factor why these men have taken the risk of dealing more openly with their own bisexuality. This atmosphere fosters healthy alternatives for dealing with their bisexuality, other than concealing or sublimating it, or attempting to live an exclusively heterosexual or gay lifestyle.

Another factor which seems to account for the decision to deal more openly with their bisexuality is the age of these men. Many of them had entered their "mid-life crisis." Questioning their basic assumptions of life, they wondered if life would be better if they had taken a different course, one which took into account what they wanted. Many tired from the burden of family responsibilities and the sex-role expectations of the traditional male role. Same-sex feelings, activities, relationships, and fantasies of leaving the marital relationship could provide an escape from these pressures, changes similar to those other men in mid-life crises have taken. This perspective, while not applicable in all cases, seems to be a significant factor in understanding the psychodynamics of these men.

Concealment, secrecy, and sublimation had negative effects on these men, although they were different for each man. Depression had been common, as were sexual compulsivity and preoccupation, "workaholism," and alcohol abuse. Secrecy and shame led to sexual addiction (Carnes, 1983) in a number of cases. Two of the men recognized their alcoholism, and their recovery involved elimination of the secrecy and shame which fueled their depression and compulsive behaviors. Developing multiple addictions had been common to mask the pain of being different.

Many of the men have suffered their own dependency problems. In their own pre-coming out stage (Coleman, 1981/1982b), they suffered underlying self-esteem problems and shame about their bisexuality. These problems caused feelings of emotional dependency. Part of the male's growth process is overcoming feelings of shame regarding their bisexual orientation and building their self-esteem. Again, the males in this study indicate this growth has taken place. This finding is further confirmed by the increased self-esteem scores from the time of the original study (Coleman, 1981/1982a).

The risk, of course, of increased self-esteem and independence for the men and the women is a recognition of their ability to begin new relationships and abandon old ones. While this increases the risk of marital dissolution, it also creates vitality and psychological health. Unfortunately, in a few cases in this study, the relationship survives because of mutual dependency needs and low self-esteem. These relationships remain chronically unhappy, without resolution or dissolution.

Finally, in regards to sexual activity, the husbands had more than their wives. The wives were clearly monogamous. This fact illustrates the double standard which exists in these relationships. Many of the wives could accept their husband's same-sex activities, but did not find that behavior acceptable in themselves. Most of the men were never confronted with their wives' sexual activity outside the relationship. However, many of the men admitted to potential discomfort with such a situation. None of the relationships developed an open-marriage contract similar to that described by Kohn and Matusow (1980) in their description of their "bisexual marriage."

The finding that the amount of emotional involvement with male partners was negatively correlated with sexual satisfaction suggests that this greater emotional involvement may interfere with the marital-sexual relationship. Yet, this has not been determined as cause and effect and must be carefully interpreted. One possible area of exploration is whether or not emotional involvement may be a factor in creating or affecting marital-sexual satisfaction. Would restricting the emotional involvement with male partners lead to greater sexual satisfaction in the marriage, and, thus, greater self-esteem and marital adjustment?

CONCLUSION

Even though this study is an improvement on earlier studies in terms of follow-up and information gathered from both the husband and the wife, longer periods of follow-up are still necessary. Many of these couples indicated uncertainty about the future; all the couples were still struggling, and it is uncertain how they will continue to adjust. Basically, this study has reinforced the notion that some marriages can survive and be relatively satisfactory, given the fact that the husband is bisexual. Positive self-esteem of the individuals seems to be related to sexual satisfaction and marital satisfaction. The hypothesis that the degree of open communication in the marital relationship is related to higher marital satisfaction was confirmed by this study. Acceptance and understanding is still an important ingredient of success. Positive self-esteem of husband and wife, independence, love, caring, respect and commitment; all of these contribute to successful adjustment. These factors can counterbalance the ongoing conflict created by the husband's bisexuality.

REFERENCES

Bozett, F. (1981). Gay fathers: Identify conflict resolution through integrative sanctioning. *Alternative Lifestyles, 4,* 90-101.

Brownfain, J. J. (1985). A study of the married bisexual male: Paradox and resolution. *Journal of Homosexuality, 11*(1/2), 173-188.

Carnes, P. (1983). *The sexual addiction.* Minneapolis, MN: Compcare Publications.

Coleman, E. (1981/1982a). Bisexual and gay men in heterosexual marriage: Conflicts and resolutions in therapy. *Journal of Homosexuality, 7*(2/3), 93-103.

Coleman, E. (1981/1982b). Developmental stages of the coming out process. *Journal of Homosexuality, 7*(2/3), 31-43.

Dank, B. M. (1973). *The development of a homosexual identity: Antecedents and consequences.* Unpublished doctoral dissertation, University of Wisconsin, Madison, WI.

Fitts, W. H. (1965). *Manual, Tennessee self-concept scale.* Nashville: Counselor Recording & Tests.

Gochros, H. (1978). Counseling gay husbands. *Journal of Sex Education and Therapy, 4,* 6-10.

Hammersmith, S. K., & Weinberg, M. S. (1973). Homosexual identity: Commitment, adjustment, and significant others. *Sociometry, 36,* 56-70.

Klein, F. (1978). *The bisexual option.* New York: Arbor House.

Kohn, B., & Matusow, A. (1980). *Barry and Alice.* Englewood Cliffs, NJ: Prentice-Hall.

Latham, J. D., & White, G. D. (1978). Coping with homosexual expression within heterosexual marriages: Five case studies. *Journal of Sex and Marital Therapy, 4,* 198-212.

Locke, H. J., & Wallace, K. M. (1959). Short marital adjustment and prediction tests: Their reliability and validity. *Marriage and Family Living, 21,* 251-255.

LoPiccolo, J., & Steger, J. C. (1974). The sexual interaction inventory. A new instrument for assessment of sexual dysfunction. *Archives of Sexual Behavior, 3,* 585-595.

Malone, J. (1980). *Straight women/Gay men.* New York: Dial Press.

Matteson, D. R. (1985). Bisexual men in marriage: Is a positive homosexual identity and stable marriage possible? *Journal of Homosexuality, 11*(1/2), 149-171.

Miller, B. (1979a). Lifestyles of gay fathers. In M. Levine (Ed.), *Gay men: The sociology of male homosexuality* (pp. 239-252). New York: Harper & Row.

Miller, B. (1979b). Gay fathers and their children. *The Family Coordinator, 28,* 544-552.

Nahas, R., & Turley, M. (1979). *The new couple: Women and gay men.* New York: Seaview Books.

Ross, H. L. (1971). Modes of adjustment and married homosexuals. *Social Problems, 188,* 385-393.

Weinberg, M. S., & Williams, C. J. (1974). *Male homosexuals: Their problems and adaptations.* New York: Oxford University Press.

Wolf, T. J. (1985). Marriages of bisexual men. *Journal of Homosexuality, 11*(1/2), 135-148.

Perceived Sexual Satisfaction and Marital Happiness of Bisexual and Heterosexual Swinging Husbands

Dwight Dixon, JD, PhD

Basic Research Service

San Diego

ABSTRACT. This study compared the sexual satisfaction and marital happiness of 50 bisexual and 50 heterosexual married male volunteers. All participants chosen were in swinging marriages. Age, length of current marriages, and socioeconomic status were matched and controlled between samples. The bisexual sample reported: (a) significantly more frequent orgasms with females, from masturbation, and from all sexual activities combined; and (b) a significantly greater incidence of orgasms from fantasies or dreams. Although both samples gave high ratings to their sexual satisfaction and marital happiness, both measures were rated significantly higher by the heterosexual males.

A demonstrated need exists (Dixon, 1984; MacDonald, 1981, 1983) for more data with which to understand persons with bisexual orientations. Almost nothing is known about how a bisexual orientation affects relationships. MacDonald (1981) observed that "we have no idea . . . to what extent a bisexual orientation facilitates or inhibits marital adjustments" (p. 24).

Most people rate marital happiness as a very important factor in their lives (Rhyne, 1981). Glenn and Weaver (1981) concluded that "the estimated contribution of marital happiness [to one's overall happiness] is far greater than the estimated contribution of any [other] kinds of satisfaction" (p. 161), and that "the most reasonable conclusion to be drawn about marriage and personal happiness in the contemporary United States is that for most adults happiness depends upon having a good marriage more than anything else" (p. 166).

Dr. Dixon is the President of the Western Region of the Society for the Scientific Study of Sex, President of the Institute for Advanced Study of Human Sexuality Alumni Association, and a principal researcher at Basic Research Service. Requests for reprints or further information may be addressed to the author, c/o Basic Research Service, P.O. Box 9591, San Diego, CA 92109.

By its nature, bisexual behavior involves contemporaneous sexual activity with more than one person, which for a married person means engaging in extramarital sex (EMS). It follows that bisexuality may pose a threat to marital happiness.

Extramarital sex is seen by many authorities (e.g., Edwards & Booth, 1976; Maykovich, 1976; Thompson, 1983; Whitehurst, 1969) to be associated with, if not indicative of, low levels of marital happiness. Furthermore, Edwards and Booth (1976), Glass and Wright (1977), and Johnson (1970) all have shown that the relationship between marital or coital dissatisfaction and EMS is stronger and more consistent for men than for women. If so, it follows that married men who are bisexually active would register greater marital dissatisfaction than would heterosexual married men not engaging in EMS. However, aside from the general correlation of EMS with greater marital dissatisfaction, there still remains the question of the influence of a husband's bisexuality on his marriage.

To control for the effect of EMS, and to isolate and assess the effect of bisexuality on men's marital happiness, the author decided to study samples from two groups of married men, one bisexual and one heterosexual, both of which regularly participated in EMS. Because sexual activity is a central ingredient in bisexual and heterosexual EMS, this study inquired into the sources from which the two samples gained sexual satisfaction, and the frequency of orgasms derived from those sources. Both samples were composed of married male subjects who, together with their respective spouses, occasionally engaged in swinging. Swinging is defined, for the purpose of this study, as an activity wherein a married couple, with each other's knowledge and consent, engage in sexual activity with one or more other persons.

Most studies of swingers agree that in the United States the population of male swingers is composed predominantly of Caucasian, middle-class, married, fairly well-educated suburbanites in their 20s and 30s, including, however, sizeable groups of exceptions to each of those categories (Bartell, 1970, 1971; Gilmartin, 1978; Margolis & Rubenstein, 1972; Smith & Smith, 1970, 1974). It was from such a population that this research drew its samples.

METHOD

Sample

Gathering

Participants were contacted at social and educational functions frequented by swingers, by answering and placing ads in swingers' contact publications, and by referrals. All participants lived in California,

Oregon, or Washington. The general purpose of the research was briefly explained to all persons contacted. They were assured that both the identities and responses of all participants would be held in strict confidence.

Instructions and Instruments

Each qualified person who participated received material which included: (a) a 27-item questionnaire designed by the author to gather the necessary demographic, behavioral, and opinion data; (b) a Bem Sex-Role Inventory designed to measure sex-role adherence (these results not reported in this article); (c) a written statement about the general purpose of the study, identifying the researcher, assuring the confidentiality of responses, and requesting the respondent not to discuss his answers with his spouse until after he had completed and returned the questionnaires.

Participants were reminded that they would remain anonymous. They were also informed that when a question asked for a definite number (like number of sex partners), they should supply only that.

In order to construct separate samples of bisexual and heterosexual respondents, the questionnaire asked all respondents to indicate whether they were bisexual (defined as relating sexually to some men and to some women), homosexual (defined as relating sexually only to men), or heterosexual (defined as relating sexually only to women). No respondent indicated a homosexual orientation.

Bisexual and Heterosexual Samples

Selection

To be included in the bisexual sample, a respondent must have positively indicated both a self-identity as a bisexual and postpubertal genital sexual experience with females in addition to his wife and with at least one male. To be included in the heterosexual sample, a respondent had to have self-identified as a heterosexual, had postpubertal genital sexual experience with females in addition to his wife, and to have reported no more than incidental (accidental or one-time) postpubertal genital sexual contact with another male. Based upon this classification scheme, all subjects were placed in either a heterosexual or a bisexual pool of respondents.

To control for the effects of age, length of current marriage, and socioeconomic status as variables, samples were used which had been matched on the basis of those three factors. As responses were received, each member of one sample was compared in terms of those factors and, if possible, matched to a member of the other sample using predetermined criteria (described below) of closeness of fit of the three factors. Also, the sample means of age, length of current marriage, and socioeconomic status, respectively, were matched until equal or nearly equal.

A total of 133 responses were received and compared before the 50 acceptable matched pairs were found and the respective group means, standard deviations, medians, and ranges for the three crucial demographic items were found to be acceptable.

Identification

For purposes of brevity, at times in this report the bisexual sample is referred to as the "Bi sample" and the heterosexual sample is referred to as the "Hetero sample."

Statistical Treatment

Because the matching was done only for purposes of matching the two samples as closely as was reasonably possible on the three mentioned demographic items, no other use of the pairs, as such, was made in this study. Because this study is not based on the use of a stratified random sample population, it is being reported and should be interpreted as a description only of the two samples involved.

All t and z values were attained using two-tailed tests. Whenever two samples are being compared using a t value, and one of the samples has a small n ($n < 30$), adjusted degrees of freedom were used.

Demographics

Ages

In the selected pairs, the maximum age difference allowed was 5 years. The maximum was acceptable only if there was a close match between the subjects on the other two demographic matching variables. Thirty percent of the pairs had less than a year's difference in ages, and only 6% had a 5-year difference. The matching produced identical age medians of 38 for both the Bi sample and the Hetero sample. The Bi-sample mean of 39.3 ($SD = 10.1$) and the Hetero-sample mean of 39.1 ($SD = 9.6$) were close to equal ($z = 0.13$, $p = .90$). Ages in the Bi sample ranged from 22 to 60, and in the Hetero sample, from 21 to 64.

Length of Current Marriages

The predetermined maximum permissible marriage-length difference between pairmates for marriages under 20 years in length was 5 years. Fifty-six percent of the pairs had a difference of one year or less in length of marriages. Just 6% of pairs had more than a 5-year difference. The matching produced identical means of 10.5 years of duration of current marriages, and Bi-sample and Hetero-sample standard deviations of 9.1 and 9.2, respectively ($z = 0.01, p = .99$). Bi-sample marriages ranged in length from 1.2 to 37.8 years, and Hetero-sample marriages ranged from 0.8 to 34.8 years.

Socioeconomic Status

A number was assigned to six categories of educational attainment and to six of total marital annual income. The lowest education and the lowest income categories were each assigned the number 1, and the highest, the number 6. Adding the two numbers together indicated the subject's socio-economic status number (SSN). The maximum permissible difference in SSNs between any two pairmates was 2.

There was no difference in SSNs in 30% of the pairs, a difference of 1 in 44% of the pairs, and a difference of 2 in 26% of the pairs. The means (3.4) and the standard deviations (1.2) of the SSNs for the Bi and Hetero samples were identical ($z = 0, p = 1.0$).

Race

Ninety-six percent of respondents in each sample were Caucasian, 4% were Black.[1] Because of the overwhelming predominance of Caucasians no analysis was based on racial breakdown.

RESULTS

Beginning Multimale Sexual Activity[2]

The Bi-sample subjects typically had not begun engaging in sexual activities with another male until the subjects were past the age of 21 ($M = 21.8, SD = 13.5$), but the ages at which that activity began varied widely (6 to 58). A mean of 18 years ($SD = 13.5$) had elapsed since that first incident; however, again a wide range was involved (1 to 50 years).

Number of Sex Partners

The Bi sample had had a mean of 5.7 ($SD = 5.5$) male sex partners in the last 12 months; the range being 1 to 30. Both samples had had much larger numbers of female sex partners in the same 12-month period. The means for female partners in the period were: Bi sample, 17.1 ($SD = 20.0$); Hetero sample, 21.4 ($SD = 38.5$). Those standard deviations and the ranges (Bi sample, 2 to 96; Hetero sample, 2 to 250) were statistically insignificant ($z = 0.43$).

Swinging Activities

In examining 11 different swinging activities, this study found only two significant differences between samples: (1) The Bi sample (88%) was more prone to engage in threesomes, involving the subject and his spouse and a third person, than was the Hetero sample (68%) ($z = 2.41$; $p = .02$); and (2) The spouses of the bisexual subjects (18%) were more likely than the spouses of the heterosexual subjects (4%) to separately date without the subject doing so ($z = 2.24$; $p = .02$).

Orgasms

In order better to isolate frequency statistics regarding orgasm from masturbation, the author asked respondents to exclude counting orgasms from masturbation when responding to questions about frequencies of orgasm in relation to activity with partners.

With Female Partners

As seen in Table 1, the Bi sample had significantly more orgasms in a typical week from both vaginal and oral sexual activities with female partners than did the Hetero sample.

The total number of orgasms reported by bisexual subjects from sexual activities with female partners ($M = 9.3$, $SD = 9.2$) was significantly higher than the number of such orgasms reported by the Hetero sample ($M = 6.6$, $SD = 4.2$; $z = 1.95$, $p = .05$).

With Male Partners: Bi Sample

Ninety percent of the Bi sample had had an orgasm in the preceding 12 months during sexual activity with male partners, while 2% had not in that time period, and another 8% had never had an orgasm from such activity. Four percent of the Bi sample had had only one orgasm in the preceding 12 months from multimale sexual activity, and another 10% reported having had only two orgasms in that period from multimale activity.

During the preceding 12-month period: (a) orgasms from multimale oral sexual activity were experienced by 86% of the Bi sample, at a mean frequency of 0.3 orgasms per week ($SD = 0.4$); (b) orgasms from multimale anal intercourse were experienced by 56% of the Bi sample, at a

Table 1

Orgasms During Last Twelve Months From Sex Activities With All
Female Sex Partners

Measure	Sample	Vaginal Intercourse	Oral Sex	Anal Intercourse	Other[a]
Active	Bi	50	48	34	26
ns	Hetero	50	44	25	19
Active					
weekly	Bi	5.5*[b]	2.8**[c]	0.4[d]	1.7[e]
mean	Hetero	4.3	1.9	0.5	0.9
	Bi	1.6	1.1	0.6	2.2
SD	Hetero	2.8	2.0	0.8	1.0
Active					
weekly	Bi	4.0	2.0	0.2	1.0
median	Hetero	4.0	1.0	0.2	0.5
Active					
weekly	Bi	1.0–35.0	Nil–15.0	Nil–9.0	Nil–11.5
range	Hetero	0.2–15.0	Nil– 8.0	Nil–4.0	Nil– 4.0

[a]Excluding masturbation. [b]$z = 2.56$. [c]$z = 2.78$. [d]$t(43) = -1.39$.
[e]$t(32) = 0.96$.
*$p = .01$. **$p = .005$

mean frequency of 0.2 orgasms a week (*SD* = 0.4); and (c) orgasms
from "other" (unspecified) multimale activities were experienced by
36% of the Bi sample, at a mean frequency of 0.2 orgasms per week
(*SD* = 0.3).

From Masturbation

A larger percentage of the Bi sample (96%) than the Hetero sample (82%) reported they had engaged in masturbation in the preceding 12 months. The weekly frequency of such orgasms ($M = 2.7$, $SD = 2.8$) is significantly greater than that reported by the Hetero sample ($M = 1.5$, $SD = 2.0$; $z = 3.70$, $p = .000$).

From Fantasy or Dreams

Significantly more members of the Bi sample (38%) than the Hetero sample (16%) ($z = 2.48$, $p = .01$) reported having had orgasms during the preceding 12 months from fantasy or dreams. However, the active weekly mean frequencies were not significantly different ($t[25] = -0.45$). Neither age ($t[15] = -0.43$) nor length of current marriage ($t[14] = -0.50$) was found to be significantly related to active incidence of orgasms from fantasy or dreams.

From Other Sources

The questionnaires also asked for frequencies of orgasms from all sources other than those previously mentioned. Specific reference in the question was made to the fact that the question included, but was not limited to, orgasms with animals. There was a significantly larger active incidence of this unspecified orgasmic activity within the Bi sample (36%) than within the Hetero sample (18%); ($z = 2.03$, $p = .04$). However, there was no significant difference in the active weekly mean frequencies reported from the two samples ($t[25] = 1.36$). A very wide range for the weekly frequency of this activity by the active Bi sample was found (nil to 28.0), whereas the corresponding range for the active Hetero sample was a more modest 0.2 to 8.0.

Total

As shown in Table 2, the Bi sample had, with or without multimale sexual activity being considered, significantly more orgasms during the preceding 12 months from all sources combined than did the Hetero sample. The wide ranges for both samples in Table 2 are striking.

Sexual Satisfaction

Five questions were asked concerning the subjects' satisfaction with various aspects of their sex lives. Four of the topics covered are noted in Table 3. The fifth topic, which concerned multimale sexual satisfaction,

Table 2

Total Orgasms During Last Twelve Months Compared without and

with Inclusion of Multimale Sexual Activity

Measure	Bisexual[a]		Heterosexual[a]
	Without Multi-male Sexual Activity	With Multi-male Sexual Activity	
Weekly mean	14.5*[b]	14.9**[c]	8.6
SD	14.0	13.9	4.7
Weekly median	10.1	10.8	8.0
Weekly range	2.4-72.1	2.4-72.2	1.9-21.5

[a]n = 50 for each.

[b]z = 2.84. [c]z = 3.03.

*p = .005. **p = .002.

is described separately below. On each question, subjects were asked to indicate on a 7-point scale the level of their satisfaction or dissatisfaction. In general, both samples rated their marital sex, extramarital heterosexual sex, swinging, and overall sex lives as "usually," or "always or almost always" satisfying, the top two categories of satisfaction.

Numerical values of 1 through 7 were assigned to the possible responses, with the value 1 indicating the least satisfaction and the value 7 the most. Because within samples the responses did not present a reasonable approximation of a normal distribution curve, a nonparametric test was used to compare the samples.

The Hetero sample registered significantly greater overall satisfaction with their sex lives, the only significant difference found. Interestingly, the Bi sample found their multimale activities the least satisfying. That relatively low level of satisfaction does not appear to be attributable to the gender of the sex partner, for a correlation was found between how satisfied a bisexual subject was with his female partners and how satisfied he was with his male partners (r = .35 p = < .02). He was apt to be as

Table 3

Sample Comparisons of Marital, Extramarital Heterosexual, Swinging, and Overall Sexual Satisfaction

Equivalent Satisfaction With	Mean Rank		z^{b}
	Bi Sample[a]	Hetero Sample[a]	
Marital sex	48.96	53.92	0.61
Extramarital heterosexual sex	49.35	51.65	0.42
Swinging sex	48.19	52.81	0.82
Overall sex life	43.37	57.63	2.64*

[a]$\underline{n}$ = 50 for each. [b]Mann-Whitney U test was used, with adjustments made for ties.

*$\underline{p}$ = .008.

satisfied or dissatisfied with his sex partners of one sex as he was with his sex partners of the other sex.

Marital Happiness

Marital happiness was assessed two ways: (a) the subjects' perceptions of how their spouses felt about their marriages, and (b) their own feelings about their spouses and their marriages.

To measure how they felt about their spouses, subjects were asked to rate the likelihood that they would again marry their spouses.

A large majority of each sample gave the two highest ratings (out of seven possible ratings) to questions about their perceptions of their own marital happiness, and about the likelihood that the subjects would again marry their spouses. However, as seen in Table 4, the Hetero sample registered significantly greater happiness and satisfaction than the Bi sample in all three categories.

DISCUSSION

The purpose of this study was to determine if a husband's bisexuality, per se, is likely to have an effect upon his sexual satisfaction and marital happiness. The results indicate that, even when the factor of extramarital sex (EMS) is controlled, some significant effects on one of four measures of sexual satisfaction and on three measures of marital happiness appear in association with a comparison of bisexuality and heterosexuality.

Table 4

Sample Comparisons of Indices of Marital Happiness

| | Mean Rank | | |
Indices Compared	Bi Sample[a]	Hetero Sample[a]	z[b]
Subjects' estimates of spouses' overall current marital happiness	42.84	58.16	2.85**
Likelihood subjects would marry spouses now if not already	44.92	56.08	2.20*
Subjects' ratings of overall marital happiness	41.15	59.85	3.50**

[a]n = 50 for each. [b]Mann-Whitney U test was used, with adjustments made for ties.

*p<.05.   **p = .000.

Sexual Satisfaction

Orgasms

The Bi sample far exceeded the Hetero sample in frequencies of orgasm derived from sexual activities with female partners, through masturbation, and from all sources combined, and in incidence of orgasms from dreams or fantasy and (unspecified) sources other than sexual partners and self-stimulation.

The 96% of the Bi sample which was currently active in masturbation activity is a spectacularly high figure when compared to Kinsey, Pomeroy, and Martin's (1948) reported data. In that study, the age group of married males (age 21 to 30) who had the greatest percent of masturbators had an active incidence of only 48%. Also, the 2.7 weekly mean frequency of that activity by the Bi sample was many times higher than the 0.45 weekly-mean masturbation frequency of the age group of males reported in the Kinsey study as most active in that regard.

It is significant, but as yet unexplained, that 8% of the Bi sample had never had an orgasm from sexual activity with a male partner.[3] The incidence of orgasms reported by the Bi sample from sources outside of those specified in the questionnaires is a finding worthy of further investigation. Over one-third of the Bi sample (36%) were regularly (more than once a week) having an orgasm from unspecified sources. Up to 28 orgasms per week from unspecified sources were reported by at least one bisexual subject.[4]

With the Bi sample having 73% more orgasms from all sources in the preceding year than did the Hetero sample, the Bi sample's mean frequency of orgasm is believed to be one of the highest recorded for a sample of males of similar age. This figure is over three and a half times the highest frequency of such orgasms reported by Kinsey et al. (1948) for males within the age parameters of this study.

Orgasmic data were sought as an aid to understanding possible differences between samples in sexual satisfaction or marital happiness. The results show that both frequency and incidence of orgasm from various sources may not (and did not in this case) predict the comparative level of either sexual satisfaction or marital happiness of bisexual and heterosexual husbands.

General

Since there is no significant difference between the Bi and Hetero samples as to satisfaction with their sexuality with female partners (including their wives) or in their swinging activities, the finding of a significantly lower level of satisfaction by the Bi sample in comparison to the

Hetero sample regarding their overall sex lives raises questions about the source of that difference.

Although this study does not answer those questions, one might speculate that the Bi sample's multimale activity may play a part in that difference. That conclusion can be supported by the fact that the Bi sample rated their multimale activities to be less satisfying than any of the other.

That lower satisfaction level for multimale sexual activity may be the result of several contributing factors: the cultural antipathy toward such activity (Ford & Beach, 1951; Klein, 1978; Spiers, 1976); the generally adverse reaction of the swinging community toward multimale sexuality (O'Neill & O'Neill, 1970; Palson & Palson, 1972; Ramey, 1972; Stephenson, 1973; Symonds, 1971; Ziskin & Ziskin, 1974); and the possibly negative reaction of some of the bisexual subjects' wives to their husbands' bisexuality. In her article elsewhere in this issue, J. K. Dixon (1985) reports that, ironically, a substantial portion of swinging wives who are themselves bisexual maintain strongly adverse views about multimale sexuality.

Marital Happiness

As might be expected from the foregoing, something did affect the marital happiness of the Bi sample, for their ratings of it were significantly lower than those of the Hetero sample. However, that is not to say that as a group the marriages in either sample were unhappy. On the contrary, both samples revealed high levels of marital happiness.

The two significant differences in swinging activities found between samples can be possibly linked to the Bi sample's lower level of marital happiness. Swinging is primarily a couple-oriented activity, yet the Bi sample was much more inclined to be active in sexual situations where either the couple or the wife alone was involved with only one other person.

Although this study did not explore the causes of the sample differences, it is hoped that knowing such differences exist will spur further research into the marital and sexual relationships of bisexual men.

NOTES

1. From the author's personal experience, those percentages fairly accurately represent the actual ratio by which those two races may be found in the global swinging population of the geographical area involved.

2. The term "multimale sexual activity" is used to refer to sexual activity involving two or more males because it is a term neutral of connotations regarding the sexual orientation or the intent of the persons involved in the acts. Refer to the article by J. K. Dixon (1985) in this issue for further explanation.

3. In an article elsewhere in this issue, J. K. Dixon (1985) reports finding in her sample of bisexual swinging wives an identical 8% who had not had an orgasm from same-sex sexual activity.

4. The questionnaire specifically mentioned that the question referred to, among other sources

not previously covered, sex with animals. Based upon the results of this study, the author is currently conducting research on the subject of bestiality. Preliminary results are indicating a preponderance of respondents are bisexual males. Another possible source for the reported orgasms is sadomasochistic activities, in which the other person involved is often not considered to be a "sex partner."

REFERENCES

Bartell, G. D. (1970). Group sex among the mid-Americans. *The Journal of Sex Research, 6,* 113-130.

Bartell, G. D. (1971). *Group sex.* New York: Peter H. Wyden.

Dixon, J. K. (1985). Sexuality and relationship changes following the commencement of bisexuality after age thirty by a sample of wives. *Journal of Homosexuality, 11*(1/2), 000-000.

Dixon, J. K. (1984). The commencement of bisexual activity in swinging married women over age thirty. *The Journal of Sex Research, 20,* 71-90.

Edwards, J. N., & Booth, A. (1976). Sexual behavior in and out of marriage: An assessment of correlates. *Journal of Marriage and the Family, 38,* 73-81.

Ford, C. S., & Beach, F. A. (1951). *Patterns of sexual behavior.* New York: Harper & Row.

Gilmartin, B. G. (1978). *The Gilmartin report.* Secaucus, NJ: Citadel.

Glass, S. P., & Wright, T. L. (1977). The relationship of extramarital sex, length of marriage and sex differences on marital satisfaction and romanticism: Athanasiou's data reanalyzed. *Journal of Marriage and the Family, 39,* 691-703.

Glenn, N. D., & Weaver, C. N. (1981). The contribution of marital happiness to global happiness. *Journal of Marriage and the Family, 43,* 161-168.

Johnson, R. E. (1970). Some correlates of extramarital coitus. *Journal of Marriage and the Family, 32,* 449-456.

Kinsey, A. C., Pomeroy, W. B., & Martin, C. E. (1948). *Sexual behavior in the human male.* Philadelphia: W. B. Saunders.

Klein, F. (1978). *The bisexual option.* New York: Arbor House.

MacDonald, A. P., Jr. (1981). Bisexuality: Some comments on research and theory. *Journal of Homosexuality, 6*(3), 21-35.

MacDonald, A. P., Jr. (1983). A little bit of lavender goes a long way: A critique of research on sexual orientation. *The Journal of Sex Research, 19,* 94-100.

Margolis, H. F., & Rubenstein, P. M. (1972). *The groupsex tapes.* New York: Paperback Library.

Maykovich, M. K. (1976). Attitudes versus behavior in extramarital sexual-relations. *Journal of Marriage and the Family, 38,* 693-699.

O'Neill, G. C., & O'Neill, N. (1970). Patterns in group sexual activity. *The Journal of Sex Research, 6,* 101-112.

Palson, C., & Palson, R. (1972). Swinging in wedlock. *Society, 9,* 28-37.

Ramey, J. W. (1972). Emerging patterns of behavior in marriage: Deviations or innovations? *The Journal of Sex Research, 8,* 6-30.

Rhyne, D. (1981). Bases of marital satisfaction among men and women. *Journal of Marriage and the Family, 43,* 941-955.

Smith, J. R., & Smith, L. G. (1970). Co-marital sex and the sexual freedom movement. *The Journal of Sex Research, 6,* 131-142.

Smith, L. G., & Smith, J. R. (Eds.). (1974). *Beyond monogamy: Recent studies of sexual alternatives in marriage.* Baltimore, MD: Johns Hopkins University Press.

Spiers, E. D. (1976). The no-man's land of the bisexual. *Journal of Behavior Technology Methods and Therapy, 22,* 6-11.

Stephenson, R. M. (1973). Involvement in deviance: An example and some theoretical implications. *Social Problems, 21,* 173-190.

Symonds, C. (1971). Sexual mate-swapping: Violations of norms and reconciliation of guilt. In J. M. Henslin (Ed.), *Studies in the sociology of sex* (pp. 81-109). New York: Appleton-Century-Crofts.

Thompson, A. P. (1983). Extramarital sex: A review of the research literature. *The Journal of Sex Research, 19,* 1-22.

Whitehurst, R. N. (1969). Extramarital sex: Alienation or extension of normal behavior. In G. Neubeck (Ed.), *Extramarital Relations* (pp. 130-157). Englewood Cliffs, NJ: Prentice-Hall.

Ziskin, J., & Ziskin, M. (1974, January). 3 in a bed: The new thrill seekers. *Sexology,* pp. 30-34.

The Bisexual Scene in New York City

Chuck Mishaan
New York City

The bisexual community is not as publicly active today as it was several years ago, a phenomenon especially true for the community as organized and directed specifically for and by people who define themselves as bisexual in preference or behavior. Organized community development seems to have matured rather quickly in the New York City area, flourishing for less than 10 years before again becoming more of an adjunct to the homosexual community. That is not to say that the major New York City bisexual groups, including the Bi-Forum, the Bisexual Center and Both Sides Now, were substantially focused on the needs of bisexual people. On the contrary, these groups were of major import in the late 1970s and early 1980s in developing, along with the gay community, an enlarged sense of what sexual orientation was about, and how to serve the needs of the substantial numbers of people who did not identify with mainstream heterosexual values.

It seems now that many of the people involved in the bisexual community have been able to develop a strong enough sense of personal identity to establish and nourish the kinds of relationships that are appropriate for themselves, and that the communal effort of identification and support has become less crucial. Of course, I am speaking of the active group of participants who, in the course of long self-examination and social contact, were able to understand themselves better, and the special needs that their style of living creates. It was, and is, true that for many people, the concept of bisexuality, even its very existence, remains obscure and elusive.

Reprint requests may be addressed to the author, 119 East 84th Street, New York, NY 10028.

The task of reaching and educating these people has been continued, to some degree, under the aegis of the gay community; specifically, the monthly rap groups at Identity House, the bisexual discussion groups headed by gay/bisexual professionals, and the thriving forum of Gay Fathers for homosexual and bisexual fathers.

Despite the experiential common ground between the gay and bisexual communities, and the amount of work that has been done in the field in the past 10 years, such a shared support network is less than satisfactory. Understanding between the two groups has not greatly increased, and the cross-nurturing which has developed has left both sides somewhat dissatisfied. I find that the clients with whom I work, who identify themselves as bisexual, do not feel that the gay community provides them with the support and contact that they seek. There remains for them the sense that the gay community will affirm only a part of their sexual identity. This problem becomes acute at different times in a person's relationship experience, and seems more acute for bisexual women than for bisexual men.

The Bisexual Forum of New York began in 1975 under the leadership of Fred Klein, MD, and Chuck Mishaan. It began as a social, educational, and support group seeking to encourage awareness of bisexual issues in a non-threatening and non-judgmental environment. Discussion groups were held weekly and other activities such as parties, workshops and lectures were added as the membership grew. In 1977, a monthly newsletter was started, and published more or less regularly for four years. At its peak in 1980, the Bi-Forum involved over 200 active members, and maintained a mailing list of several thousand. The last official meeting of the Bisexual Forum took place in May of 1983. Many of the Forum participants have maintained informal contact, but no formal programs exist at the present time.

One of the great accomplishments of the gay movement in the recent past has been the strong and effective move toward political action and influence. This dramatic change in the politics of sex has helped to provide a protective umbrella of awareness and community, if not yet strong legal shelter, under which the individual could explore and affirm his or her sexuality. It is important to note that, very consistently, the bisexual community, at least outside of San Francisco, has refused to become politically identified and active. The strong consensus at meetings of the Bi-Forum, for instance, was that political action or commitment would polarize and weaken a coalition of people whose only unifying theme was its bisexual identity. Forum participants ranged widely across the Kinsey scale in terms of self-identity, interest and behavior, and many individuals became uncomfortable with the idea of political alliance outside the sphere of intimate relationships. The legacy of this reluctance has been the absence of an organized bisexual movement.

One could easily, but perhaps hastily, conclude that these remarks confirm the image of the bisexual person as an uncommitted individual more interested in casual intimacy than in directed, mobilized activity and relationships. I must caution against this conclusion since, the bisexual who has seriously sought for identity and community among others similarly identified, the challenge and the journey has led rather to the understanding of the special nature of his or her situation. To model one's relationships and choices according to one's special needs and circumstances is difficult because each situation is different. Even with the support and sharing of others, a person must make very individual, and sometimes complex, choices.

In summary, it seems natural that a bisexual community would not be long-lived as an organized, focused effort, and would appear that the New York experience has confirmed this. That other communities have been able to generate greater momentum speaks to the youth of our understanding. There are many individuals who have become self-aware and active in the exploration of their social and sexual lives, and who consider themselves bisexual, but yet do not consider themselves part of an identified bisexual community. They are, to a large extent, however, integrating a complex sexuality into their lives, an achievement that can be traced to the once active bisexual community.

A Profile of
the San Francisco Bisexual Center

Maggi Rubenstein, PhD
Cynthia Ann Slater
San Francisco

To promote a more sex-positive environment for bisexual persons, a bisexual center was started in San Francisco in 1976. Prior to that time many bisexual persons in the San Francisco Bay Area had hoped for the formation of a center, but felt it was impossible because of the lack of time, energy and funding. Dr. Rubenstein's meeting with Dr. Leve early in 1976 began to change that view.

Dr. Leve had been searching for a place to meet and talk to bisexual women and men, but was unable to find one apart from established homosexual or heterosexual organizations. As they talked about this lack of community service for bisexual people, they realized that they already knew many bisexual women and men in the Bay Area who might be interested in working together. Leve offered financial help and assistance, and he and Rubenstein committed themselves to work for at least a year or two on developing the center. They called friends and associates together to see how interested they might be in supporting such a venture. Out of this first meeting grew the Bisexual Center, offering a base of support and a sense of community for people who were either defining themselves as bisexual, or exploring bisexuality as a possible option.

Multi-disciplinary services, with counseling, discussion groups, social programs, a newsletter, and speakers' bureau would be offered, and for those ends a working committee was begun. Its first activities took place in rented office space and private homes. Many letters were received in response to press releases that were mailed to various newspapers in the San Francisco Bay Area. The Center began in September of 1976 and became official in November of that year with the publication of its first newsletter. Its progressive public statement declared:

> The Bisexual Center is united in struggling for the rights of all women and men to develop as whole, androgynous beings. We support relationships between persons of the same as well as the other

Reprint requests may be sent c/o Dr. Rubenstein, 1523 Franklin Street, San Francisco, CA 94109.

sex. These relationships may include relating spiritually, socially, emotionally, sensually, sexually and intellectually. We also support the choice of a celibate lifestyle. We support people who have been oppressed because of sexual preference, gender, age or ethnic group. We encourage and support people struggling to bring about equality in areas of employment, housing, medical care, and complete sexual information and for the right to engage in the free expression of consenting sexual activity. We support the open expression of affection and touch among people, without such expression necessarily having sexual implications.

On June 30, 1977, the Center held its first press conference. Speakers included Dr. Benjamin Spock, Dr. Harriet Leve, Dr. Phyllis Lyon, Ruth Falk, and Dr. Claude Steiner. These persons spoke out against Anita Bryant's efforts to bar homosexuals from employment as school teachers, and discussed other civil rights issues. Emphasizing that gay concerns were also bisexual concerns, Dr. Leve stated: "It is imperative for bisexuals to support and form a unity with our gay sisters and brothers in order to demand what is rightfully ours." This press conference was featured on two local TV evening news programs and was reported by several radio stations. It also generated articles in *The San Francisco Examiner, The Oakland Tribune*, and *The Bay Area Reporter*. Membership soared to 435 in the next month; the Bisexual Center was on its way.

During the first year of its existence, the Center held its general meetings in members' homes, with some activities held at other locations, such as the National Sex Forum. It began its second year with a meeting at its new office on Market Street. In 1978, it moved to its present headquarters on Hayes Street. The bi-monthly newsletter, groups and workshops, general meetings and panel discussions, counseling referrals, research, and a speakers bureau have continued since then.

The Bisexual Center is run by a Board of Directors. Its bylaws require that this board consist of nine to twenty members, including the President, the Vice President, Treasurer, Secretary, and Chairs of various committees. These committees include the newsletter staff, rap group staff, and social committee. All staff positions are on a volunteer basis. Funding continues to be derived from a mix of private donations, membership fees, newsletter subscriptions, and admission fees to the Center's social events.

Sharing the Center's space and rent is Bisexual Counseling Services, a separate organization. Bisexual Counseling Services consists of interns, residents, and counselors, all of whom must identify as bisexual. Its staff facilitates rap groups, leads workshops, and designs educational programs on bisexuality, as well as provides speakers to many colleges and community and public service organizations throughout the Bay Area.

The Bisexual Counseling Sevice also helps individuals who are having problems involving bisexual issues, provides accurate information, and helps the clients generate a support community.

Within its internal community, the Center has been fairly successful in implementing its objectives, and has also begun to reach out to other communities. The Center provides a place for bisexuals to be together and give each other mutual support, while the various workshops, presentations, and other sponsored activities facilitate communication both between individuals and between the bisexual community and the larger society. Due to the Center's initiative, several local hospitals and community organizations now include education about bisexuality in their training programs. Bay Area colleges and churches find the Center a good source of guest speakers.

The future goals of the Center are more specific: first, to develop theories and techniques for dealing with the problems and concerns of bisexual-identified persons; and second, to have the American Psychological and Psychiatric Associations recognize bisexuality as a valid state of being, rather than as an indication of neurosis.

The major strengths of the Bisexual Center are its relevance in the face of community need, the enthusiasm and diversity of its members, and its non-judgemental policies toward members of the community. The strengths of Bisexual Counseling Services also include its social relevance, innovative approaches, and humanistic stances. Major weaknesses of the Bisexual Center include its exclusive reliance on volunteer resources and its lack of extensive financial resources.

The clientele of the Bisexual Center and Bisexual Counseling Services is multi-cultural and multi-racial: 70% Caucasian, 10% Black, 15% Latino, and 5% Asian. Members come from a wide range of socio-economic backgrounds, and their incomes range from welfare levels to above $50,000 annually. Educational levels tend to be higher than those of the general population: a 1978 survey of 100 male members of the Center revealed that 56% had post-graduate degrees.

Parents and relatives of bisexuals often seek help from the Center or from Bisexual Counseling Services. Counselors, researchers, therapists, educators, and others in the helping professions also turn to the Center for information and aid.

The needs and problems of those individuals who use the services of the Bisexual Center or Bisexual Counseling Services are many and varied. Some people seek help in developing social skills, in dealing with relationship concerns. Others address problems involving sexual orientation conflict and transition, as well as other emotional disturbances and conflicts related to bisexual issues.

In the spring of 1983, a new group, Bi-Pol, was formed to address specifically political concerns. Additionally, the Center itself will continue to stimulate development of bisexual-oriented resources in the United Staes and worldwide. Recently, Dr. Rubenstein was invited to speak at the Lesbian/Gay Freedom Day Parade, evidence that The Bisexual Center is dedicated to building coalitions between many communities.

As of 1982, the Bisexual Center of San Francisco was the largest bisexual organization in the United States, with over 550 paid members. David Lourea, President of the Board of Directors of the Bisexual Center, recently stated: "We have actively given support, encouragement and guidelines to newly forming bisexual organizations throughout the country, and to people doing research or doctoral dissertations on bisexual topics." Of the Center's future role, he stated: "Our dream is that there will eventually be a bi-positive, thriving, supporting environment in every major city in the U.S."

Now in 1984, as bisexuals face the AIDS crisis, we need each other more than ever in order to combat homophobia and biphobia and to educate ourselves in a positive way about safe sexual practices.

Chicago Bi-Ways:
An Informal History

George Barr
Chicago

There are many ways to write a history. A factual chronology seems in part appropriate, but to many of us at Chicago Bi-Ways the valuable memories involve times spent with special people willing to share openly their deeper selves. We usually think of an organization as a structure, but often our administrative functions materialized over a cup of coffee, while putting together a newsletter, or meeting somewhere near the train stop.

Like many organizations, Bi-Ways started with a single individual, and a conviction he held concerning individual honesty and freedom of expression. Don was acquainted with the Bisexual Center in San Francisco; upon moving to Chicago, he missed the quality of interpersonal contact and honesty he had experienced in San Francisco. He wondered whether such an organization would be possible in Chicago. He placed an ad in the *Reader* (a weekly free paper) stating that anyone, either bisexual or interested in bisexuality, should respond. From the people who wrote in, Don put together a sheet of quotations, personal reflections, and the possible goals of a bisexual organization.

As background, what is bisexuality? Fundamental to bisexuality is the belief that in each of us there is a masculine-feminine polarity, a masculine side and a feminine side, whatever our gender. Most people, both heterosexuals and homosexuals, go through life attempting to deny this masculine-feminine polarity. They try to complete themselves by finding someone of the opposite (or same) sex who is playing the same game. Such relationships are extremely limited in potential, at best, and are usually unfulfilling. Many argue that the differences between men and women are mostly illusionary, burdensome, restrictive roles that close doors to new ways of relating, and stand in the way of living a more fulfilling life.

Most persons interested in bisexuality support development of relationships with both females and males. These may include spiritual, social, emotional, sensual, sexual, and intellectual ties. Although the

Reprint requests may be sent to the author, c/o Chicago Bi-Ways, P.O. Box A3330, Chicago, IL 60690.

231

open expression of affection and touch among people can occur in these relationships, it does not necessarily have sexual implications. Persons interested in bisexuality also support people who have been oppressed because of sexual preferences, gender, age, or ethnic group.

The first bisexual organizational meeting took place on December 15, 1978. This was followed by a second in January, less than a month later, a sign that interest was growing. The third meeting in March solicited ideas and feedback. In preparation for that meeting, a letter was composed which suggested these goals: (1) publish a bisexual newsletter; (2) hold regular meetings; (3) form a steering committee; (4) provide a responsive ear to those with concerns about sexual orientation; (5) become politically active; and (6) organize social activities.

Attendance at the March meeting was not good, nor at the picnic/beach party. During August, a letter was issued asking for more support, and brought up the issue of funds to cover costs of publishing and mailing.

A new approach took the form of a newsletter. Mary's name not only began to appear in the letters, but she also sponsored a women's group. During the months of October and November, seven activities were held, including women's and mixed drop-in groups, a Halloween Party, a Thanksgiving buffet, and a get-away weekend.

What would we call ourselves? The members were asked:

> It's been suggested that we try to give ourselves a name for our first anniversary. There are two nominations thus far. BOTH—standing for Becoming Our Total Humanity and Bi-Us for Bisexuality—individuality, unity, self. Or we could select something like Chicago Bisexual Forum, TAOS (Together Accepting Our Sensuality); or Chicago Bi-Ways. What do you think?

In addition to the regular monthly activities, a "Christmas with Friends Party" was held December 22. Christmas was remembered, but our first birthday was forgotten, and was not mentioned in the newsletter.

Chicago Bi-Ways is most proud of the members' willingness to help each other. Mary was helped with her moving and subsequently threw a thank you party in her empty apartment. Such feelings of goodwill are often seen in the group.

Activities in March and April of 1980 doubled. They included a pot luck dinner party and spring celebration at Blackhawk Ridge. Events became successes and our fame spread. Letters poured in from Detroit, Indonesia, and Skokie. The letter from Indonesia was from a student in a major university asking to correspond with Bi-Ways because there was no one in Indonesia he could talk with. The established activities continued even as new ones developed. We helped support the Gay Pride Parade, organized a picnic, watched the *Rocky Horror Picture Show*, and afterward stopped at "His and Hers"—a bar that caters to homosexual men and women.

The year 1981 marked the beginning of the third year of Chicago Bi-Ways, and did not go unnoticed. At the January drop-in members shared a cake topped with the words, "By Gosh, By Golly: Bi-Gals, Bi-Guys." The women's support group was rekindled and seasonal activities emerged (e.g., a Valentine's Day Party). There was even a free weekend retreat at the Indiana State Park. Massage parties emerged as another activity. Variations flourished. A "We Welcome the Curious" meeting was held on March 1.

No history is complete without a little romance. Thanksgiving weekend was the wedding of Don, our founder, and Susan, whom he met at a Bi-Ways meeting.

In December of 1981, Chicago Bi-Ways adopted a mascot. His name was Ron, and became known as "Bi-Ron." He was a precocious fellow with a girlfriend called Ronette. A contest was run to determine his looks and character.

In 1982, Bi-Ways started changing its internal organization. Newsletter production changed from an individual to a team task. Each team was responsible for three newsletters. As the organization grew, Chicago Bi-Ways was listed in the directory of Self-Help/Mutual Aid Groups in the Chicago metro area.

On February 1, 1982, Bi-Ways co-sponsored an on-tour lecture by Barry Kohn, co-author of the book, *Barry and Alice: Portrait of a Bisexual Marriage*. He discussed independence within a long-term relationship, and the issues of jealousy, trust, and third persons.

Many Bi-Ways members enjoyed "heated" discussions, but not the kind encountered at Billy and Estelle's Valentine's Day party. During the meeting a fire was discovered in the hall, forcing evacuation of the building. Members helped carry out prized possessions. Two Bi-Ways members broke a window, and helped rescue two small children who may otherwise have been statistics. Members helped Billy and Estelle relocate and took up a collection at the next meeting.

Summer brought outdoor activities. Jerome sponsored a successful jacuzzi party. Barry Kohn returned to Chicago for the Phil Donahue Show, and four Bi-Ways members attended. Don was interviewed about bisexuality, along with the group Review, on a Sunday broadcast on WFYR.

As social activities continued, a committee was formed to consider possibilities of formal governance. The first governance committee meeting took place April 1982. The four major issues were: (1) form an ongoing committee to handle Bi-Ways business, work and finances; (2) produce graphically up-to-date newsletters; (3) open a Bi-Ways checking account to handle funds; and (4) find a larger meeting space for the events that Bi-Ways would officially sponsor. All members met in August to discuss and amend the Committee's proposed charter which was approved. In addition, many personal conflicts arose. The one-time informal social group was turning into an official organization with growing pains. The election of five board members, in accordance with the newly adopted charter, was held in October.

In the spring of 1983, we had our first bi-baby. Don and Susan gave birth to a baby girl on March 25.

The committee of five started out like a dynamo after the election. However, by the following July, no one was taking primary responsibility for activities of the organization. Consequently, there were none during July, August, September and October of 1983. The Board got together for a final time in August, at which time three of the five members chose not to serve another term.

The number of Board members was reduced to three which allowed for better communication. In addition, Charlene arranged for Bi-Ways to utilize space, and the use of a switchboard, with a Chicago homosexual organization that encouraged regular meetings.

The need for support for bisexuals and bisexuality in the Chicago area has given birth to yet another group. Even in some feminist circles, bisexuality is frowned upon. To answer an unmet need, several women got together to develop a feminist-oriented group to meet their special needs concerning bisexuality. Calling themselves "Action Bi-Women," members have sponsored discussion groups and pot luck dinners. There has been exchange and interaction between the two groups; it feels good not to be alone.

A Bibliography on Bisexuality

Charles Steir
Bronx, New York

Aaron, W. (pseudonym). (1972). *Straight: A heterosexual talks about his homosexual past*. New York: Doubleday.

Abrahamsen, D. (1946). *The mind and death of a genius*. New York: Columbia University Press.

Adams, P. (1970). Bisexual conflicts of adolescents with school phobia. *Psychiatry Digest, 31*, 47-49.

Adams, P. (1966). School phobia and bisexual conflict. *American Journal of Psychiatry, 123*, 541-547.

Adler, A. (1910). Der psychische hermaphroditismus in leben und in der neurose. *Fortschritte der Medizin, 38*, 486-493.

Alexander, F. (1933). Bisexual conflict in homosexuality. *Psychoanalytic Quarterly, 2*, 197-201.

Allen, S. (1973, April). Bisexuality: The best of both worlds. *Spare Rib*, pp. 25-26.

Altman, D. (1971). *Homosexual: Oppression and liberation*. New York: Outerbridge & Dienstfrey.

Anderson, S. (1971). *The young bisexuals*. Los Angeles: Centurion Press.

Anxieu, D. (1973, Spring). La bisexualité dans l'autoanalyse de Freud. *Nouvelle Revue Psychoanalyse*, p. 7.

Arce, H. (1979). *The secret life of Tyrone Power: The drama of a bisexual in the spotlight*. New York: Morrow.

Arduin. (1900). Die Frauenfrage und die sexuellen Zwischenstufen. *Jahrbuch für sexuellen Zwischenstufen, 2*, 211-223.

Arieti, S. (Ed.). (1974-75). *American handbook of psychiatry* (2nd Ed.). New York: Basic Books.

Arnaud-Lefoulon, D. (1961). Bisexualité des dieux dans la mythologie hindouaste. *Arcadie, 86*, 82-85.

Bak, R. (1969). The phallic woman: The unbiquitous fantasy in perversions. *Psychoanalytic Quarterly, 38*, 516.
It appears in *Psychoanalytic Study of the Child* (1968). pp. 23, 15-36, with discussion by Greenacre on p. 46.

Reprint requests may be addressed to the author, 3875 Waldo Avenue, Bronx, NY 10463.

Balint, M. (1963). The younger sister and prince charming. *International Journal of Psychoanalysis, 44*, 226-227.

Bartlett, J. (1966). A bisexual fantasy associated with the testes. *Bulletin of the Psychoanalytic Association of New York, 6*(2/3), 23-24.

Bazin, N. (1974). The concept of androgyny: A working bibliography. *Women's Studies, 2*, 217-235.

Bazlin, N. (1977). *Virginia Woolf and the androgynous vision.* New Jersey: Rutgers University Press.

Bell, A. P., & Weinberg, M. S. (1978). *Homosexualities: A study of diversity among men and women.* New York: Simon & Schuster.

Bell, A. P., Weinberg, M. S., & Hammersmith, S. K. (1981). *Sexual preferences: Its development in men and women.* Bloomington, IN: Indiana University Press.

Bell, A. P., (1968). Additional aspects of passivity and female identification in the male. *International Journal of Psychoanalysis, 49*, 640-647.

Benedek, T. (1959). Sexual functions in women and their disturbance. In S. Arieti (Ed.), *American handbook of psychiatry* (pp. 727-748). New York: Basic Books.

Benedek, T. (1973). *Psychoanalytic investigations: Selected papers.* New York: Times Books.

Berezin, M. (1954). Enuresis and bisexual identification. *Journal of the American Psychoanalytic Association, 2*, 509-513.

Bergenson, R. (1983). *Die Bisexuelle Frau.* Munich: Moewig.

Bern, S. (1974). The measurement of psychological androgyny. *Journal of Consulting and Clinical Psychology, 42*, 155-162.

Bern, S. (1977). On the unity of alternative procedures for assessing psychological androgyny. *Journal of Consulting and Clinical Psychology, 45*, 196-205.

Bieber, I. (1969). The married male homosexual. *Medical aspects of human sexuality, 3*(5), 76-84.

Bieler, H., & Nichols, S. (1972). *Dr. Bieler's natural way to sexual health.* Los Angeles: Charles.
    See pp. 169-172 on ambisexual persons.

Binstock, W. (1973). On the two forms of intimacy. *Journal of the American Psychoanalytic Association, 21*, 93-107.

Bird, B. (1958). A study of the bisexual meaning of foreskin. *Journal of the American Psychoanalytic Association, 6*, 278-286.

Bird, C. (1968). *Born female.* New York: Pocket Books.

Bisexual chic: Anyone goes. (1974, May 27). *Newsweek Magazine*, p. 90.

Bishop, G. (1964). *The bisexuals.* Los Angeles: Century Publishing.

Blair, R. (1974). Counseling concerns and bisexual behavior. *The Homosexual Counseling Journal, 1*(2), 26-30.

Blos, P. (1965). The initial stage of male adolescence. *Psychosomatic study of the child, 20*, 145-164.

Blos, P. (1979). *The adolescent passage: Developmental issues.* New York: IU Press.

Blueher, H. (1912). *Niels Lyhne* von J. P. Jakobsen und das Problem der bisexualität (J. P. Jakobsen's *Niels Lyhne* and the problems of bisexuality). *Imago, 1*, 386-400.

Blumstein, P. W., & Schwartz, P. (1974). Lesbianism and bisexuality. *Archives of Sexual Behavior, 5*, 171-181.

Blumstein, P. W., & Schwartz, P. (1976). Bisexual women. In J. Wiseman (Ed.), *The social psychology of sex* (pp. 154-162). New York: Harper & Row.

Blumstein, P. W., & Schartz, P. (1976). Bisexuality in men. *Urban Life, 5*, 339-358.

Blumstein, P. W., & Schwartz, P. (1976). Bisexuality in women. *Archives of Sexual Behavior, 5*, 171-181.

Blumstein, P. W., & Schwartz, P. (1977). Bisexuality: Some social psychological issues. *Journal of Social Issues, 33*, 30-45.

Bode, J. (1976). View from another closet. *Exploring bisexuality in women.* New York: Hawthorn Books.

Bonaparte, M., Freud, A., & Kris, E. (Eds.). (1954). *Origins of psychoanalysis: Letters to Wilhelm Fliess, drafts and notes: 1887-1902.* New York: Basic Books.

Bonaparte, M. (1935). Passivity, masochism and femininity. *International Journal of Psychoanalysis, 16,* 325-333.

Boswell, J. (1980). *Christianity, social tolerance and homosexuality.* Chicago: University of Chicago Press.

Bozett, F. (1981). Gay fathers: Identify conflict resolution through integrative sanctioning. *Alternative Lifestyles, 4,* 90-101.

Bram, J. R. (1979). Sex reversal in the ancient world. In M. C. Nelson & J. Ikenberry (Eds.), *Psychosexual imperatives: Their role in identity formation* (pp. 91-106). New York: Human Sciences Press.

Breger, L. (1981). *Freud's unfinished journey.* London: Routledge & Kegan Paul.

Breitner, B. (1951). *Das Problem der Bisexualität.* Wien: Verlag Wilhelm Maundrich.

Brody, E. (1978). Intimacy and the fantasy of becoming both sexes. *Journal of the American Academy of Psychoanalysis, 6,* 521-531.

Brody, J. (1974, March 24). Bisexual life-style appears to be spreading, and not necessarily among swingers. *New York Times,* p. 57.

Based on a study done at the University of Washington, the *Times* article has comments by Drs. Green, Hatterer, Money, Myers, Schwartz, Shainess, and Spiers.

Broughton, J. (1977). *The androgyne journal.* Oakland, CA: Scrimshaw Press.

Brown, R. (1965). *Social psychology.* New York: Free Press.

An excellent commentary on Freud's concept of identification vis-à-vis bisexuality, pp. 278-279.

Bryan, D. (1930). Bisexuality. *International Journal of Psychoanalysis, 11,* 150-166.

Burnside, J. (1963, August). Bisexuality and its possibilities as a way of life. *One Magazine,* pp. 6-9.

Buzzacott, F., & Wymore, M. (1912). *Bi-sexual man, or evolution of the sexes.* Chicago: M. A. Donahue.

Campbell, C. (1958). *Induced delusions: The psychopathy of Freudism.* Chicago: Regent House.

One chapter attacks Freud's concept of bisexuality.

Caprio, F. (1955). *The adequate male.* New York: Medical Research Press.

Carpenter, E. (1919). *Intermediate types among primitive folk* (2nd Ed.). London: Allen & Unwin. (Originally published 1914)

Cass, V. (1979). Homosexual identity formation: A theoretical model. *Journal of Homosexuality, 4,* 219-233.

Cauldwell, D. (1948). *Bisexuality in patterns of human behavior: A study of individuals who indulge in both heterosexual and homosexual practices, with comparative data on hermaphrodites, the human intersex.* Girard, KS: Haldeman-Julius Publications.

Childs, E. (1976). Women's sexuality: A feminist view. In S. Cox (Ed.), *Female psychology: The emerging self.* Chicago: Science Research Associates.

Christy, R. (1968). *The intermediate gender: The sex that can't make up its mind.* Van Nuys, CA: Triumph.

Churchill, W. (1967). *Homosexual behavior among males: A cross-cultural and cross-species investigation.* New York: Hawthorn Books.

Clark, D. (Ed.). (1973). Symposium: AC/DC: The bisexual. *The Humanist, 33*(4), 15-20.

Clark's article includes contributions by A. Ellis, C. Margolis, J. Margolis, and E. van de Haag.

Coleman, E. (1981/1982). Bisexual and gay men in heterosexual marriage: Conflicts and resolutions in therapy. *Journal of Homosexuality, 7*(2/3), 93-103.

Colton, N. (1954). Salvation: An expression of bisexuality. *Bulletin of the Philadelphia Association of Psychoanalysts, 4,* 36-37.

Comfort, A. (1972). *The joy of sex.* New York: Crown.

Comfort, A. (1974). *More joy of sex.* New York: Crown.

Coons, F. (1972). Ambisexuality as an alternative adaptation. *Journal of the American College Health Association, 21,* 142-144.

Coriat, I. (1917). Hermaphroditic dreams. *Psychoanalytic Review, 40,* 88-92.

Corvo, B. (1953). *The desire and pursuit of the whole.* New York: New Directions.

Cory, D., & LeRoy, J. (1963). *The homosexual and his society.* New York: Citadel Press.

Cucchiari, S. (1981). The gender revolution and the transition from bisexual horde to patrilocal band. In Ortner & Whitenead (Eds.), *Sexual meanings* (pp. 31-79). New York: Cambridge University Press.

Dank, B. (1972). Why homosexuals marry women. *Medical aspects of human sexuality, 6,* 614-627.

Darwin, C. (1871). *The descent of man, and selection in relation to sex* (Vol. 1). London: John Murray.

David, C. (1975). La bisexualité psychique: Éléments d'une réevaluation. *Revue Française de Psychoanalyse, 39,* 713-757.

David, C. (1977). Psychic bisexuality: Clinical and theoretical considerations. *International Psychoanalytic Association Newsletter, 9*(1), 33.

Davis, C. (1968). *AC/DC.* Los Angeles: Classic Publications.

Deb, S. (1979). On bisexuality: An overview. *Samiska, 33*(2), 53-57.

De Cecco, J. P. (1981). Definition and meaning of sexual orientation. *Journal of Homosexuality, 6*(4), 51-67.

Delcourt, M. (1961). *Hermaphrodite: The bisexual figure in myth and ritual.* London: Studio Books. (Originally published in French, 1956)

De Lora, J., & Warren, C. (1977). *Understanding sexual interaction.* Boston: Houghton Mifflin.

Denniston, R. (1980). Ambisexuality in animals. In J. Marmor (Ed.), *Homosexual behavior* (pp. 25-40). New York: Basic Books.

DeRiver, J. P. (1958). *Crime and the sexual psychopath.* Springfield, IL: C. C. Thomas.

Dervin, D. (1980). Rainbow, phoenix and plumed serpent: D. H. Lawrence's great composite symbols and their vicissitudes. *Psychoanalytic Review, 67,* 515-541.

Deutsch, H. (1944). *The psychology of women.* New York: Grune & Stratton.

Deutsch, H. (1968). Bisexuality and immortality in the Dionysis myth. *Psychoanalytic Quarterly, 37,* 321-322.

Deutsch, H. (1967). *Selected problems of adolescence with special emphasis on group formation.* New York: International Universities Press.

Dickes, R. (1971). Factors in the development of male homosexuality. In M. Kanzer (Ed.), *The unconscious today* (pp. 25-273). New York: International Universities Press.

Dixon, J. (1982). *The confusion about preferences and orientations regarding sex of sex partners.* Unpublished manuscript.

Douglas, J. (1970). *Bisexuality.* London: Canova Press, Ltd.

Eglinton, J. Z. (1965). *Greek love.* New York: Oliver Layton Press.

Eissler, K. R. (1971). *Talent and genius: The fictitious case of Tausk contra Freud.* New York: Quadrangle.

Ellenberger, H. F. (1970). *The discovery of the unconscious.* New York: Basic Books.

Faithfull, T. J. (1927). *Bisexuality: An essay on extraversion and introversion.* London: John Bale, Sons & Danielson, Ltd.

Falk, R. (1975). *Women loving: A journey toward becoming an independent woman.* New York: Random House.

Fast, I. (1978). Developments in gender identity: The original matrix. *International Review of Psychoanalysis, 5*(3), 265-273.

Fast, J., & Wells, H. (1975). *Bisexual living.* New York: Evans.

Fineman, J. (1979). Psychoanalysis, bisexuality, and the difference before the sexes. In M. C. Nelson & J. Ikenberry (Eds.), *Psychosexual imperatives: Their role in identity formation* (pp. 109-145). New York: Human Sciences Press.

Fisher, P. (1972). *The gay mystique: The myth and reality.* New York: Stein & Day.

Fodor, N. (1946). The search for the beloved. *Psychiatric Quarterly, 20,* 294-306.

Fodor, N. (1954). Dreams of masculine regret. In A. M. Krich (Ed.), *The homosexual* (pp. 25-28). New York: Citadel Press.

Ford, C. S., & Beach, F. A. (1951). *Patterns of sexual behavior.* New York: Harper.

Forman, M. (1976, March). *The bisexual phallic narcissistic phase of development, sexual identity and the cohesive.* Paper presented at the sixth Regional Conference of the Chicago Psychoanalytic Society, Chicago, IL.

Fraser-Harris, D. F. (1933). Bisexual mentality. *Hibbert Journal, 31,* 571-581.

Freud, E. (1960). *The letters of Sigmund Freud.* New York: Basic Books.
See especially the portion of letter 122, pp. 250-251, written to Karl Kraus, dealing with the Fleiss/Weininger/Svoboda controversy; and see letter 209, pp. 350-352, to Fritz Wittels, written 1924, about Wittels' Freud biography and the Fliess controversy.

Freud, S. (1961). Analysis terminable and interminable. In J. Strachey (Ed. and Trans.), *The standard edition of the complete psychological works of Sigmund Freud* (Vol. 23, Part 8). London: Hogarth Press. (Original work publisehd 1937)

Freud, S. (1961). Femininity. In J. Strachey (Ed. and Trans.), *The standard edition of the complete psychological works of Sigmund Freud* (Vol. 22, pp. 112-135). London: Hogarth Press. (Original work published 1923)

Freud, S. (1961). Hysterical phantasies and their relation to bisexuality. In J. Strachey (Ed. and Trans.), *The standard edition of the complete psychological works of Sigmund Freud* (Vol. 9, pp. 157-160). London: Hogarth Press. (Original work published 1923)

Freud, S. (1961). Notes on a case of obsessional neurosis. In J. Strachey (Ed. and Trans.), *The standard edition of the complete psychological works of Sigmund Freud* (Vol. 10, pp. 153-320). London: Hogarth Press. (Original work published 1923)

Freud, S. (1961). Psychoanalytic notes upon an autobiographical account of a case of paranoia. In J. Strachey (Ed. and Trans.), *The standard edition of the complete psychological works of Sigmund Freud* (Vol. 12, pp. 9-82). London: Hogarth Press. (Original work published 1923)

Freud, S. (1961). The psychoanalysis of a case of homosexuality in a woman. In J. Strachey (Ed. and Trans.), *The standard edition of the complete psychological works of Sigmund Freud* (Vol. 18, pp. 146-154). London: Hogarth Press. (Original work published 1923)

Freud, S. (1961). Three essays on the theory of sexuality. In J. Strachey (Ed. and Trans.), *The standard edition of the complete psychological works of Sigmund Freud* (Vol. 7, inclusive). London: Hogarth Press. (Original work published 1905)

Freund, K. (1974). Male homosexuality. An analysis of the pattern. In J. A. Loraine (Ed.), *Understanding homosexuality: Its biological and psychological bases* (pp. 25-81). New York: American Elsevier.

Freund, K., & Langevin, R. (1976). Bisexuality in homosexual pedophilia. *Archives of Sexual Behavior, 5,* 415-424.

Freund, K., Scher, H., Chan, S., & Ben-Aron, M. (1982). Experimental analysis of pedophilia. *Behavior Research and Therapy, 20,* 105-112.

Friedman, S. (1976). On the umbilicus as bisexual genital. *Psychoanalytic Quarterly, 45,* 296-298.

Frosch, J. (1981). The role of unconscious homosexuality in the paranoid constellation. *Psychoanalytic Quarterly, 50,* 587-613.

Galland, V. R. (1975). Bisexual women. Doctoral dissertation, California School of Professional Psychology. *Dissertation Abstracts International*, Vol. 36 (6-B), 3037-3038.

Galt, W. E. (1943). The male-female dichotomy in human behavior: A phylobiological evaluation. *Psychiatry Journal of the Biology and Pathology of Interpersonal Relations, 6*(1), 1-14.

Gagnon, J. (1977). *Human sexualities*. Glenview, IL: Scott Foresman.

Gault, O., & Smith, R. M. (1961). *Sex clinic*. Hollywood, CA: All Star Classic Books.

Gay America. (1983, August 8). *Newsweek Magazine*, pp. 30-36.

Gebhard, P. H. (1972). Incidence of overt homosexuality in the U.S. and Western Europe. In J. M. Livingood (Ed.), *NIMH task force on homosexuality: Final report and papers* (#HSM 72-9116). Rockville, MD: Department of Health, Education, and Welfare.

Gebhard, P. H., & Johnson, A. B. (1979). *The Kinsey data: Marginal tabulations of the 1938-1963 interviews conducted by the Institute for Sex Research*. Philadelphia: W. B. Saunders.

Gilmore, M. M., & Gilmore, D. D. (1979). Machismo: A psychodynamic approach. *Journal of Psychological Anthropology, 23*, 281-299.

Gochros, H. L. (1978). Counseling gay husbands. *Journal of Sex and Marital Therapy, 5*, 142-151.

Gonsiorek, J. C., Paul, W., Weinrich, J. D., & Hotvedt, M. E. (Eds.). (1982). *Homosexuality: Social, psychological and biological issues*. Beverly Hills: Sage Publications.

Gottman, J. M. (1979). *Marital interaction: Experimental investigations*. Chicago: Academic Press.

Goy, R. W. (1974, June). *Comparative aspects of bisexuality in mammals*. Paper presented at the research Workshop on Future Directions in Research in Human Sexuality. State University of New York, Stony Brook, NY.
    Available from Bloomington, IN: Alfred C. Kinsey Institute (Mimeo, 24 pp.).

Graves, A. (1942). *The eclipse of a mind*. New York: Medical Journal Press.

Greenacre, P. (1952). *Trauma, growth and personality*. New York: Norton.

Greenson, R. (1964). Bisexuality and gender identity. *International Journal of Psychoanalysis, 45*, 217-219.

Grossman, W. I. (1976). Discussion of "Freud and female sexuality." *International Journal of Psychoanalysis, 57*, 301-306.

Guttman, S. A. (1955). Bisexuality in symbolism. *Journal of the American Psychoanalytic Association, 3*, 280-284.

Harley, M. (1963). A secret in prepuberty (its sexual aspects). *Psychoanalytic Quarterly, 32*, 616-617.

Harris, D. A. (1977). *Social-psychological characteristics of ambisexuals*. Unpublished doctoral dissertation, University of Tennessee, Knoxville, TN.
    Available from University Microfilms, Ann Arbor, Michigan, order #78-2004, 525.

Harriman, P. (1964). *Bisexuality: Normal or not?* North Hollywood: Dominion.

Harrison, B. G. (1974, April). Sexual chic, sexual fascism, and sexual confusion. *New York Magazine*, pp. 31-36.

Harry, J., & De Vall, W. (1978). *The social organization of gay males*. New York: Praeger.

Hartman, J. J., & Gilbard, G. S. (1973). Bisexual fantasy and group process. Contemporary Psychoanalysis, 93, 303-326.

Harwell, J. L. (1976). *Bisexuality: Persistent lifestyle or transitional state?* Doctoral dissertation, International University, Independence, MO.
    Available from University Microfilms, Ann Arbor, Michigan. Order #76-22, 384.

Hathaway, B. (1974). *Bisexuality: An annotated bibliography*. Unpublished manuscript. Available at Kinsey Institute for Sex Research.

Hatterer, M. S. (1974). The problems of women married to homosexual men. *American Journal of Psychiatry, 131*, 275-278.

Heilbrun, C. G. (1973). *Towards a recognition of bisexuality.* New York: Knopf.

Helmreich, R. L., Spence, J. T., & Holahan, C. K. Psychological androgyny and sex role flexibility: A test of two hypotheses. *Journal of Personality and Social Psychology, 37*, 1631-1644.

Henry, G. W. (1955). *All the sexes: A study of masculinity and femininity.* New York: Rinehart.

Hinkle, B. M. (1922). *The re-creating of the individual.* New York: Harcourt Brace.

Hirschfeld, M. (1906). *Die gestohlene bisexualität.* Vienna: (n.p.).

Hirschfeld, M. (1912). *Naturgesetze der Liebe* (The nature of love). Berlin: Pulvermacher. (Published earlier in Leipzig in 1895 and 1906)

Hodges, A., & Hutter, D. (1979). *With downcast gays: Aspects of homosexual self-oppression* (2nd Ed.). Toronto: Pink Triangle Press.

Hoffman, M. (1976). *The gay world: Male homosexuality and the social creation of evil.* New York: Basic Books.

Horney, K. (1967). *Feminine psychology.* New York: Norton.

Humphreys, L. (1970). *Tearoom trade: Impersonal sex in public places.* New York: Aldine.

Humphreys, L., & Miller, B. (1970). Identities in the emerging gay culture. In J. Marmor (Ed.), *Homosexual behavior: A modern-reappraisal.* New York; Basic Books.

Hunt, M. B. (1974). *Sexual behavior in the 1970's.* Chicago: Playboy Press.

Hurwood, B. J. (1974). *The bisexuals.* Greenwich: Fawcett.

Imielinski, K. (1970). *Milieubedingte einstehung der homo- und bisexualität: Eine theorie der geschlechtsorientierung.* (Situational origin of homosexuality and bisexuality: A theory of sexual orientation). Munich & Basel: Ernst Reinhardt Verlag. This appears to be a translation to German of the original Polish work. There is no English translation, but the German edition is still available.

Institute for Sex Research Information Service. (1979). *Bisexuality.* (Annotated bibliography). Bloomington, IN: Author.

Jardine, J., & Whyte, S. (1971). *The bisexual female.* Los Angeles: Centurion Press.

Jay, K., & Young, A. (1979). *The gay report.* New York: Summit.

Kalcheim, C., Szechtman, H., & Koch, Y. (1981). Bisexual behavior in male rats treated neonatally with antibodies to luteinizing hormone-releasing hormone. *Journal of Comparative and Physiological Psychology, 95*(1), 36-44.

Kantrowitz, A. (1977, May 4). Bosom buddies. *The Advocate*, pp. 31-32.

Kaplan, A., & Sedney, M. A. (1980). *Psychology & sex roles: An androgynous perspective.* Boston: Little, Brown.

Kardiner, A., Karush, A., & Ovesey, L. (1959). A methodological study of Freudian theory. *Journal of Nervous and Mental Diseases, 129*, 11-19, 133-143, 207-221, 341-346.

Karlen, A. (1971). *Sexuality and homosexuality: A new view.* New York: Norton.

Katan, M. (1955). Those wrecked by success, bisexual conflicts, and ego defense.*The Psychoanalytic Quarterly, 24*, 477-478.

Kelly, G. F. (1974). Bisexuality and youth culture. *The Homosexual Counseling Journal, 1*(2), 16-25.

Kempf, E. J. (1945). Ontogeny of bisexual differentiation in man. *Journal of Clinical Psychopathology, 7*, 213.

Kempf, E. J. (1949). Bisexual factors in curable schizophrenia. *Journal of Abnormal and Social Psychology, 44*, 414-419.

Kestenberg, J., & Marcus, H. (1979). Hypothetical monosex and bisexuality. In M. C. Nelson & J. Ikenberry (Eds.), *Psychosexual imperatives: Their role in identity formation.* New York: Human Sciences Press.

Khan, M., & Masud, R. (1974). Ego orgasm and bisexual love. *International Review of Psychoanalysis, 1*, 143-149.

Khan, M., & Masud, R. (1979). *Alienation in perversion*. London: Hogarth Press.

Kiernan, J. G. (1884). Insanity: Lecture XXVI—Sexual perversion. *Detroit Lancet, 7*, 481-484.

Kiernan, J. G. (1891). Psychological aspects of the sexual appetite. *The Alienist and Neurologist, 12*, 188-219.

Kinsey, A. C., Pomeroy, W. B., Martin, C. E., & Gebhard, P. E. (1948). *Sexual behavior in the human male*. Philadelphia: W. B. Saunders.

Kinsey, A. C., Pomeroy, W. B., Martin, C. E., & Gebhard, P. E. (1953). *Sexual behavior in the human female*. Philadelphia: W. B. Saunders.

Kisker, G. W. (1972). *The disorganized personality* (2nd Ed.). New York: McGraw-Hill.

Klein, F. (1978). *The bisexual option*. New York: Arbor House.

Klein, F. (1980, December). Are you sure you're heterosexual? or homosexual? or even bisexual? *Forum Magazine*, pp. 41-45.

Kleinberg, S. (1980). *Alienated affections: Being gay in America*. New York: St. Martin's Press.

Klemsrud, J. (1974, April 1). The bisexuals. *New York Magazine*, pp. 37-38.

Knox, L. (1974, July). The bisexual phenomenon. *Viva Magazine*, pp. 42-45.

Kohn, B., & Matusow, A. (1980). *Barry & Alice: Portrait of a bisexual marriage*. New York: Prentice-Hall.

Korber, H. (1913). Die Bisexualität als Grundlage der Sexualforschung (Bisexuality as a basis for sexual research). *Neue Generation, 9*, 73.

Kraft-Ebing, R. von (1965). *Psychopathia sexualis*. London: Staples Press. The 10th edition was published in London by Rebman in 1899.

Kraus, Julius. (1906). Otto Weininger, plagiarist. *Die Wage, 43*, 970.

Krich, A. M. (Ed.) (1954). *The homosexuals*. New York: Citadel Press.

Krim, S. (1968). *Views of a near-sighted cannoner*. New York: Dutton.

Kubie, L. S. (1974). The drive to become both sexes. *Psychoanalytic Quarterly, 43*, 349-426.

Lampl-De Groot, J. (1967). On obstacles in the way of psychoanalytic cure. *Psychoanalytic Study of the Child, 22*, 20-35.

Lang, T. (1971). *The difference between a man and a woman*. New York: John Day.

LaPlanche, J. (1974). Panel on hysteria today. *International Journal of Psychoanalysis, 5*, 198-212.

Latham, J. D., & White, G. D. (1978). Coping with homosexual expression within heterosexual marriages: Five case studies. *Journal of Sex and Marital Therapy, 4*, 198-212.

La Torre, R. A. (1979). *Sexual identity: Implications for mental health*. Chicago: Nelson-Hall.

A lesbian encounter. (1975, September). *Human Response, 1*(7), 34-40.

Lewis, S. G. (1974, October 23). Bisexuals are "healthy," researchers conclude. *The Advocate*, p. 20.

Limentani, A. (1976). Object choice and actual bisexuality. *International Journal of Psychoanalytic Psychotherapy, 5*, 205-218. (Originally appeared as Le choix d'objet dans la bisexualité actuelle, *Revue Française de Psychoanalyse*, 1975, *5*, 857-868.)

Limentani, A. (1979). Clinical types of homosexuality. In I. Rosen (Ed.), *Sexual deviation* (2nd Ed.) (pp. 195-205). New York: Oxford University Press.

Lorand, S. (1931). *Morbid personality*. New York: Knopf.

Lynne, D. (1967). *The bisexual woman*. New York: Midweek.

Macalpine, I., & Hunter, R. A. (1955). *Daniel Paul Schreber: Memoirs of my nervous illness*. London: Dawson.

MacDonald, A. P. (1981). An annotated subject-indexed bibliography of research on bisexuality, lesbianism and male homosexuality (1975-1978). *Catalog of Selected Documents in Psychology, 11*(16), Ms. 2206.

MacDonald, A. P. (1983). A little bit of lavender goes a long way: A critique of research on sexual orientation. *Journal of Sex Research, 19*, 94-100.

MacInnes, C. (1973). *Loving them both: A study in bisexuality and bisexuals*. London: Martin Bran & O'Keefe.

Maddox, B. (1982). *Married and gay: What hapens when a gay man marries a lesbian?* New York: Harcourt Brace Jovanovich.

Malone, J. (1980). *Straight women/gay men: A special relationship*. New York: Dial Press.

Margold, J. (1974, June). Bisexuality: The newest sex-style. *Cosmopolitan Magazine*, pp. 189-192.

Markus, E. (1981). An examination of psychological adjustment and sexual preference in the female. Doctoral dissertation, University of Missouri (1980). *Dissertation Abstracts International, 41*, 4338-A.

Marmor, J. (Ed.). (1965). *Sexual inversion: The multiple roots of homosexuality*. New York: Basic Books.

Masters, W. H., & Johnson, V. E. (1979). *Homosexuality in perspective*. Boston: Little, Brown.

Matthews, J. (1969). Bisexuality in the male. *The Journal of Sex Research, 5*, 126-129.

McCary, J. L. (1971). *Sexual myths and fallacies*. New York: Van Nostrand Reinhold.

McConaghy, N. (1978). Heterosexual experience, marital status, and orientation of homosexual males. *Archives of Sexual Behavior, 7*, 575-582.

McConaghy, N., et al. (1979). The incidence of bisexual feelings and opposite sex behavior in medical students. *Journal of Nervous and Mental Disease, 67*, 685-688.

McMurtie, D. C. (1913). The theory of bisexuality: A review and critique. *Lancet Clinic, 109*, 370-372.

Mead, M. (1976, January). Bisexuality: What is it all about? *Redbook Magazine*, pp. 29-31.

Melukx, I. U. (1976). Discussion of Freud and female sexuality. *International Journal of Psychoanalysis, 75*, 307-310.

Mendola, M. (1980). *The Mendola report: A new look at gay couples*. New York: Crown.

Meyerson, S. (1975). *Adolescence: The crisis of adjustment*. Winchester, MA: Allen & Unwin.

Money, J. (1977). Bisexual, homosexual and heterosexual: Society, law and medicine. *Journal of Homosexuality, 2*, 229-233.

Money, J. (1978). Human hermaphroditism. In F. A. Beach (Ed.), *Human sexuality in four perspectives* (pp. 62-86). Baltimore: Johns Hopkins University Press.

Money, J. (1980). *Love and love sickness*. Baltimore: Johns Hopkins University Press.

Money, J. (1974, May 13). The new bisexual. *Time Magazine*, pp. 79-80.

Money, J. (1972). Pubertal hormones and homosexuality, bisexuality and heterosexuality. In *National Institute of Mental Health Task Force on Homosexuality: Final Report and Background Papers*. Washington D.C.: U.S. Government Printing Office.

Money, J. (1974). Two names, two wardrobes, two personalities. *Journal of Homosexuality, 1*, 65-70.

Money, J., & Ehrhardt, A. A. (1972). *Man & woman/boy & girl*. Baltimore: Johns Hopkins University Press.

Money, J., & Tucker, P. (1975). *Sexual signatures: On being a man or a woman*. Boston: Little, Brown.

Money-Kryle, R. (1952). *The development of sexual impulses.* London: Routledge & Kegan Paul. (Original work published 1932)

Moore, B. E. (1976). Freud and female sexuality: A current view. *International Journal of Psychoanalysis, 57,* 287-300.

Murphy, W. F. (1965). *The tactics of psychotherapy.* New York: International University Press.

Myer, L. (1976). *Bisexual behavior.* Unpublished paper. Indiana University, Alfred A. Kinsey Institute, Bloomington, IN.

Myerson, A., & Neustadt, R. (1942). Bisexuality and male homosexuality: Their biological and medical aspects. *Clinic, 1,* 932-957.

Nacke, P. (1906). Some psychiatric experiences in support of bisexual vestiges in mankind. *Jahrbuch für Sexualzwischenstufen (Annual for Sexual Intermediate Stages), 8,* 583-603.
This is apparently available only in the German original.

Nahas, R., & Turley, M. (1979). *The new couple: Women and gay men.* New York: Seaview Books.

Narlett, J. W. (1966). A bisexual fantasy associated with the testes. *Bulletin of the Psychoanalytic Association of New York, 6,* 23-24.

Nelson, M. C., & Ikenberry, J. (Eds.). (1979). *Psychosexual imperatives: Their role in identity formation.* New York: Human Sciences Press.
See contributions by Bram, Fineman, Kestenberg & Marcus.

Newman, L. E., & Stoller, R. F. (1969). Spider symbolism and bisexuality. *Journal of the American Psychoanalytic Association, 17,* 862-872.

Nunberg, H. (1949). *Problems of bisexuality as reflected in circumcision.* London: Imago.

Nunberg, H. (1968). Homosexuality, magic and aggression. *International Journal of Psychoanalysis, 19,* 1-16.

Nurius, P. S. (1983). Mental health implications of sexual orientation. *Journal of Sex Research, 19,* 119-136.

O'Flaherty, W. D. (1980). *Women, androgynes, and other mythical beasts.* Chicago & London: The University of Chicago Press.

Ogden, J. (1969). Mono-, bi-, and polysexuality. *Ladder, 9/10,* 32-34.

O'Neil, N., & O'Neil, G. (1968). *Open marriage.* New York: Avon Books.

Orgel, S. Z. (1957). The problem of bisexuality as reflected in circumcision. *Journal of Hillside Hospital, 5,* 375-383.

Palm, R. (1957). A note on the bisexual origin of man. *Psychoanalysis, 5,* 77-82.

Parker, E. (1968). *Spanish fly.* Los Angeles: Echelon.

Parker, M. (1973). *The two-way swingers.* California: Barclay House.

Patry, F. L. (1928). Theories of bisexuality with report of a case. *Psychoanalytic Review, 15,* 417-439.

Philipp, E. (1968). Homosexuality as seen in a New Zealand city practice. New Zealand Medical Journal, 67, 397-401.

Philips, W. B. (1969). *The fourth sex: Bisexual.* Chatsworth, CA: Barclay House.

Playboy Readers Sex Survey. (1983, May). *Playboy Magazine,* pp. 126-128, 136, 210-220.

Pudor, H. (1906). *Bisexualität.* Berlin: (n. p.)

Rado, S. (1956 & 1962). *Psychoanalysis of behavior.* New York: Grune.
Also in Marmor, J. (Ed., 1965), *Sexual inversion* (pp. 175-189). New York: Basic Books. (Originally appeared in *Psychoanalytic Medicine* (1940), 2, pp. 459-467.)
For 25 years this negative critique of the concept of bisexuality was the most frequently cited piece in the journal literature, at a time when Stekel's inconclusive work (see below) was the most frequently cited book. An alternative literature began to develop only in the late 1960s.

Rangell, L. (1963). On friendship. *Journal of the American Psychoanalytic Association, 11*, 3-54.

Raven, S. (1960). Boys will be boys. *Encounter, 20*, 19-24.
On p. 20, in discussing a young British guardsman who sells sexual favors and who denies that is at all "queer," Raven asserts, "that he is, in fact, bisexual . . ." and briefly supports this position.

Richardson, F. (1972). *Napoleon: Bisexual emperor.* New York: Horizon Press.

Richmond, L., & Noguera, G. (Eds.). (1973). *The gay liberation book.* San Francisco: Ramparts Press.

Roazen, P. (1969). *Brother animal: The story of Freud and Tausk.* New York: Knopf.
See especially the section "Plagiarism," on the Fleiss-Weininger affairs. Kurt Eissler (see above) wrote a book to refute Roazen's book.

Robertiello, R. C. (1978). The "fag hag." *Journal of Contemporary Psychotherapy, 10*, 10-11.
Discusses women who sought out lovers who were homosexual, bisexual or extremely passive men.

Robbins, B. (1967). *The fourth sex.* Canoga Park, CA: Viceroy Books.

Rochlin, G. (1980). *The masculine dilemma: A psychology of masculinity.* Boston: Little, Brown.

Roessler, T., & Deisher, R. W. (1972). Youthful male homosexuality. *Journal of the American Medical Association, 219*, 1018-1023.

Rogers, C. (1967). *Impulsive bi-sexuality.* Buffalo: Unique Books.

Rohrbaugh, J. F. (1979). *Women: Psychology's puzzle.* New York: Basic Books.

Rokeach, M. (1964). *The three Christs of Ypsilanti.* New York: Knopf.

Rosen, I. (1964). *The pathology and treatment of sexual deviation.* London: Oxford University Press.

Rosenberger, J. B. (1970). *Men and women who go both ways.* Los Angeles: Media Books.

Ross, H. L. (1971). Modes of adjustment of married homosexuals. *Social Problems, 18*, 385-393.

Ross, M. (1979). Bisexuality: Fact or fallacy? *British Journal of Sexual Medicine, 6*, 49-50.

Rosenzweig, S. (1973). Human sexual autonomy as an evolutionary attainment, anticipating proceptive sex choice and idiodynamic bisexuality. In J. Zubin & J. Money (Eds.), *Contemporary sexual behavior* (pp. 189-230). Baltimore: Johns Hopkins University Press.

Roy, D., & Rustum, J. (1972). Is monogamy outdated? In J. Delora & J. Delora (Eds.), *Intimate life styles.* Pacific Palisades, CA: Goodyear Publishing.

Rubenstein, M. (1982). *An in-depth study of bisexuality and its relation to self-esteem.* Unpublished doctoral dissertation, Institute for Advanced Study of Human Sexuality, San Francisco, CA.

Rubin, I. (1961). *The third sex.* New York: New Book.

Ruitenbeek, H. M. (1970). *Sexuality and identity.* New York: Delta.

Ruitenbeek, H. M. (Ed.). (1973). *Homosexuality: A changing picture.* London: Souvenir.

Russ, J. (1975). *The female man.* New York: Bantam Books.

Saliba, P. (1982). Research project on sexual orientation. *The Bi-Monthly Newsletter of the Bisexual Center of San Francisco, 6*(5), 3-6.

Salzman, L. (1980). Latent homosexuality. In J. Marmor (Ed.), *Homosexual behavior* (pp. 312-324). New York: Basic Books.

Sarlin, L. (1963). Feminine identity. *Journal of the American Psychoanalytic Association, 11*, 790-816.

Saul, L. (1951). Wood as a bisexual symbol. *Psychoanalytic Quarterly, 20*, 616.

Sawyer, E. (1965, September). *A study of a public lesbian community.* Paper presented to the Sociology-Anthropology Department of George Washington University, Washington, D. C. Available at the Alfred C. Kinsey Institute.

Schafer, S. (1975). Sexuelle und soziale Probleme von Lesbierinnin in der DBR (Sexual and social problems among lesbians in the German Democratic Republic). In E. Schorsch & G. Schmidt (Eds.), *Ergebnisse zur sexual forschung* (pp. 299-325). Köln: Wissenschafts-Verlag.

Schafer, S. (1977). Sociosexual behavior in male and female homosexuals: A study in sex differences. *Archives of Sexual Behavior, 6,* 355-364.

Schecter, D. E. (1968). Identification and individuation, *Journal of the American Psychoanalytic Association, 16,* 48-80.

Schuster, D. (1969). Bisexuality, and body as phallus. *Psychoanalytic Quarterly, 38,* 72-80.

Schwartz, P., & Blumstein, P. W. (1976, November). Bisexuals: When love speaks louder than labels. *Ms. Magazine,* pp. 80-81.

Scott, J. (pseud.). (1978). *Wives who love women.* New York: Walker.

Simeon, A. T. W. (1961). *Man's presumptuous brain.* New York: Dutton.

Singer, J. (1977). *Androgyny: Toward a new theory of sexuality.* New York: Doubleday.

Sisley, E. L., & Harris, B. (1977). *The joy of lesbian sex.* New York: Crown.

Smith, D. C. (1981). *The naked child: The long-range effects of family and social nudity.* Saratoga, CA: Twenty-one Publishing.

Smith-Rosenberg, C. (1975). The female world of love and ritual: Relations between women in nineteenth century America. *Signs: Journal of Women in Culture and Society, 1*(1), 1-29.

Socarides, C. W. (1963). The historical development of theoretical and clinical concepts of overt female homosexuality. *Journal of the American Psychoanalytic Association, 11,* 385-414.

Socarides, C. W. (1968). Homosexuality in the male: A report of a psychiatric study group. *International Journal of Psychiatry, 11,* 460-469.

Socarides, C. W. (1968). *The overt homosexual.* New York: Grune & Stratton.

Sours, J. A. (1974). Growth and development in childhood. In A. Arieti (Ed.), *American handbook of psychiatry* (Vol. 1). New York: Basic Books.

Spada, J. (1979). *The Spada report.* New York: New American Library.

Sperling, M. (1971). Spider phobias and spider fantasies: A clinical contribution to the study of symbol and symptom choice. *Journal of the American Psychoanalytic Association, 19,* 472-498.

Spiers, D. E. (1976). The no-man's land of the bisexual. *Psychiatry, 22*(3), 6-11.

Spruiell, V. (1978). Groddeck's children. *Journal of the Philadelphia Association for Psychoanalysis, 6,* 175-181.

Starkweather, D. (1974, August 15). Bisexuality is not succotash. *Village Voice,* p. 27.

Stearn, J. (1964). *The grapevine: A report on the secret world of the lesbian.* New York: Doubleday.

Stearn, J. (1962). *The sixth man.* Philadelphia: McFadden.

Stekel, W. (1944). *Bisexual love.* New York: Emerson Books. (First English edition published 1922)

Stimpson, C. (1974). The androgyne and the homosexual. *Women's studies, 2,* 237-247.

Stoller, R. J. (1968). *Sex and gender: On the development of masculinity and femininity* (Vol. 1). New York: Aronson.

Stoller, R. J. (1972). The bedrock of masculinity and femininity: Bisexuality. *Archives of General Psychiatry, 26,* 207-212.

Stoller, R. J. (1973). The impact of new advances in sex research on psychoanalytic theory. *American Journal of Psychiatry, 130,* 241-251.

Stoller, R. J. (1973). *Splitting: A case of female masculinity.* New York: Quadrangle.

Stoller, R. J. (1974). Facts and fancies: An examination of Freud's concept of bisexuality. In J. Strouse (Ed.), *Women and analysis* (pp. 343-364). New York: Viking.

Stoller, R. J. (1975). *Perversion: The erotic form of hatred.* New York: Pantheon.

Stoller, R. J. (1976). Primary femininity. *Journal of the American Psychoanalytic Association* (supplement), *24*, 59-78.

Stoller, R. J. (1979). *Sexual excitement: Dynamics of erotic life.* New York: Pantheon.

Stoller, R. J. (1980). A different view of Oedipal conflict. In S. Greenspan & G. Pollock (Eds.), *The course of life* (Vol. 1) (pp. 589-602). City: publisher.

Stoller, R. J., & Newman, L. E. (1971). The bisexual identity of transsexuals: Two case examples. *Archives of Sexual Behavior, 1*, 17-28.

Stone, L. (1981, October). Women who live with gay men. *Ms. Magazine*, pp. 103-104.

Storms, M. D. (1980). Theories of sexual orientation. *Journal of Personality and Social Psychology, 38*, 783-792.

Strutt, M. (1970). *Bisexual swapping.* Chatsworth, CA: Barclay House.

Sulloway, F. J. (1979). *Freud, biologist of the mind: Beyond the psychoanalytic legend.* New York: Basic Books.
Extremely informative on the Freud/Fliess controversy and has an excellent presentation of early theorizing on bisexuality in the late 1800s.

Summer, W. (1955, July/August). On the bisexuality of man. *Mattachine Review*, pp. 16-18.

Thornton, N. (1948). Why American homosexuals marry. *Neurotica, 1*(1), 24-28.

Tripp, C. A. (1976). *The homosexual matrix.* New York: McGraw-Hill.

Vassi, M. (1975). *Metasex, myth and madness.* New York: Penthouse Press.

Vidal, G. (1973). Bisexual politics. In L. Richmond & G. Noguera (Eds.), *The gay liberation book* (pp. 134-137). San Francisco: Ramparts Press.

Vorhaus, M. (1959). *Adam's rib: An analysis of normal bisexuality in each of us.* New York: Horizon Press.

Warren, C. A. B. (1974). *Identity and community in the gay world.* New York: John Wiley & Sons.

Weinberg, G. (1972). *Society and the healthy homosexual.* New York: St. Martin's Press.

Weinberg, M. S., & Williams, C. J. (1974). *Male homosexuals: Their problems and adaptations.* New York: Oxford University Press.

Weinberg, T. S. (1977, September). *On "doing" and "being" Gay: Sexual behavior and homosexual self-identity.* Paper presented at the annual meeting of the Society for the Study of Social Problems, Alfred C. Kinsey Institute, Bloomington, IN.

Weininger, O. (n.d.). *Sex and character* (6th Ed.). London: Heinemann, and New York: Putnam's. (First edition published as *Geschlecht und Charakter*, Vienna, 1903)

Weiss, E. (1958). Bisexuality and ego structure. *International Journal of Psychoanalysis, 39*, 91-97.

Weissman, P. (1962). Structural considerations in overt male bisexuality. *International Journal of Psychoanalysis, 42*, 159-168.

West, D. J. (1977). *Homosexuality re-examined.* (Minneapolis: University of Minnesota Press.

Westwood, G. (1960). *A minority—A report on the life of the male homosexual in Great Britain.* London: Longmans, Green.

Willis, D. (1974). Bisexuality: A personal view. *Women: A Journal of liberation, 4*(1), 10.

Wise, D. (1971). *Understanding bisexuality.* Los Angeles: Centurion Press.

Wise, D., & Jardine, J. (1971). *The bisexual male.* Los Angeles: Centurion Press.

Wittels, F. (1929). *Critique of love.* New York: Macaulay.

Wittels, F. (1934). Motherhood and bisexuality. *Psychoanalytic Review, 21*, 180-193.

Wittels, F. (1954). Heinrich von Kleist: A Prussian Junker and creative genius: A study in bisexuality. *American Imago, 11*, 11-31.

Wittels, F. (1934). Mona Lisa and feminine beauty: A study in bisexuality. *International Journal of Psychoanalysis, 15*, 25-40.

Wolf, T. J. (1982). *Selected social and psychological aspects of male homosexual be-*

havior in marriage. Unpublished doctoral dissertation, United States International University, San Diego, CA.

Wolfe, C. (1977). *Bisexuality: A study.* London: Quartet Books.

Wolfenden, J. (1957). *Report on the committee on homosexual offenses and prostitution.* London: H. M. Stationery Office.

Wolman, B. (Ed.). (1977). *International encyclopedia of psychiatry, psychology and psychoanalysis.* New York: Van Nostrand Reinhold.

Wooden, W., & Parker, J. (1982). *Men behind bars: Sexual exploitation in prison.* New York & London: Plenum Press.

Wyckoff, H. (1973). In behalf of bisexuality. *Issues in Radical Therapy, 1*(3), 10-13.

Wysor, B. (1974). *The lesbian myth.* New York: Random House.

Yankelovich, D. (1981, April). New rules in American life: Searching for self-fulfillment in a world turned upside down. *Psychology Today*, pp. 67-75.

Zinik, G. (1983). *The sexual orientation inventory.* Unpublished manuscript, University of California, Santa Barbara, CA.

Zolla, E. (1981). *The androgyne: The creative tension of male and female.* New York: Crossword Publishing.

Index

adolescents, homosexual period of 46
age factors
  in bisexual marriages 145-146,170,203,204
  in female bisexuality 119
alcohol abuse 205
amantes 79
ambisexuality 176
American Psychiatric Association 64
American Psychological Association 64
amiga 79
anal intercourse 77,79,123-124
androgyny 55-56,64,175
Anglo-Americans, bisexuality of 81,83-84
anxiety 16,68,71
attentional difficulties 67-68,70-71

Baez, Joan 13
Barry and Alice: Portrait of a Bisexual
  Marriage (Kohn) 233
behavior therapy, PLISSIT model 52
Bem Sex Role Inventory 64
bestiality 216,221-222 n.
biological factors, in homosexuality 24-25,28
Bi-Pol 229
birth control, anal intercourse as 79
bisexual centers
  in Chicago 231-234
  in New York City 223
  in San Francisco 227-230
Bisexual Counseling Service 228-229
Bisexual Forum 223,224
bisexual identity, 29-32
  as bisexuality criterion 8
  conflict in 9
  development of 97
Bisexual Option, The (Klein) 176
bisexuality
  as arrested development 46
  clinical/empirical studies 14-17
  concept of 2,174-176
  concurrent 8-9
  conflict in 2,9,12,15
  conflict model of 9-11
  confusion in 2,12,15,53-54
  counseling issues for 51-62
    androgyny 55-56
    "coming out" 53,54-55
    conceptualization 54
    confusion 53-54
    homosexual transition 56
    problem differentiation 52-53

  sex role stereotyping 55-56
  cultural factors in 75-85
  definitions of 8-9,64,174
    problems of 1-6
  emotional characteristics of 15
  fantasy in 15,36,41,122-123,129,200,216
  "fashionable" nature of 13
  in females, *see* female bisexuality
  of fetus 25
  flexibility model of 11-13
  Freud's theory of 12,36,116,174
  heterosexuality in 3
  heterosexuals, relationships with 56-61,
    see also marriage
    children in 59-60
    "coming out" 60-61
    communication skills in 59
    counseling for 56-61
    homophobia in 57
    insecurity in 58
    monogamy in 58-59
    sexual choice in 57-58
  homosexuality in 3-4,63-64
  homosexuals' attitudes towards 2,11,30
  identity conflict in 9
  incidence of 7,13-14,36
  isolation in 65
  Jung's theory of 174
  Kinsey scale of 3-4,5,13-14,37-38,163,199,
    200
  Klein Sexual Orientation Grid of 38-48,64
  learned 14
  in males, *see* male bisexuality
  personality factors in 63-73,163,167,168,169
  promiscuity in 3
  psychological factors in 16-17,63-73
  research errors in 3-4
  self-acceptance of 167,169
  self-esteem in 15,65,67-68,71,199-200,
    201-202,205
  self-labeling of 2,37,42,44,45,46,47,64,
    131,147
  serial 9
  sexual dichotomization and 10,11-12,13,
    21-22,35-36,76,116
  sexual orientation in 8,15,163,166
  sexual partner availability and 76-77
  Sexual Screening Questionnaire of 65-66,70
  simultaneous 8
  social attitudes towards 10,11,12-13,30,65
  social stigmatization of 10,16

genitality 2
guilt 17

hermaphroditism, psychic 24
heterosexuality
  in bisexuality 3
  bisexuals, relationships with 56-61,
      see also marriage
    children in 59-60
    "coming out" 60-61
    communication skills in 59
    counseling for 56-61
    homophobia in 57
    insecurity in 58
    monogamy in 58-59
    sexual choice in 57-58
  fantasies of 15
  Freud's theory of 36
  homosexual orientation in 45,46
  incidence of 13,37
  Kinsey scale of 1-2,37-38
  Klein Sexual Orientation Grid of 38-48
  as latent homosexuality 25-26
  marital satisfaction and 209-210,218-219,
      221
  personality factors in 63-73
  self-labeling 37
  sexual satisfaction and 209-210,217-218,
      219-221
homophobia 57
homosexual identity, *see also* gay identity
  adoption of 29
  androgyny in 64
  bisexual identity and 29-30
  delayed formation of 96-97
  of married male bisexuals 162-163,167
homosexual role 28-29
homosexuality
  as arrested development 46
  biological factors in 24-25,28
  in bisexuality 3-4,63-64
  cultural factors in 75-85
  decriminalization of 24-25
  development of 14,46
  as deviant behavior 24-25,36
  DSM-II classification of 36
  effeminacy and 78,81,82,84
  ego-dystonic 64
  fantasies in 15
  in females, *see* lesbians
  Freud's theory of 25,36
  heterosexual orientation in 45,46
  historical context of 23-27
  incidence of 7,13-14,37,63,135
  innate vs acquired 24-25
  Kinsey scale of 2,37
  Klein Sexual Orientation Grid of 38-48
  latent 25-26,116
  learned 14

in Mexico 77-78,80-85
misuse of term 116
as normal behavior 64
patent 116
personality factors in 63-73
predispositional 14
in pre-pubertal boys 81-82
self-labeling 26,29-30,31-32,37
social life in 28
social stigmatization of 10
sociobiological basis of 36
transition to bisexuality 56
Homosexuality in Perspective (Masters and
    Johnson) 176
homosexuals
  attitudes towards bisexuality 2,11,30
  life adjustment of 36-37
  married, 88,89,135,136, *see also* male
    bisexuality, in marriage
hostility 16
husbands
  bisexual, *see* male bisexuality, in marriage
  of bisexual women 91-92,97,124-126,128
  in swinging marriages
    marital satisfaction of 209-210,218-219,
      221
    sexual satisfaction of 209-210,217-218,
      219-221

identity crisis 9,109
Identity House 224
insecurity 58
intersex 24
Intimate Enemy, The (Bach) 59
inverts 24
isolation 65,109

Jagger, Mick 13
Joplin, Janis 13
Jung, Carl 174

King, Billy Jean 13
Kinsey, Alfred 7,46
Kinsey Heterosexual-Homosexual Scale
    (KHHS) 37-38
Kinsey scales 1-2
  of bisexuality 3-4,5,13-14,37-38,163,199,
      200
  of heterosexuality 1-2,37-38
  of homosexuality 2,37
Klein, Fred 224
Klein Sexual Orientation Grid 38-48,64,137,
    145,147
Kohn, Barry 233

labeling 26, *see also* self-labeling
learning 45
lesbian identity 96-97